ƒP

THINKING INSIDE THE BOX

*The 12 Timeless Rules for
Managing a Successful Business*

KIRK CHEYFITZ

Free Press
NEW YORK LONDON TORONTO SYDNEY SINGAPORE

FREE PRESS
A Division of Simon & Schuster, Inc.
1230 Avenue of the Americas
New York, NY 10020

For information regarding special discounts for bulk purchases,
please contact Simon & Schuster Special Sales at 1-800-456-6798
or business@simonandschuster.com

DESIGNED BY PAUL DIPPOLITO

Manufactured in the United States of America

10 9 8 7 6 5 4 3 2 1

Library of Congress Cataloging-in-Publication Data
Cheyfitz, Kirk.
Thinking inside the box : the 12 timeless rules for managing a
successful business / Kirk Cheyfitz.
 p. cm.
Includes bibliographical references and index.
1. Industrial management. I. Title.
HD31.C4723 2003
658—dc21 2002045588

ISBN 978-0-7432-3576-1

*For my wife, Ellen, who knows
the most important rules*

CONTENTS

THINKING
INSIDE
THE BOX

Read This First

DON'T DO ANYTHING STUPID

By early 2002, many of the world's major media companies (along with quite a few telecommunications companies, investment firms, and various other businesses) were in big trouble. Vivendi Universal, AOL Time Warner, and Bertelsmann all ousted top managers after suffering disastrous reversals in market value. It was during this dismaying period that Mel Karmazin, president and COO of media giant Viacom, devised the most reassuring message he could muster to calm the fears of his jittery investors.

Karmazin's message contained none of the ideas that had set the business world on fire during the previous decade. It was not a pledge to change relentlessly with changing times, or a hymn to thinking outside the box, or a nod to the revolutionary power of technology, or an invocation of the godlike qualities of his CEO. Instead, displayed bravely on the T-shirt Karmazin wore for a conference call with his big institutional investors was the promise: "We won't do anything stupid."[1]

As modest as it was, no message could have been more welcome and appropriate in the post-new-economy agony of the time. Simply by avoiding stupid moves, Karmazin and his boss, Sumner Redstone, Viacom's chairman and controlling shareholder, had steered the corporation into the top spot among media conglomerates. In mid-2002, Viacom—owner of such leading entertainment brands as Paramount, MTV, CBS, Blockbuster Video, and Simon & Schuster (the publisher of this book)—was the most valuable media company on the planet, mostly because it had avoided expensive gambles on unproven fads.[2]

During the 1990s, Viacom turned down the opportunity to pour money into countless Internet-based start-ups, and Redstone turned

away the hyper-expensive America Online deal that Time Warner later swallowed, much to its shareholders' ultimate regret. In short, Viacom stuck to the tried-and-true basics of its businesses, and Viacom's managers kept their thinking firmly inside the box.

In undertaking the research for this book, I found it impossible to avoid the conclusion that much of the business world essentially lost its head during the 1990s, making a series of moves so stupid that it seems—in retrospect, at least—they should have been obvious to anyone. It is clear that this recent stupidity was both a reprise of past stupidity and a total failure to heed the lessons of commercial or human history. Almost without exception, the biggest errors were based on the notion that the foundations of sound business were being radically altered by technological and social change. But that notion, which has been briefly entertained by virtually every generation of humanity, has always proven to be a monumental overstatement. This latest time around was no exception.

Consider for a moment the groundbreaking work of Herbert A. Simon, one of the twentieth century's outstanding economic thinkers. Born in 1916 in Milwaukee, educated in the public schools, Simon found himself during the Great Depression at the University of Chicago, where he latched onto the notion that would form the center of his life's work: "The social sciences, I thought, needed the same kind of rigor and the same mathematical underpinnings that had made the 'hard' sciences so brilliantly successful," he wrote years later. So he set about training himself to be "a mathematical social scientist." An undergraduate term paper on decision-making in business organizations led to graduate work on the same topic and then to a research fellowship at the University of California at Berkeley.[3] As one culmination of his research, Simon published a book in 1947 titled, simply, *Administrative Behavior*, which created a firm foundation for understanding the complex ways in which decisions are made inside corporations and other "economic organizations." When the Royal Swedish Academy of Sciences explained in 1978 its reasons for honoring Simon with the Nobel Prize in economics, it cited *Administrative Behavior*, calling it an "epoch-making book."

The ideas expressed in Simon's work are fascinating—he rejects

the notion of the omnipotent CEO and replaces it with a model of multiple decision-makers limited by their knowledge and their loyalties. But what is even more fascinating is the unwavering persistence of his ideas. Writing the introduction to the fourth edition of *Administrative Behavior*, which was published on the book's fiftieth anniversary, Simon has this to say: "In this fourth edition, as in the previous ones, the text of the original work is kept intact, for there is essentially nothing in it that I wish to retract."

As Simon explains, his book hasn't changed in more than half a century because people and the way they make decisions haven't changed. "Human organizations, quite large ones, have been with us for at least four thousand years," he writes. "Although the physical technology a modern army employs is wholly different from the technology employed by the armies of Nineveh or Egypt or X'ian, the processes people used in these ancient armies to make decisions or to manage people appear quite familiar to us and largely unchanged over the centuries."[4]

It is the premise of this book that, in business, the recurring disenchantment with so-called old ideas is completely misguided; the search for some revolution that will change everything is essentially wasteful; the relentless insistence on "thinking outside the box" is wrongheaded.

I began this book with the conviction that we can't think outside the box or even inside the box unless we have a very precise idea of what the box is. A look at business past and present reveals the existence of certain unchanging, timeless rules—the rules that I collectively call "The Box." Among the planks that make up The Box, for example, are the millennia-old rules of organizational decision-making uncovered by Simon. Ignoring the established rules of The Box is neither innovative nor entrepreneurial nor revolutionary. It is, to borrow a word from Mel Karmazin's T-shirt, stupid. Plain and simple.

The welcome corollary of this premise is that there is no substance to the myth of the Oz-like CEO. Managing an enterprise requires neither genius nor constant invention (let alone reinvention). Rather, good management largely consists of paying attention to history and present reality while applying hard work and prudence. This is the

gospel of business—that management is a set of skills to be learned, not a matter of divine inspiration or magical foresight, and that the list of requisite skills has been consistent over a long period of time. Given the right set of rules, we can all manage from one quarter to the next, providing something useful to society and making a reasonable profit in return, while avoiding doing too much that is stupid. That's what this book is about.

CHAPTER 1

The Basic Box:
Some Things Never Change

> *Know the difference between what will change and*
> *what won't, and pay attention to the former.*

So, What Was New About the "New Economy"?

The official end of the "new economy" began shortly after the dawn of the new millennium, on January 29, 2001, when one of the nation's most prestigious academic think tanks publicly announced its roster of research fellows for the coming term. The Joan Shorenstein Center on the Press, Politics and Public Policy, a creature of Harvard University's John F. Kennedy School of Government (no less), trotted out its version of the usual suspects—a short list of visiting fellows, all prominent journalists and authors.

One of the center's fellows for spring 2001, economics writer Jeffrey Madrick, would "examine how today's media have reported, analyzed and questioned the new economy," the center announced.[1]

From the practical viewpoint of the marketplace, the promised critique of the so-called new economy—what Wall Street, the press, and even Alan Greenspan had promoted as an unprecedented, fundamental change in economic reality in the 1990s—might have been more welcome if it had come just a little sooner. Already the so-called new economy had come to represent a series of excesses and blind follies that made it seem as if the business world had lost both its head and its way in the prior decade. The stock market had seemingly discarded such straightforward benchmarks as price/earnings ratios.

Prices no longer needed to be related to earnings in the new economy, and the world could set aside the old-economy idea that the value of a company's shares is nothing more nor less than the net present value of the future cash flow to be generated by the company. Having freed business from constraining realities like P/E ratios and the need for profits, the new economy meant the bull market could rage on forever. Or so it seemed.

It is probably appropriate that the Shorenstein Center should be the first quasi-official arm of government and academia to plumb the myth of the new economy. The center was established by great wealth earned in one of the oldest of economic endeavors (no, not that one): real estate development and speculation. Walter H. Shorenstein of San Francisco, a big-time Democratic contributor and founder of one of America's largest commercial real estate empires, endowed the center in 1986 to honor his late journalist daughter, Joan. It has been devoted ever since to researching the shady-gray nexus where journalists, politicos, and historians rub elbows and slap each other's backs. Despite all its evident conflicts of interest, it has backed some excellent research.

Shorenstein fellow Madrick, editor of the bimonthly economics journal *Challenge* and a regular columnist for *The New York Times*, had once professed belief in a new economy. "I think there is a new economy," Madrick told Microsoft's online zine *Salon* in a spring 1998 interview.[2] "What I don't think is that it's going to result in the same kind of productivity growth that the old economy generated," he added. But by December 2001, when Madrick published his research, he was convinced that there "was, in truth, little empirical support . . . for a new economy that was unprecedented in any meaningful way."[3]

Previously, Madrick had written in his column in *The New York Times* that people had put their faith in a lot of so-called new economies since the 1970s and that the phrase had been used to describe a lot of very different economic events, including some very, very bad times (the stagflation of the 1970s), just okay times (the corporate restructuring of the 1980s), and unbelievably good times (the dot-boom of the 1990s). "Sometimes it was about computer technology. But it has also been used to describe a service economy, globalization, the

two-worker family, stagnating wages, the rise of small companies, deindustrialization and corporate restructuring," Madrick wrote.[4]

The research could have gone back a lot farther. A single afternoon amid the computerized stacks of the New York Public Library reveals that so-called new economies have been dreamed of and cited by writers at least as far back as the last century. The earliest reference found in a casual search was to the work of Laurence Gronlund, a radical American economic theorist who published a book of prophecy called *The New Economy*. Gronlund's work debuted in 1898, a year before his death and more than a century before Madrick's appointment as a Shorenstein fellow. For Gronlund, the phrase defined the organization of production and distribution under socialism, which he fervently believed was just around the corner.

But Madrick's central point was not how often history had seen the rise and fall of false new economies. Rather, it was that in its most recent incarnation in the 1990s, a false belief in fundamental economic change had wasted billions in wealth to no purpose. "The broad faith in a new economy ultimately did a lot of damage," he concluded in his research.[5]

Journalists, trend-of-the-minute authors, true believers, and starry-eyed social activists, of course, cannot be stopped from running amok, dreaming up new economies that never existed. But businesspeople take such folks seriously only at their own dire economic peril. The most recent (and, therefore, most vivid) examples of this truth have been provided by the great telecom collapse of 2000 and 2001, an unmitigated disaster that destroyed half a million jobs in the Western world as company after company—Worldcom, Global Crossing, Winstar, Marconi, and so on—succumbed to insolvency after losing big bets on the future need for high-speed transmission equipment and wireless systems to carry voice and Internet traffic. All in all, the telecom crash incinerated more than a trillion dollars of capital, and single-handedly edged the world economy to the brink of full-fledged recession after the longest period of expansion in modern history.[6] Unfortunately, building the new economy envisioned by the captains of the telecom revolution required violating virtually every single principle of sound business.

Before the telecom cataclysm, there was the much more widely understood and lamented collapse of the dot-coms, the Internet-generated version of a new economy that seemed so plausible in the late 1990s. And on top of all that, there was the massive collapse of Enron, a series of frauds masquerading as a new-economy venture that supposedly had redefined trading in power and energy.

But these are just the most recent examples among many fleeting "new economies" throughout history. And we can be certain there will be more in the future. No matter what the elements of their supposed newness, they share one fate: They invariably have proven the most poisonous kind of nonsense for a real businessperson—or a real economist or historian, for that matter—to swallow.

Business-Building Tools That Just Don't Quit

The facts, unanimously ignored by the headline writers of the new economies, tell us the world economy in which we all live and do business has been essentially unchanged for at least the past three centuries.

What this means is that the basic rules for business-building—the rules that form the operating framework I've nicknamed "The Box"— simply don't change much. Absolutely never over months or weeks, certainly not much over years, probably not significantly over decades or centuries, arguably not even over millennia.

In this chapter and the eleven that follow, I describe what I see as the twelve planks in The Box, offering examples, tales from the front lines of commerce, comments from real live managers about their best moves and their worst, fragments of historical context, and other helpful information.

Thinking Inside The Box is not a path to revolution or a get-rich-quick scheme. It's not even fail-safe. Execute a bad idea flawlessly and it will still fail, most likely. But the underlying argument is that these pages contain a practical blueprint for building profitable and longer-lasting enterprises, given the investment of sufficient vigilance and hard work (which is what doing business mostly consists of). Once

understood and remembered, The Box's planks can be utilized reliably no matter what snake oil might be getting sold on Wall Street on any given day; no matter what passing fad or fashion might be gripping the short attention span of the press, the politicians, the business gurus, and the general public; and no matter what temporary disaster—economic, social, or political—might befall your neighborhood, country, hemisphere, or world.

Successful enterprises throughout time have profited from keeping these rules in practice. Every businessperson trying to compete in the current era of unremitting uncertainty also can profit by keeping these relatively immutable rules in mind all the time. In a sea of technological, social, and political change, The Box is a sea-anchor that can keep enterprises headed reliably toward economic gain.

The Basics of Business: Some Stuff Never Changes

Two great modern scholars, anthropologist Eric Wolf and sociologist Immanuel Wallerstein, both find the world of the late 1300s dominated by a global capitalist market in goods and services. To paint the picture of early global capitalism, Wolf lays out a tantalizing chronology of a few early trading voyages, some still famed, most forgotten: From Venice, beginning in 1271, the Polo family (merchant brothers Niccolo and Maffeo, along with Niccolo's everlastingly celebrated son Marco) sailed the seas and trekked the old Silk Road to Peking, finally voyaging home in 1295; a Moroccan official and scholar journeyed through eastern Europe to India and China, arriving home again in 1349 to dictate a travelogue; in the early 1400s, a Chinese admiral sailed numerous times to the east African coast; and of course, there was the much heralded voyage in 1492 of "a Genoese sea captain in the employ of the Queen of Aragon" who, seeing the New World for the first time, thought he had arrived in Asia (and continued to think so through three more voyages).[7]

"These voyages were not isolated adventures but manifestations of forces that were drawing the continents into more encompassing relationships and would soon make the world a unified stage for

human action," Wolf writes in his masterpiece *Europe and the People without History*. Wolf goes on to draw a vivid and detailed picture of the commercial world of 1400, when the Old World (Europe, Asia, and Africa) was crisscrossed with well-trodden trade routes connecting a few regions of agricultural riches with the raw materials and manufactures of the known globe. From Venice to Constantinople to Kashgar to Peking, from Canton to Calcutta to the east coast of southern Africa, the trade routes cover the old globe. And the merchants traveling these sea and land routes, Wolf writes, "would have followed in the footsteps of innumerable traders who, for millennia, had labored to construct far-flung commercial networks between widely separate regions." Wolf did not casually employ the phrase "for millennia."[8] One of the old-world trade routes, the Silk Road linking the Mediterranean and the South China Sea, existed as early as two hundred years before Christ.

Powered by the human desire for gain and novelty, untold varieties and quantities of trade goods were transported and exchanged over these ancient routes. Items as simple as seeds and agricultural tools, and as complex as newly built ships, were traded.

Summing up Wallerstein and other economics theorists and scholars, Wolf explains, "This world economy, originating in the late fifteenth and early sixteenth centuries, constitutes a global market characterized by a global division of labor. Firms (be they individuals, enterprises, or regions) meet in this market to exchange the goods they have produced in the hope of realizing a profit."[9] This global marketplace of six centuries ago came complete with low-wage regions, which supplied the bulk of the world's labor and raw materials, and high-wage regions, which supplied the technology and the capital. Firms involved in trade made complex decisions about sourcing labor, materials, and finished products based on price and availability, just like today. In virtually all the fundamental ways that matter economically, transactions conducted in the worldwide marketplace of 1400 would have seemed completely familiar on the front of the "Marketplace" section of *The Wall Street Journal* circa 2000.

The point—that there is absolutely nothing new about the economy—might be made by stopping there, some six hundred years ago,

in the global, highly competitive, profit-oriented marketplace of the 1400s. But there are other researchers who take this line of inquiry a few steps farther back.

At the heart of any economic matter is the notion of exchange. And that notion appears to have existed as long as there have been creatures recognizable as human beings. "The Neanderthals conducted trade over long distances," says Lawrence Hirschfeld, the University of Michigan anthropologist. Hirschfeld points out that one of the strongest theories of anthropology is "that, basically, all you need is the notion of reciprocity in exchange to kick start culture." In other words, the starting point for social interaction, culture, and economics, as we now know it, is the idea of giving something to another individual and then getting back something roughly equivalent in value. But Hirschfeld adds, "It's not simple exchange. It's indirect exchange."[10]

The ultimate facilitator of indirect exchange, of course, is money, which allows an individual to turn labor, for example, into any needed commodity. When it comes to indirect exchange, says Hirschfeld, "humans are very good at that and other species are not." In fact, we're so good at it that we've built a global economy on the concept of indirect exchange and we've sustained it for centuries.

Hirschfeld, who has done a lot of study on human development, cites some research on infants showing that even tiny babies pay attention to exchanges. Infants will watch the giving and taking of gifts and will register interest or surprise if the direction of the exchange changes—if the gift-giver becomes a gift-receiver. The sum total of this and other similar research suggests that the notion of exchange—the central idea behind our economy—is hardwired into the human brain. We have, in effect, an inborn instinct for doing business.

As far as anyone can tell, only people possess these instincts for economic relationships. "Chimpanzees will cooperate to do things like hunt," says Hirschfeld, citing relatively recent research findings. And chimps who pair off to groom each other have also been shown to share food. "It's kind of like cementing friendships" with exchanges, Hirschfeld explains. But even though individual chimps apparently share food with other individuals based on their relation-

ship or on what each chimp "owes" the other, they have no notion of how to create systems of exchange for doing things like dividing the products of a hunt among an entire band. "Humans, of course, spend fifty hours before they go on a hunt deciding how they're going to divvy up whatever they catch," says Hirschfeld. And human culture is based on systems of sharing (exchange) that extend far beyond the local band or tribe or nation.

"Chimps have very complex social structures, surely the most complex of any nonhuman animal," Hirschfeld says. But their exchanges are limited to direct sharing between two individuals. Humans, however, have a natural talent for indirect exchanges involving many more individuals—where person A gives something to person B, who gives something else to person C, who completes the exchange by giving something different (but equivalent) to person A. The path-breaking French anthropologist Claude Levi-Strauss "showed that with little more than this relationship, particularly when B and C don't live in A's village, you can generate very complex societies," Hirschfeld points out. And that is exactly what human beings have been doing for tens of thousands of years.

History and social science, in sum, not only teach us that there is nothing new in the new economy. Even more important, they teach us *it is not possible for there to be anything really new in the economy.*

This does not mean that technology isn't critically important. Every significant technological innovation from the wheel to the Internet, including the invention of the steam engine and the resulting Industrial Revolution, has changed our culture, our social organization, and our daily lives in enduring and irreversible ways. Technology always heavily impacts the shape of some businesses—the steam engine ultimately put the horse out of business, just as diesel power ultimately killed steam; the computer put hand-cranked adding machines out of business; and so on.

But none of this has changed the fundamental operation of the economy—the exchange of goods and services for gain. It is important not to confuse our technology and our economy just because they both end in *y.* Yes, certainly, technology will change—anyone who doesn't expect constant technological change is probably brain-dead.

Walking, inevitably, will give way to carts and horseback riding and bicycles and, eventually, to the faster-than-sound, suborbital, intercontinental rocket. Painting on cave walls will lead to paper and movable type and, eventually, to broadband delivery of digital, multimedia extravaganzas at light speed. But while rockets and broadband will revolutionize movement and communications, they will not fundamentally alter the economy or the notions of exchange that underlie the economy. The rule the world seemingly forgot when the Internet was going to "change everything" is that the way our economy is organized—the way we perceive and execute the exchange of labor and goods—has not ever been and shows no signs that it ever will be changed in any fundamental way by advances in technology.

"Evolution has invested a fair amount of time and energy in developing conceptual and perceptual tools that facilitate exchange and ways of regulating it, and it's probably not an accident that our economies are built today the way they are. Because the ways we imagine exchange to be possible and reasonable have their roots in our evolutionary history," says Hirschfeld.

Our evolutionary history is as much as 5.8 million years old right now, as far as the paleoanthropologists can tell.[11] So much for the newness of the new economy.

This is not just academic mumbo-jumbo. This is important stuff for managers of all ranks and ideologies, from imperial CEOs of global conglomerates to middle managers to start-up entrepreneurs. Because it is absolutely critical in business to know which things will change and which won't—to know the difference between what is coming next and what will always be.

This knowledge is the route to understanding the unchanging nature of the fundamental rules that make business work, while also appreciating the constantly changing nature of the infinite factors that influence all businesses. It also is the single most critical element in allocating your intellectual resources and attention properly. When addressing a pressing business problem, there is no greater waste of time than to try tinkering with something that cannot be altered. Because while you try to change the unchangeable, of course, you are

distracted from your real job, which is to anticipate the things that must change and to stay ahead of them.

Beware of Biz-Book Gurus Bearing "Revolutionary New" Theories Involving Free Lunches

Now flash forward a few thousand millennia.

The past few years have been the era of "out-of-the-box" thinking. Every manager in the world has been urged to think *revolutionary* thoughts. And the results have been pretty disastrous, on the whole, because not one of the geniuses afflicting modern business with their out-of-the-box theories has actually defined the "box" we are supposed to think outside of.

Gary Hamel, the consultant and biz school prof cum business-book guru, is a good case in point. Hamel, a smart and well-read fellow, shot to the top of the business-book bestseller list in 2000 with *Leading the Revolution*.[12] His thesis, riding the dot-com comet's blazing tail of overinflated hype, was that business was entering more than a new economy, it was beginning a "new era." But his thesis falls apart under scrutiny precisely because it pays no attention to the difference between the changeable and the unchangeable.

With the benefit of hindsight, it now may be enough to point out that Hamel's leading example of the perfect new-era company was Enron, which he praised lavishly and at great length for having a "genius for innovation."[13] But the flaws in Hamel's thesis were more fundamental than his misplaced admiration for Enron.

"Never has incumbency been worth less," Hamel trumpeted (in large red type) on page six of his 333-page tome. This was the essential point of Hamel's book. He proposed the intentionally heretical—and, time would prove, totally false—claim that there was suddenly little or no advantage to having an established enterprise because the new economy had changed the rules to favor newness. For the sake of this punchy, sexy, simple, saleable message, Hamel simply ignored anything contradictory. (Thus, Hamel never noticed, or intentionally overlooked, the powerful pro-incumbency forces, led by Goldman

Sachs, that in 2000 launched the iFormation Group, a $300 million investment company based on the perception, voiced by Gene Sykes, a Goldman managing director, that "incumbents were going to be the driving force" behind most financially successful innovation.)[14]

Hamel wove his notion about the supremacy of newness and the necessity for revolution into a web of warnings about the coming end for companies big and small that failed to employ what he called "radical innovation." As a seer, Hamel saved his most dire (and most inaccurate) visions for the future of retailers whose lack of foresight, in Hamel's view, had led them into the terrible error of actually building and relying on real brick-and-mortar stores. "The Internet has turned bricks and mortar into millstones," he wrote, ignoring the facts of retail shopping, the well-documented love affair between American consumers and stores, and the centuries-old rule that strong locations confer strong advantages on retail establishments.

To unprove Hamel's point, one need look no further than Webvan, the online grocer without a single real store. Webvan dumped $1.2 billion down the drain on high-tech warehouses and fulfillment systems before it finally and inevitably went broke in early 2001. People, it turns out, actually prefer to shop for their groceries in grocery stores.

To prove his point in his book, Hamel turned to a British company called Freeserve, PLC, an Internet service provider, or "ISP." It is worth examining Freeserve in some detail because the company turns out to be a prime example of the delusions, excesses, and illogic of the new economy era—an era in which American business and finance went searching for the holy grail of out-of-the-box thinking and temporarily forgot the immutable rules of business.

Launched in September 1998 by the consumer electronics chain Dixon's (the United Kingdom's equivalent of Best Buy or Circuit City), Freeserve offered the public "free" Internet access. Freeserve's offer, aimed largely at individual consumers using computers in their homes, depended on the way phone calls were priced in Europe. Unlike the United States, where most local residential service had been available since 1997 for a cheap flat fee no matter how many hours were spent on the phone, all local calls in Europe were still being billed by the minute. This meant that spending a long time

online, even with a local dial-up, cost a lot. So Freeserve decided to get its money by sharing a small portion of the phone charges, supplemented by whatever advertising and e-commerce revenues it could bring in. Incumbent America Online, then the UK's number-one ISP, was charging a monthly subscription fee (on top of the bills from the phone company) for its Web access, so Freeserve's approach seemed a powerful competitive offer. And it was . . . for a while.

Freeserve's "free" offer, needless to say, proved initially popular with consumers and the stock market. More than one million Britons signed on to Freeserve in its first five months, as the free service surpassed AOL UK and took over leadership among the U.K.'s ISPs. Ten months after opening its doors, Freeserve "floated" (as they call an initial public stock offering in Britain), with Dixon's selling a minority share of the company for £135 million (roughly $200 million) or about £1.50 per share, a price that valued the total fledgling concern at an amazing £1.51 billion.[15]

Hamel's book revels in the skyrocketing share price of Freeserve's early days and boldly declares, "What is indisputable is that revolutionaries like AOL are just as vulnerable to radical new business models as flabby geriatrics, and that speed is no substitute for rule-breaking new business concepts."

What's the Difference Between a Revolutionary New Business Concept and an Old-fashioned Price Cut? Well, It Depends . . .

What's fascinating about this sweeping statement is not that Gary Hamel was being stupid or venal. He appears to be neither. The important thing is that so much of the global business world believed exactly what Hamel concluded—and believed it based upon the same scanty and ultimately unconvincing evidence of barely eighteen months of operating history. Most of the business world, including the business press, saw in Freeserve what they wanted to see—a revolutionary, rule-breaking new business concept. But subsequent events proved, just a short time later, that the life and death of free Internet

service was merely a brief descent into a nonproductive, old-fashioned price war that ended with the demise of the "free" concept.

Some very "old economy" problems soon overtook Freeserve. The "free" ISP idea quickly spawned dozens of imitators, none of which ever made a penny. Freeserve maintained its substantial lead in customers, and by August 1999, it had even forced AOL to launch a separately branded "free" service in Britain called Netscape Online,[16] a move that was seen then as extremely significant. But Freeserve's losses mounted at the same time from just over £1 million in all of 1999 to nearly £18.5 million in roughly the first quarter of 2000, when its market value peaked. By mid-2000, after less than a two-year run, free Internet service had become a dying notion and Freeserve's value had begun to slide precipitously.

There were a lot of reasons for Freeserve's collapse in market value. Freeserve was undercapitalized, had no clear route to profitability, and was starving for cash to sustain itself. In late 2000, Freeserve was swallowed by its huge rival Wanadoo, the French Internet concern whose principal owner is the telecommunications giant France Telecom. At the time it was sold, Freeserve had racked up additional pretax losses of £17.8 million in June, July, and August, a rate that would have exhausted its cash within a year.[17]

But the real problem with Freeserve was that it had failed to follow one of the most fundamental rules in all of business—give the customers what they want. Freeserve had eliminated Internet access fees, but it had left the consumer to cope with the uncomfortable uncertainties of the ever-ticking meter represented by their pay-by-the-minute phone bills. What the consumer *really* wanted was not "free" access that wasn't free; consumers wanted certainty. In this case, that meant unlimited access to the Internet for a fixed, strictly limited, and dependable monthly charge that included the phone, the ISP, and everything else. And that's exactly what AOL set out to give them.

As Freeserve's losses mounted, AOL took the tack of joining a consumer revolt already in progress. It added its voice to those pressuring European government regulators to create a flat-rate tariff for Internet connections, just like in the United States, to encourage Internet usage and e-commerce.

AOL's move was not rocket science, but it was very smart, traditional business thinking on three counts:

1. First and foremost, it aimed to provide what consumers really wanted by making it unnecessary for them to nervously count the minutes while surfing the Web.

2. It cut off the "free" competitors at the knees by eliminating the high, pay-by-the-minute phone charges, a slice of which had provided their meager revenue.

3. And most important for AOL, it allowed AOL's proven and profitable subscription-fee service to take root in Europe as it had in the States.

By the end of 2000, AOL's old-fashioned business model had won the battle. "The future clearly lies with subscription-based access," wrote Andrew Fisher of London's *Financial Times*, the world's most widespread business daily, known affectionately as the FT. But by then it was no secret that the old, tried-and-true model of selling Internet access for a fee was going to win out after all, despite the hype accorded the free services. The FT had begun writing the epitaph for Freeserve's marketing ploy six months earlier, declaring that "barely two years after the free access phenomenon burst onto the online scene and pushed aside subscription-based services, its future is now in doubt."

Very simply, the so-called free ISPs had been doomed from the start. Their slice of the phone bill proved inadequate to ever make them profitable, and other hoped-for revenues (from ads and online sales) just weren't materializing. Problems with the sustainability of online advertising in particular would soon be causing horrendous problems for AOL's mothership in the United States. But AOL's method of charging for Internet service—more reminiscent of a newspaper subscription than a revolution—would prove a durable winner.

The death knell for the free ISPs was sounded, in the final analysis, by those pesky customers. After having had a chance to think it over, consumers decided they much preferred paying a fixed fee for Internet access as opposed to paying minute by minute to the phone company. Europe's telecom regulators heard their citizens, as well as

AOL's lobbyists, and began to create flat-rate local phone tariffs for ISPs. The U.K. was the first to fall, followed by the Netherlands, France, and Italy. German regulators got onboard, too, but Deutsche Telecom, the German phone company, stalled with appeals.

As a triumphant Matt Peacock, communications director of AOL UK, said at the time, "We knew the biggest single inhibitor of wider Internet use by the public was fear of the phone bill. Customers want to know where they stand, what they're paying for. They hate to sign up and realize there are hidden charges."[18]

In the end, Freeserve proved to be a hugely successful investment for Dixon's, its parent company, and a hugely unsuccessful one for nearly everybody else. When Freeserve was sold to Wanadoo for about £1.6 billion in late 2000, the price was approximately the same as the value placed on Freeserve at its initial public offering some eighteen months earlier. During those eighteen months, however, Freeserve's value had climbed more than 500 percent before crashing to the ground again. So all the unfortunates who bought in after the initial float were losers on the deal. And as for Freeserve's radical new business model? Under its new ownership, Freeserve turned its attention to converting its "free" customers into fee-paying customers, an arduous process at best.[19]

Freeserve's permanent business "revolution," heralded so loudly in 1999 and 2000, looked by 2001 like a very old-fashioned price war that had been terminated because it was completely unprofitable. The demise of this sure-fail scheme was only hastened when the competition applied some smarter analysis and street-smart politics to the problem.

Writing at the end of 2000, as the old millennium slipped quietly away, the FT's Andrew Fisher summed it up nicely in a line that would serve well as the cautionary moral to the whole new-economy debacle: "Everyone likes a free lunch, but it is usually worth looking for the catch."[20]

Everything Makes More Sense in Context

An ancient belief shared by East and West alike is that the present reflects the past and knowing something of history can save present-

day leaders from repeating old mistakes. It was expressed by the father of Western history, Herodotus, long before Christ, and it is the motive for the eleventh century writings of the father of Chinese history, Ssu-ma Kuang.[21]

Historical context also offers a flip side, embodied in the more forward-looking adage chiseled over the entrance to the National Archives in Washington, D.C. "The past is prologue," it says in stone letters; the past merits scrutiny because it leads inevitably to the future. And then there is the favorite saying of anyone who has ever attended a meeting about management process or corporate reengineering: "Let's not reinvent the wheel here." Once the wheel has been invented, of course, it's really not ever necessary to invent it again. But to avoid time-wasting reinvention, you must be aware of all previous inventions and how well they have worked.

Paying attention to history, in short, can save a lot of time and pain and produce a lot of gain. In a corporate world where lots of managers switch jobs every eighteen to twenty-four months, most businesspeople pay entirely too little attention to history, and many pay for it handsomely.

HOW TO BUILD THE BOX

THE FIRST PLANK

1. From time to time, everyone will believe that the economy is changing in some fundamental way, but this has never been true.
2. Don't waste time trying to create a "new business model." There aren't any.
3. The fundamental rules of commerce never change. So don't worry about how to change them.
4. Use your time to focus on how your customers' lives are changing and how you can serve their emerging needs with new products and services (delivered using the same old business models).

CHAPTER 2

The Jack in The Box: Profits

The first business of business is making money.

It's All about Profits and Planning

In the fall of 1996, when the new economy still engendered more be-
lief than disbelief and life was full of infinite promise, an obscure en-
trepreneur named Jason Olim was talking to a newspaper reporter
about his business, CDnow, which sold music CDs on a Web site. At
that moment, Olim sounded as if he felt absolutely certain he had
worked out a set of revolutionary new business principles that would
rock the world. Then twenty-seven years old and the president and
cofounder (along with his twin brother) of CDnow, located in Fort
Washington, Pennsylvania, Olim summed up his approach as follows:
"My thought is that profitability shows a lack of creativity."[1] By this
measure, no one will ever accuse Olim of being uncreative, because, as
it turned out, his venture would remain unprofitable forever.*[2]

Turning our attention away from Fort Washington and the late
nineties, we next encounter a set of attitudes and circumstances

*Three weeks after this interview with *Newsday,* perhaps chastened by negative
attention he'd generated with his disdain for profit, Olim told *BusinessWeek* how
important cost control was, adding, "It's simply the discipline of having to be
profitable to survive." But his subsequent conduct of his company's business
turned out to be more consistent with the attitude displayed in the *Newsday* inter-
view than the *BusinessWeek* story.

totally foreign to Jason Olim's frame of reference. It was 1971, Memphis, Tennessee. A rich young man (also, coincidentally, twenty-seven years old) named Frederick W. Smith was founding a new company to be called the Federal Express Corporation.[3] Like Jason Olim, Fred Smith planned to raise a great deal of money and then lose a lot of it in launching his novel operation. But unlike Olim, Smith had put together a tight business plan, based on a detailed analysis of the opportunities and obstacles he faced. Complete with financial projections that included a breakeven point and future profits. Smith built his plan on the market research and extensive analysis of two independent consulting firms, both of which assessed the business's financial assumptions and the realities of the marketplace and neither of which knew the other was performing the same assignment. Thirty years later, having become the leader of a $20 billion global business, Smith traveled to the luxurious Casa de Campo resort on the shores of the Dominican Republic to share with a conference of entrepreneurs his five "secrets" of success. One of the five turned out to be "a conservative business plan" with detailed assumptions backed by hard numbers, including (everyone take a deep breath and prepare for a shock) "revenue, expenses, projected profits."[4]

In some sense, this discussion of the most fundamental plank of The Box can be seen as a tale of two companies, two twenty-seven-year-old kids, and two eras. CDnow (along with a few other enterprises from the late 1990s) is here to show us how not to start a company. It also will serve as an icon for a disastrous era when too many managers and investors were somehow easily persuaded that there was no need to plan for or achieve profitability—at least not anytime soon. FedEx, one of the greatest entrepreneurial success stories of the twentieth century, is here to demonstrate and stand for exactly the opposite, even though, like many great start-ups, it almost went out of business several times during its frenetic and relatively brief initial search for profitability.

The principle that profits are what enterprises in a capitalist system are all about should be noncontroversial. It has been true for thousands of years. As early as the twenty-sixth century B.C., some 4,600 years ago, mankind's earliest alphabet, cuneiform, was being incised

into wet clay tablets by ancient Iraqi scribes and sealed inside clay envelopes to document and preserve signed contracts, account ledgers, and other mercantile economic information.[5] Hundreds of thousands of cuneiform tablets have been unearthed. Thus far, the vast majority are concerned with running households and businesses, with recording commercial transactions, all in the pursuit of gain. Looking at more contemporary records, only 800 to 900 years old, anthropologists and historians like Eric Wolf have pointed out relentlessly that virtually every voyage of discovery from the thirteenth to the sixteenth centuries was set in motion in hopes of profit through trade.

If there were just a single fundamental rule of economic activity, the one about profits being primary would seem a likely candidate. Even having to state that economic activity is about gain would sound impossibly simpleminded if we had not recently survived, just barely, an international debate over the relative unimportance of profitability.

For a time in the late nineties, having profitability in your business plan was an open invitation to having your stock undervalued as an "old economy" play. It got so bad, and the business world so completely lost its way for a time, that *Business 2.0*, a fairly respectable business magazine now owned by Time, Inc., actually published an article in its April 2000 issue titled "Do Profits Matter?"—as if that were a real question the answer to which was in doubt.[6] Even more terrifying is the fact that thirty-two businesspeople, consultants, and academics—fairly substantial types like Michael Bloomberg, the billionaire founder of Bloomberg LP (whose next job would be mayor of New York); Michael Moritz, a partner at venture firm Sequoia Capital; and the poster child of the new economy, Amazon.com founder and CEO Jeff Bezos himself—took the question seriously enough to participate in the article. But the ultimate nightmare, of course, is this: Based on a reading of the responses (some of which were none too clear and one of which was completely opaque), it appears only half the folks answered yes, profits do, in fact, matter. Nine definitely said no (including Bezos) and one more apparently said no. Five went into a category I labeled "eventually"; they seemed to feel profits would be important some unknown time in the future, but not now. And one response was so weasel-worded, it cannot be categorized.

Such was the state of our common confusion in spring 2000, and so it had been for a few years. So it is almost understandable in this bizarre business landscape, somehow untethered from millennia of prior economic reality, that Jason Olim, young head of CDnow and proprietor of its e-commerce site, felt free to express disdain for profit as the hobgoblin of small, uncreative minds.

In early summer 2000, four years after Olim declared profits to be uncreative, following a public offering and continual losses, Olim's cash-starved company was picked off by German media giant Bertelsmann, which folded the music e-tailer into its own much larger but also struggling Web business. The deal "saves the struggling online music retailer from joining the ranks of failed dot-com companies," reported the *San Jose Mercury News*, the daily newspaper of record for Silicon Valley.[7]

Bertelsmann paid about $99 million for CDnow, plus some loans and advances to pay down debt and provide operating capital.[8] The total payments from Bertelsmann amounted to a fraction of the company's former value. The Germans paid $3 a share for CDnow, a scant 4 percent over its last public trade before the offer and some 86 percent off its high a year earlier.

But more important, true to Olim's initial vision about never making money, Bertelsmann's deal represented a fraction of the cash CDnow had lost in building up sales and fighting with the inevitable rivals who entered the music e-tailing business after it did. All in all, Olim spent some $212 million of his investors' cash in six years and got less than $141 million in cash and debt assumption from Bertelsmann[9]—not a winning equation in business.

From CDnow's founding to its sale, Olim saw his company's annual revenues skyrocket from $2.2 million in 1995 to $147 million in 1999, a spectacular increase of nearly 6,600 percent. But sales were wildly outpaced by the nearly 61,000 percent growth in annual operating losses. CDnow's losses spiraled from $200,000 in 1995 to $121 million in 1999. Losses grew nine times faster than revenues, in fact—a startling record. During the first five years of its existence, CDnow accumulated just under $180 million in total losses—and at the accelerating rate it was losing money in early 2000, it was on a course to

end up some $350 million in the hole if it had managed to keep going as an independent through the end of the year.

Those numbers, and CDnow's desperate lack of cash, explain why Bertelsmann, in the view of analysts, was able to buy the company for far less money than it would have taken the German media conglomerate to build its own online music retailer. But the acquisition of CDnow, even at a fire-sale price, proved to be a terrible deal for Bertelsmann. The company's Web ventures, including CDnow, were such a massive failure that the losses eventually provoked the dismissal of the company's CEO, Thomas Middelhoff, in mid-2002. Not even Bertelsmann's size and enormous cash flow could turn the music e-tailer around or make its other ill-conceived online stores generate profits.[10]

Even though CDnow had thousands of shareholders who collectively lost millions of dollars, even though its failure helped bring down a high-flying superstar of global media, the story of Jason Olim might not be worth repeating if the basic story line itself had not been repeated over and over again during the 1990s, perpetuated by financiers, investment banks, reporters, and business gurus who all knew (or should have known) better.

The same 1996 newspaper story that led with Jason Olim's disdain for profits culminated with a nod of agreement from Leslie Koch, then vice president of marketing for no less an authority on profitability than Amazon.com.

As the New York *Newsday* story put it in that hot July of '96, "Like Olim, Koch feels that the time is not right to start skimming money off the top of the sales stream. . . . 'We're not trying to be profitable,' she said. 'We're building a business. We would be making a mistake if we were trying to be profitable.'"[11]

Some four years after that statement, when *Business 2.0* asked if profits really mattered, Amazon CEO Bezos essentially confirmed they still didn't. Despite growing pressure on Amazon to cut costs, pay attention to operations, and finally make some money, Bezos said, "I believe if we're investing in something and if it works, then we should invest more. Profitability is important to us, but it's long-term profitability that's important, not short-term profitability."

By the end of 2001, Amazon, founded in mid-1995, had an unbro-

ken record of annual losses and a cumulative five-year operating loss of $2.85 billion since its debut as a public company in 1997.[12] After operating for twenty-six quarters, Amazon had made a net profit in only one—$5.1 million in the fourth quarter of 2001. The one-time profit was much ballyhooed in the press and on Wall Street. But it amounted to a profit margin of less than one-half of one percent.[13] And it was widely acknowledged that this was a miracle not to be repeated, at best, for some time to come.

So how does one define a business as "working" when it's lost about three billion bucks since its inception and its best quarter showed a microscopic margin of profit? When does "building a business" end and throwing money down a rat hole begin? These questions are not that hard to answer when business fundamentals are kept in mind. After seven straight years of heavy annual losses, with the company and analysts predicting continued losses for at least two more years, informed skeptical observers of the online marketing scene see Amazon's prospects for independent survival ranging between slim and none. Jeffrey Madrick, the well-known economics writer, expert on the dot-com crash, and one-time Shorenstein research fellow on the fiction of the new economy, said in a brief phone conversation, "I'm still not convinced Amazon will survive."[14] Like him, many people, including me, see Amazon's future, if it has one, as the online appendage of a strong bricks-and-mortar merchant or merchants.

So the world will see, inevitably, whether Amazon has been building a business or just digging a hole. But the fate of so many of Amazon's fellow dot-com-ic enterprises proves beyond a doubt that beginning an enterprise without a due regard for profit is not apt to be a long-lived exercise.

Beware of "Other" Metrics

Long after the absorption of CDnow into Bertelsmann, in a retrospective interview, the brash Jason Olim who disregarded profit has been replaced by a more statesmanlike Jason Olim.[15] "It all depends on

your frame of reference whether it was a failure or a success," Olim says of CDnow. He wouldn't talk about exactly how much he made personally on the Bertelsmann deal, but said he did well. An academic business newsletter confirms this, reporting that Jason and his twin brother got $17.4 million out of the deal.[16] This is a whole lot better than most of their shareholders and confirms Olim's contention that assessing his late venture depends on one's frame of reference.

The most telling statement in Olim's retelling of the 1990s is that while profit was always thought to be an important future objective, it became *secondary* in the white-hot redefining frenzy of the so-called new economy. "These companies and their investors always believed that profitability was the cornerstone of a valid investment and a good company," Olim said. But he added, "What happened was that other metrics became more important to the leaders of these companies and their investors as near-term indicators."

"Other metrics" were among the great fictions of the era just past. Remember when "eyeballs" were supposed to be a measure of success? This metric went hand in hand with the bizarre notion that "branding" was nothing more than the overnight creation of corporate notoriety or celebrity and that such a "branding" exercise could put new enterprises on a par with established companies whose brand names had accreted trust, respect, and a well-defined public persona over years of investment and performance. At various times in various places, the proposed metric of success has been market share or penetration of "new markets" or undercutting competitors or any one of a myriad of excuses for failing to make money.

FedEx's Fred Smith has this to say about the measurements he used in founding and launching Federal Express: Any business plan "must include the basic metrics—revenue, expenses, projected profits and so on."[17] These are the metrics that have always counted and continue to count. It doesn't matter whether you are a CEO of an established business, an entrepreneur with a speculative venture, a senior manager with a new product or service, or a middle manager creating a departmental plan for the year. It doesn't matter whether you are launching a new company, a new division, a new product, or just a new marketing plan. No matter what you're up to in business, as Fred

Smith tells us, revenue, expenses, and profits are the basic metrics that will always count. As the entire decade of the nineties attests, anything else is delusional.

"The way I see it," Jason Olim said in early 2002, "there were two types of companies" in the Internet bubble. The second type, he opined, were the survivors who decided to "hoard our cash." He puts his own former company into this category. But the first kind of company that Olim describes actually sounds more like the CDnow that is found in SEC filings and news stories: "They were going to take a straight shot to the top, spend like mad to get there. If the market held, they'd be fine. If it collapsed, they'd be in trouble. I'd put Pets.com and Amazon in this category."

The Branding Triumph That Didn't

Amazon's story is still unfolding. But as Olim suggests, the very much completed story of the publicly traded, now defunct corporation called (at time of its demise) IPET Holdings, Inc., is a cautionary tale for our time. But not so much for its spectacular failure as for its incredible success.

IPET began life in November 1998 as Pets.com, a start-up venture launched by an Internet incubator in Pasadena, California, called Web Magic. The goal was to get a slice of the $23 billion that Americans lavish on their pets annually; the strategy was to offer consumers a huge variety of items on a convenient Web site. The venture began auspiciously enough, attracting the attention and the cash of the World Wide Web's most visible promoter, Jeff Bezos, whose Amazon.com was the lead investor, ultimately putting up $60 million for a 30 percent stake in the business.[18] Bezos was joined by the venerable San Francisco venture capital firm Hummer Winblad Venture Partners. Bezos personally issued a statement on the spring 1999 day when the first round of private financing closed, officially launching Pets.com as a place where you could find "a great customer experience."[19] He didn't mention the kind of experience the investors might have.

Pets.com was the first to enter the online pet supply fray, but fully expected half a dozen rivals to crop up soon. Even without more Web stores, the field was already plenty crowded with brick-and-mortar superstore chains, some of which were allied with Pets.com's nascent online competitors. Julia Wainwright, the company's newly hired CEO, speaking presciently about the forthcoming online competition, said, "I've never seen so many companies in a category . . . It'll be a bloodbath with huge cash outlays and low margins. It's a tough business."[20]

Considering her description, one had to wonder why anyone would want to get into the online pet supply business in the first place. The pet supply business is huge, but the margins would make most CFOs weep—2 to 4 percent for traditional pet supply retailers. And as far as anyone can tell, there was never a scrap of independent market research to indicate there really was any substantial place in the market for an Internet pet store. Nevertheless, despite her seeming understanding of the terrain, nonexistent margins and all, Wainwright and her backers chose the high-cost strategy of extremely heavy ad spending to blanket America in the Pets.com "brand." In doing so, they were missing the point of what makes a brand powerful, seeing branding merely as a form of celebrity. But in doing so, they were following the conventional wisdom of the moment: Establish the brand and the profits will follow.

Wainwright pursued her so-called branding strategy doggedly (excuse the pun) and succeeded beyond anyone's wildest dreams. Otherwise, the short unhappy life of Pets.com, despite its famous backers, wouldn't be worth a single sentence in the history books, let alone the few paragraphs devoted to it here.

To begin, Pets.com hired the San Francisco office of one of the great creative shops in the ad business, TBWA/Chiat/Day, the same folks who had created the phenomenon of the Taco Bell Chihuahua. To represent Pets.com to the American people, TBWA invented a spokescreature called the Sock Puppet—a fuzzy brown-and-white concoction with cute button eyes and a big red mouth. It looked vaguely like a dog and, in keeping with its persona as a TV spokesdog, carried a large microphone in one paw. Launched in TV campaigns in August 1999, the

Sock Puppet raced around in a delivery van, explaining that Pets.com delivered "because Pets can't drive."

Within a year, propelled by off-tune singing and vaudeville-like one-liners, the creation had "crossed over," in the jargon of the marketing business, from a fiction of advertising to a reality of pop culture. "Not since Kermit and Kukla (Fran and Ollie's friend) has a puppet been so popular," wrote The New York Times.[21] The Wall Street Journal enthused that the Sock Puppet had been "thrust . . . into the international arena." Within a few months, even the magical kingdom of Disney, attracted by all the hoopla, saw magic in the Sock Puppet and made an investment of undisclosed size in Pets.com through its Internet arm, Go.com.[22]

The Sock Puppet was ubiquitous. During its first (and last) year as a corporate icon, the Sock Puppet starred in some ten commercials and appeared on most of television's talk shows. For a cost estimated at $200,000, it became a thirty-six-foot balloon and floated down Broadway as a star of the 1999 Macy's Thanksgiving Day Parade. And its TV career peaked with one $2 million spot that aired during the 2000 Super Bowl. The Sock Puppet was getting thousands of requests each month to appear in person at weddings and graduations. Responding to popular demand, Pets.com CEO Wainwright and her marketing people devoted weeks during the summer of 1999 to creating a six-page biography for the puppet, and Wainwright herself began issuing silly-sounding statements about the puppet's life and habits.

Pushed by the Sock Puppet, Pets.com skyrocketed in the popular consciousness. The company credited the puppet with moving its customer base from 15,000 to somewhere around 300,000. While revenue in the two fiscal quarters prior to the puppet's 1999 birth had been a scant $600,000, revenue in the puppet-propelled two quarters following the advertising launch rose a miraculous 2,100 percent, reaching $13 million, the company said.[23] By the spring of 2000, Pets.com was among the top five online retailers, according to a PCData online survey. Buoyed by this wave of consumer fanaticism, Wainwright signed a national licensing deal for Sock Puppet toys and apparel with the same man who had engineered nine-figure T-shirt

and tchotchke sales for Taco Bell's bilingual Chihuahua. Wainwright was hoping for a small percentage of some $50 million in projected sales. Wainwright gushed, "This is a company's dream."[24]

With no dissenters, Pets.com was declared the hands-down gold medal winner of the great 2000 "branding" competition. It had created and sustained a universally recognized and loved character. It had established a brand personality that resonated with pet lovers and non–pet lovers alike.

The only problem was that Pets.com, despite its great celebrity, was going out of business rapidly. And in the process, it was proving beyond any lingering doubt that branding without a workable business plan is one of the most futile and misguided exercises the business world will ever see.

While Pets.com was "building the brand" and attracting eyeballs, it also was losing phenomenal amounts of money. In its first fiscal year—seven months of operations from February through September 1999—it generated operating losses of more than $20 million on revenues of only $619,000. A brief look at the financials shows that Pets.com was selling merchandise for roughly one-third what it cost the company to buy the same goods, meaning Pets.com lost money on virtually every sale without counting any other expenses at all. Then, to make things orders of magnitude worse, it spent $11.8 million on marketing—an amount more than nineteen times its total revenue.[25]

For the same period in the following year, the numbers were much bigger but the story was essentially the same. Although revenue went up nearly forty-two-fold, the cost of goods sold still exceeded the selling price by some 27 percent, producing a loss again on virtually every sale. Marketing costs, meanwhile, zoomed to $60.7 million, more than twice total revenue.

In enthusiastically endorsing the need for all businesses, including Internet businesses, to focus on and produce profits, Frederick E. Davis, a leading technology journalist and consultant, once said, "The old joke is no joke: You can't lose money on every customer and make it back on volume."[26] But what Pets.com had done, essentially, was live out the old joke.

You Can't Make It Up on Volume

Even though the numbers are as dismal as numbers can get, the disaster of Pets.com is so fundamental that it's hard for onlookers to comprehend using numbers alone. Pets.com was not just a failure of execution, it was a monumental failure of thinking—a failure that could only be achieved by ignoring the fundamental idea that profit always matters. The problem, according to many analysts and reporters, was that Pets.com had failed from the outset to calculate the high shipping costs it would bear to deliver heavy, low-margin items like pet food cans and kitty litter bags. To make money on selling and delivering such low-cost staples, the Web site would have had to charge a premium over retail store prices; instead it threw discounts at its customers. It was hoping to build a customer list and generate sales of lighter, higher-margin items like leashes and toys, but those never materialized. So the more successful its branding effort, the more money it lost.

Throughout its active corporate life, Pets.com outspent its rivals two to one on advertising, arguably created at least the beginning of a new brand, and put the Sock Puppet on the map as one of America's favorite corporate icons. But this exceptionally successful advertising exercise produced one of the shortest-lived public companies on record—268 days, to be precise, from closing its initial public offering to closing its doors.

The demise of Pets.com on November 7, 2000, marked the waste of more than $300 million in investment capital—the $200 million it had raised in public and private markets plus the $110 million that had capitalized Petstore.com, which Pets.com acquired in an all-stock deal in the summer of 2000.[27, 28]

In the end, Pets.com's most expensive asset, the Sock Puppet, product of tens of millions in advertising expenditures, was sold by the bankrupt e-tailer for a paltry $125,000.[29] The charming puppet had taught the world a critical commercial lesson: When you build a brand that makes no money, what you get in return is nothing.

The Right Metrics at Federal Express

Coincidentally, the $300 million-plus that was invested in Pets.com, adjusted for inflation, is roughly equivalent to the $90 million that Fred Smith had to raise to launch Federal Express Corporation some thirty years earlier. There, however, any similarity between the two ventures ends.

The lesson to be learned from FedEx's beginnings is not the story of a heroic entrepreneur, not even the story of a new idea. Rather, if you can separate out the ever present elements of luck and timing over which no businessperson exercises much control, the start-up of Federal Express is the story of a man who found an emerging industry, identified it as something he wanted to do, and then created and executed a plan to make it profitable as quickly as possible. If he and his management team hadn't focused on reaching the necessary critical mass for profitability, today's FedEx undoubtedly wouldn't exist. Because even with his unusually elaborate planning and manic drive, Smith just barely made it.

Christopher Lovelock wrote the authoritative case studies of Federal Express as a Harvard Business School professor in the 1970s and 1980s. Years later, while teaching at Yale's School of Management, Lovelock recalled that Federal Express was the largest start-up in U.S. history when Smith incorporated it in 1971. "The problem was that you had to start out fairly large. You couldn't start with two aircraft and work your way up. It had to start out as a national operation," Lovelock said.[30]

Smith, heir to the multimillion-dollar fortune created by the Dixie Greyhound Bus Lines and a chain of hamburger joints called the Toddle House,[31] had been nursing an idea for quite some time. In 1965, he had written an economics term paper about it as a Yale undergraduate. At the time, most air freight in the U.S. was being shipped in the bellies of passenger aircraft. Smith, whose family bus business had been one method of getting small packages from town to town, believed passenger airline route systems didn't serve the needs of air freight very well. Packages, he proposed, needed an airline of their own with routes and schedules tailored to freight, not people. And a

package airline needed to work fast to move shipments that were required immediately. "The original concept for FedEx was built around moving very high-priority parts for the electronic and medical industries," Smith said in a later interview.[32] It has become legendary that Smith got a barely passing C on the paper, along with a mildly disparaging note from his professor about the idea's being unfeasible.[33] But the truth is that the idea was not exactly novel in the way most people now think it was.

The original hub-and-spokes concept of the FedEx distribution system resulted from "borrowing a concept developed by United Parcel Service," one Harvard Business School case stated.[34] In fact, the "United" in the UPS name stands for the idea of sorting packages at a central point and consolidating or uniting in a single delivery vehicle all the items destined for a particular neighborhood. When it was first put into practice by UPS in the teens of the twentieth century, the hub-and-spokes system vastly increased the efficiency with which both manpower and vehicles were used.[35]

The real power behind Smith's approach was the way he covered the fundamental bases on his way to raising more start-up capital than anyone had ever raised before. It didn't hurt that he was rich and could inspire confidence by putting up his entire net worth and then investing another $8 million into the enterprise from the family corporation that he virtually controlled.[36] But what made the start-up possible was his disciplined approach to researching the market for overnight air freight, validating his financial assumptions, and, finally, establishing a defensible business plan for achieving profitability.

Smith began the serious pursuit of his goal by hiring two independent consulting firms, one a nationally known management consultant, A. T. Kearney, and the other a specialist in aviation management. Smith asked them both to assess the feasibility of his proposed new business[37] and he paid them $75,000 each for their reports. The consultants confirmed what Smith had believed: only 10 percent of commercial airliners were operating after 10 P.M., which made the passenger airlines useless to companies that wanted packages picked up in the afternoon and delivered the next day. The consultants also found that while 60 percent of all airline traffic moved among the

nation's twenty-five biggest cities, "over 80 percent of small, urgent shipments originated or terminated outside the 25 top markets."[38] Furthermore, the entire $700 million–plus market for air shipping high-priority, small packages to their destinations in two days or less was growing at roughly 20 percent each year—an impressive rate.[39]

The consultants concluded that Smith's fledgling Federal Express could fill the gap created by the total lack of overnight delivery service between more than 100 big city airports. And if he could capture less than 1 percent of the nation's air freight business, they said, he could make money at it.

The plan said Smith would need less than $16 million in start-up capital and "could expect to be generating earnings within six to twelve months after inaugurating the package service." Breakeven would come when annual volume hit 1.6 million packages a year—or an average of about 6,200 packages every working night.[40]

Once the consulting studies were done, Smith promptly hired the best of the consultants and put together the detailed business plan for his venture. The amount he ultimately raised was roughly $90 million, with $40 million coming from six major corporate investors and another $40 million coming from bank loans to finance the purchase of small jet aircraft.[41] It should go without saying, but it is apparently necessary to point out, that in the world of the 1970s, in sharp contrast to the world of the 1990s, Smith never would have raised a dime without demonstrating that profits would appear before the investment capital disappeared.

As it turned out, Smith's business plan, like virtually every other start-up business plan ever devised, was optimistic by more than half. But Smith's focus and fanatical devotion to his plan got the job done. A conversation with a prospective employee in the early days of Federal Express vividly depicts the founding spirit of FedEx.

"Why do you want to work for me?" Smith asked the applicant, an aircraft expert who would rise to a senior position at FedEx.

"I like airplanes," the man answered.

"Hell," Smith responded, "don't you want to make some money? I like airplanes, too, but I'd like to make some money, too."[42]

On April 17, 1973, Federal Express went into operation with four-

teen little French Falcon jets flying out of Memphis Municipal Airport. "On that night, Federal Express delivered 186 packages to 25 U.S. cities—from Rochester, N.Y. to Miami, Florida," according to the official corporate history. As one can imagine, the losses that night were heavy, and the company continued to lose money for twenty-six months.

Near the end of that start-up period, Federal Express, like many new ventures before and since, ran out money. A Harvard Business School study called FedEx "technically bankrupt," adding, "While top management worked desperately to renegotiate loans, couriers deposited their watches as security when obtaining gas for company trucks, the president sold his personal aircraft, and base personnel hid the Falcons to keep sheriffs from serving attachment papers and chaining the little jets to the ramps."[43]

But along the way, the company moved frenetically toward its carefully planned goals, hoarded whatever cash it could, got the maximum impact from a modest $150,000 advertising campaign, and pushed volume to an average of 11,000 packages per night by 1975, when it passed the breakeven point in midyear.

When three decades had passed since FedEx's founding and Fred Smith revealed his "secrets" to an entrepreneurs conference in the Caribbean, he told them his metrics for success included three main measures: revenue, expenses, and profits. With those firmly in mind, it is instructive to review the metrics of Federal Express's first five years:

FEDERAL EXPRESS OPERATING RESULTS—FIRST FIVE YEARS

Fiscal Year Ending May 31

	1974	1975	1976	1977	1978	Five-Year Average Growth
Operating Revenue	$17,292	$43,489	$75,055	$109,210	$160,301	
Percent change		151.5%	72.6%	45.5%	46.8%	79.09%
Operating Expenses	$26,137	$47,613	$65,210	$95,608	$134,024	
Percent change		82.2%	37.0%	46.6%	40.2%	51.48%
Pre-tax income/(loss)	$(8,845)	$(4,124)	$9,845	$13,602	$26,277	
Percent change		53.4%	338.7%	38.2%	93.2%	130.86%

Source: "Federal Express Corporate Financial Summary, 1974–78" as presented in "Federal Express: Customer Service Department (A)," a case prepared by Penny Pittman Merliss, research assistant, under the direction of Associate Professor Christopher H. Lovelock, Harvard Business School, 1980; revised January 1983, page 17.

On average, the metrics that count for every business moved in exactly the right directions during the very tight launch of one of the world's most successful companies. Revenue rose nearly 80 percent per year on average; while expenses, with the exception of one year only, rose at a much slower pace. As a result, the first-year loss was cut in half by the second year, and profits, on average, more than doubled each year.

So profits are not the creation of an uncreative mind, nor are they an aspirational goal, like human enlightenment, to be achieved only in some dim and distant future. Profits, in fact, are both the product and progenitor of all corporate creativity. And, according to this self-evident plank of The Box, they have to be achieved as quickly as possible or the possibility of achieving them goes away forever.

If you ever again face an era when someone seriously asks, "Do profits matter?" just remember this: By disregarding profit, Pets.com took roughly $300 million and turned it into nothing—no jobs, no assets, no productivity, zero. By executing a profit-focused business plan, Fred Smith took roughly the same amount of capital and turned it into $16.4 billion in market capitalization and more than 200,000 jobs. Which path makes more sense? Please FedEx all arguments to me.

HOW TO BUILD THE BOX

THE SECOND PLANK

1. Always judge a business first by its true revenues, expenses, and profits. Measured appropriately, these are the only meaningful metrics.
2. When starting anything new, always create profits as quickly as possible.
3. When managing any ongoing business, always focus on increasing profits.
4. Investing in something new and losing money at first are good business tactics only if there is a tight business plan that produces profits within a defined time span.

The Money Box: Cash Is Everything

If you don't manage your cash, you won't be managing anything for long.

Lessin's Lesson: Never Run Out of Cash

Now set aside the primary importance of profit. Instead, think about this: Profit is theoretically of no concern whatsoever to a business so long as the business has access to an infinite supply of cash.

Unfortunately, as a practical matter, no bottomless money wells have been discovered. That's the only real reason profit is paramount—it is the sole inexhaustible supply of cash known to business.

Sometimes, as in the nineties' technology boom, it may appear that the cash well has no bottom, but history (both modern and ancient) teaches that every supply of money has an end. This is even more immediately apparent in bad times—during economic downturns, when raising money from the usual sources becomes impossible; when it's hard to find venture capital, difficult to underwrite a public stock offering, and the banks just won't lend. Such bad times, however, can teach good lessons. Even to legends and superstars.

The distinct impression created by the majority of his press clippings is that Robert H. Lessin has led a charmed financial life, that he has had one of those career paths that go nowhere but up. He graduated magna cum laude from Harvard in 1977; earned a Harvard Business School M.B.A the following year; became the youngest partner in Morgan Stanley's history in 1987 when he was barely into his thirties;

was made vice chairman of Morgan's Investment Banking Operating Committee in 1990, and vice chairman and head of investment banking at Smith Barney in 1993. He even bounced back from a stroke in 1994 and went on to be heralded as a wildly successful technology venture capitalist. It is emblematic of his wealth and preeminence in the world of technology and money that inside the high-tech, 100,000-square-foot Harvard computer science building named for Bill Gates's and Steve Ballmer's mothers—the Maxwell Dworkin Building—the largest interior space, a multimedia meeting room, is named after Lessin and his wife.

But in 1998, Lessin left the world of big-time investment banking to become chairman of Wit Capital, a tiny Internet stock-trading pioneer born from the initial public offering of a New York microbrewery.[1] At Wit, Lessin acquired investment banker SoundView Technology Group and became chairman and CEO of the merged Wit SoundView Group, Inc. Then, after all that uphill cruising, things got very bumpy for Lessin. As 2000 turned to 2001, Wit's retail brokerage business shuttered as one more failed Internet experiment. He then had to watch SoundView's numbers go hundreds of millions of dollars into the red before giving up his top job with the firm and virtually disappearing from the headlines.[2] Relatively early in these hard times, after seeing his firm's NASDAQ-listed stock slide from a high of $38 to less than $3 a share, Lessin offered this sobering advice in early 2001, before anyone had seen the bottom of the market's downhill ride:

"When CEOs ask, 'What's the secret to venture capital?' I say, 'Not running out of money.' Don't get cute with capital. Presume that you'll never raise another dime, and run your business accordingly."[3] This is Lessin's Lesson. In a very important sense, it is the basis of all cash flow management.

Seated in the sunny public space of the Sony Building in New York in the spring of 2002, Bob Lessin seems none the worse for wear. There's a touch of gray in his brown hair, but there's still something of the wunderkind about him. He has on his trademark khakis and open-necked shirt, bringing a bit of Silicon Valley fashion to Madison Avenue.

Lessin's main business now is managing a $270 million venture fund, Dawntreader II, that specializes in early-stage tech companies.[4]

But his message is universally applicable to all business. "Anyone who's been in the capital markets—and I've been in the capital markets for a quarter of a century—understands that capital markets shut down and, when they shut down, it's binary," he says, meaning there's no middle way, it's either on or off, just like binary computer code. "Anyone who bets on the assumption that there will be . . . additional capital as part of their growth strategy is brain-dead."[5]

Lessin followed his own advice. Despite the disasters that rocked Wit SoundView from its inception in the late nineties, forcing the shutdown of its online brokerage business and the elimination of the Wit name, the company still entered 2002 with $150 million in cash,[6] a hoard that has kept SoundView alive, if not exactly well, through 2002, despite some $385 million in cumulative losses.[7]

Whether your company's ultimate source of emergency cash is a private venture capital fund or public junk bonds or short-term commercial paper or a new stock offering or your personal MasterCard, running out of cash invariably brings on very ugly outcomes. In the worst cases, of course, your company or division or department is either shut down or taken away from you. But even in the best cases, it generally means your share of the company goes down drastically and your ability to manage your own fate goes away in exchange for the cash to stay alive.

The people left in charge, of course, will be whomever you had to go to for the cash you needed to survive. If you have to get more equity capital from new investors, they will drive a very hard bargain and take the lion's share of your venture's equity. If you have to go to bankers or creditors to renegotiate loans and outstanding bills, they, too, may wind up owning big chunks of your company, restricting your ability to make management decisions and, ultimately, calling the shots. If you run a division or a department and are forced to go to your parent company or your boss for unanticipated cash needs, you will probably be fired.

Thinking inside the box is all about sticking to fundamentals, and next to profit, there is nothing more fundamental in The Box than cash. As any basic business course should quickly point out, profits all by themselves will not do the trick. The trick to surviving in busi-

ness is not merely to arrange things so that more money comes in than goes out. The real trick is to make sure that the money coming into an enterprise arrives in the right quantities and at the right times to make it possible to cover your bills on time. This means being able to cover all the necessary costs of operating the business, from payroll to rent to the phone bill to the price of that new factory. Making the timing work is not as easy as it sounds, and a lot of businesses, even big ones with long histories, have screwed it up seriously from time to time because they forgot this plank in The Box.

Cash flow problems can stem from all kinds of causes. Lack of profitability, of course, inevitably leads to terminal cash shortages, sooner or later, as we have seen. But a profitable company that is growing very fast is also a prime candidate for a cash crunch, as is any business with large investment needs, such as companies that must spend heavily on technology or machinery in order to do what they do. Particularly vulnerable to cash shortages are companies that have borrowed heavily in the past, perhaps during a time when credit was easy, and now face big loan payments during a time when credit suddenly has dried up.

Prior to the late 1980s, thinking about cash flow was merely good business. By 1987, it had become mandatory. That was the year the Financial Accounting Standards Board, which defines the rules of accounting in the United States, issued rule No. 95, requiring companies to include a "statement of cash flows" with their financials. By 1989, the Securities and Exchange Commission, which regulates the sale of stock and other corporate securities in the United States, had jumped on the bandwagon by issuing a detailed set of rules requiring companies to make sure that "management discussion and analysis" narratives—management's explanation of the numbers, required in the quarterly reports of public companies—also include a section describing current and future cash needs.[8]

The Cash Crunch That Ate Portugal

One of history's greatest cash shortages inspired (partly) one of the modern world's greatest novels, *Baltazar and Blimunda,* a tale of two

peasant lovers set in the squalor and splendor of eighteenth-century Portugal.[9] José Saramago, the Nobel-Prize-winning Portuguese writer, wraps his tale around the real-life historical figure of Dom João V, king of Portugal and ruler of its enormous New World possessions in South America. Dom João's 200-year-old story provides a classic example of cash flow mismanagement on a global scale, and his massive mistiming of revenue and expense proves conclusively that the problems inherent in managing cash are nothing new.

Dom João was obsessed with constructing a massive convent and palace in the graceless village of Mafra on a featureless plain northwest of Lisbon. In pursuit of his vision, beginning in 1717, João pressed virtually the entire working population of Portugal into service. To please the king, some 40,000 peasants labored for decades to build the palatial stone edifice, occupying some 650,000 square feet. Portugal, with its powerful navy, was then one of the world's great colonial powers. In the end, however, the cash outlays for the *convento* at Mafra outstripped even the vast income pouring in from Brazil, and the Portuguese royal treasury was exhausted.

The result of Dom João's cash crisis, according to a number of historians, was nothing less than the beginning of the decline of the Portuguese empire, a deterioration that persisted throughout the rest of the century. You can still tour the vast monument that cost Dom João V all his available cash, and while waiting in line for your ticket, you can view a wonderful portrait of the porcine, opulent sovereign. For keeping one alert about cash, a visit to Dom João's Mafra is probably the moral equivalent of a semester of hard study at Wharton.

How John F. McDonnell
Wound Up Managing Nothing

It's hard to beat the drama of a cash flow crisis that ate a kingdom, but flashing forward a couple of centuries brings us to the 1990s and a more instructive cash crunch that took a healthy bite out of the Pentagon and ended the reign of one of America's wealthy industrial families. This cash crisis involved a higher-tech endeavor than stone-

masonry, and it also involved numerous violations of the rules of cash management and management in general. But most arresting is the fact that one company's very public failures provided a rare opportunity to attend a government-sponsored course on cash management—an open classroom that can be particularly helpful for all managers.

McDonnell Douglas, the giant aircraft company that resulted from the 1967 merger of McDonnell Aircraft and Douglas Aircraft, entered the last decade of the last century with a pair of glorious histories behind it. McDonnell, in addition to being the builder of America's first manned spacecraft, was the creator of the world's most successful flying weapon, the F-4 Phantom II fighter jet. Since its introduction in 1958, the F-4 has seen service in all American wars and skirmishes from Vietnam to Desert Storm, creating the era of the supersonic fighter and delivering vast wealth to McDonnell in the process. Douglas, beginning with the venerable DC-2 in the 1930s, launched the succession of passenger aircraft that served to build the business of military transport and commercial aviation in America and the world.[10] Feeding at the bottomless trough of military spending during the Cold War, McDonnell Douglas grew fat and happy and became the U.S. armed services' biggest supplier.[11]

As McDonnell Douglas entered the 1990s, its profits, as portrayed on the corporate financial statement, still appeared very healthy. The company reported earnings of $350 million in 1988, $250 million in 1989, and $306 million in 1990.[12] But numerous factors were creating cracks in the company's financial foundation. For example, 1990's profit would have been a $105 million loss without a one-time gain not connected with operations.[13] So despite appearances, the company was in the midst of a steep three-year downturn.

The not-very-pretty picture featured a rapidly slowing economy that was falling into full-fledged recession. This was combined with heavy borrowing and spending on developing new planes and massive, multibillion-dollar cost overruns on fixed-price military projects for which McDonnell Douglas's contracts required it to eat any overruns. Making matters worse, these problems coincided with the definitive end of the Cold War and a brand new atmosphere in Congress

that was suddenly hostile to many defense programs and excessive military spending. The Berlin Wall had come down in 1989. The Soviet Union was in the process of falling to pieces, literally, and would cease to exist within a couple of years.

Considering all these political and economic factors, the Senate Armed Services Committee voted in 1990 to make an "unprecedented $18 billion cut in the defense budget."[14] The bottomless trough of Pentagon spending suddenly had developed a bottom. But unfortunately, not only was McDonnell Douglas incapable of thinking inside The Box when it came to cash, it had never learned Lessin's Lesson and was not prepared for this day.

In January 1991, *Forbes* chided McDonnell Douglas, saying its 1990 earnings were "a paper entry that may never be turned into cash."[15] The company's debt at that moment was $3 billion, and it was estimated that McDonnell Douglas would need at least another billion in cash just to get through the year. Cash flow for the year past, *Forbes* pointed out, was tens of millions in the red despite earnings supposedly being hundreds of millions in the black. To top it off, all three of McDonnell Douglas's most important new airplane programs were being curtailed by the defense cutbacks.[16] And the IRS was threatening to bill McDonnell Douglas for some $500 million in back taxes dating from the early 1980s.[17]

As time would tell, things were actually far worse than they appeared because the company was illegally hiding about $1 billion in losses on another military program, a violation that was to earn McDonnell Douglas a stern reprimand and a fine from the Securities and Exchange Commission in 1996. (Presaging the Enron disaster that was still some five years in the future, and proving once more that there is nothing new under the economic sun, *The New York Times* commented that the SEC's investigation of McDonnell Douglas showed the company had seriously exaggerated its profits, proving "how a determined management can put out the figures it wants" no matter what really happened.)[18]

Moved, at last, by the crunch it was in, McDonnell Douglas took a unique approach to cash management—an approach that would occur only to a defense contractor. It secretly asked the Pentagon for a whole

host of cash-saving breaks, including a billion-dollar "advance."[19] In a letter to an undersecretary of Defense on January 24, 1991, McDonnell Douglas Chairman and CEO John McDonnell wrote that "our near-term cash requirements remain very tight" and added that the company was finding "borrowing from traditional sources very difficult."[20]

McDonnell's request, later withdrawn when the Pentagon started asking the company about cost-saving measures, was made at a most inopportune moment. It followed by only two weeks the news that then-Defense Secretary Dick Cheney had signed the single largest contract cancellation in military history, telling McDonnell Douglas and defense contractor General Dynamics that their $4.78 billion project to develop the A-12 stealth jet for the Navy and Marines was being terminated because they were over budget (the government had spent $3 billion on the A-12 and had yet to see a single plane), a year behind schedule, and out of ideas to fix things. Cheney also told the companies that they jointly owed the government $1.35 billion for work that had never been approved, adding almost $700 million to McDonnell Douglas's cash problems.[21] (The two companies sued to keep the money. A decade later, in the summer of 2001, the Pentagon ultimately prevailed in court.)[22]

So with all these problems multiplying, the Pentagon and the U.S. Congress began to fear the imminent bankruptcy and collapse of America's biggest weapons builder.[23] McDonnell Douglas was losing money on all its operations—both military and civilian projects—and clearly lacked the cash to run its shop, let alone repay the Defense Department for the A-12 debacle or pay its back taxes. This rolling cash-management disaster came to a head on October 3, 1991, at 10:30 A.M., in Room 2123 of the Rayburn House Office Building in Washington, D.C. This was the moment when the U.S. House of Representatives subcommittee charged with overseeing government spending opened its inquiry into the problems at McDonnell Douglas. The subcommittee chairman, Michigan Democrat John Dingell, set the tone for the proceedings in his opening statement, saying, "Dismal mismanagement is the major cause of McDonnell Douglas's problems." Despite numerous invitations, no company representative was there and no one rose to contradict Dingell's assessment.

The hearings both represented and revealed one of the more amazing turnabouts in U.S. corporate history. The Pentagon, frequently derided for buying $642 toilet seats (from McDonnell Douglas, actually) and not generally known as the home of frugal and fastidious management, had written a letter to McDonnell Douglas suggesting some prudent actions the aircraft company could take to manage its serious cash problems.

The letter was dispatched on March 20, 1991, from Donald J. Yockey, a former Rockwell executive[24] who was then the undersecretary of Defense in charge of buying weapons systems, to McDonnell CEO John McDonnell. "I am concerned," Yockey wrote, "that McDonnell Douglas Corporation has not yet demonstrated it has initiated those difficult but critical austerity measures necessary to overcome very serious cash-flow problems."[25] Commenting on the Yockey letter, an unnamed defense "official" later told the authoritative trade magazine *Aviation Week & Space Technology* that the Defense Department was instructing McDonnell Douglas "how to tighten its belt and run the company."[26]

Yockey's letter came to light during the congressional hearings on McDonnell Douglas, in an exchange between Jim Slattery, then a Democratic congressman from Kansas, and Eleanor Spector, the Defense Department's procurement director. Slattery, paraphrasing Yockey's letter, said, "In that letter, he suggested that John McDonnell take a number of cost and cash outlay reductions" in virtually every area of the business, from construction to salaries. The Defense Department's Spector told the congressman that all the issues cited by Yockey were seen as important for McDonnell Douglas to address. "Mr. Yockey sent this letter to them and it seems to have had some effect," Spector said.

As it turned out, despite the Pentagon's miserable record for managing its own (make that *your* own) cash, the Defense Department letter was on target about how to manage McDonnell Douglas's cash. And Undersecretary Yockey's letter to the company remains one of the better textbooks of cash management.

Yockey understood something that apparently had eluded McDonnell Douglas's senior management: Cash management, unlike developing stealth bombers, isn't rocket science, and there are only a

few things one can do to manage cash in a crisis. Given the ten-figure magnitude of McDonnell Douglas's problem, it was a good idea to try them all. (Asking your biggest customer for a $1 billion advance, by the way, was not on Yockey's list, although it was certainly worth the try that McDonnell Douglas gave it.)

As Yockey evidently understood, the realistic possibilities open to McDonnell Douglas were exactly the same actions open to any company. Those possibilities can be summed up by the following list:

Things That Can Be Done About Cash Shortages

1. Borrow money or sell stock or find some similar new source of capital.

2. Speed up collecting money that's owed to the company (known as "reducing receivables," in the language of the accounting types).

3. Slow down paying bills that the company owes (increase payables).

4. Postpone spending on capital projects, like new buildings and equipment.

5. Cut everyday operating expenses (to the bone).

6. Sell nonessential assets.

If managers were more scrupulous about reviewing this list on a regular basis, a lot of cash problems would be avoided. By the time there's a cash crisis, it's usually too late to manage cash.

Don't Just Sit There, Do Everything

The Defense Department prudently suggested to its troubled, largest vendor that everything on the list *should* be done. The Yockey letter detailed a multitude of measures designed to reduce the bleeding of cash. Essentially, it was the same list that every company must confront when trying to conserve cash:

BORROWING MONEY McDonnell Douglas had already tried to borrow more money and its banks had said no. CEO McDonnell had

admitted as much in his letter asking Defense for an advance. And the middle of a recession, on the heels of a major cutback in defense spending, with the company in a severe cash crisis, while illegally hiding a billion-dollar loss from shareholders, was not a prime time to be selling more shares of a defense stock to the public. So option number one was out.

SPEEDING UP COLLECTIONS FROM CUSTOMERS While this is generally a good idea, it didn't look feasible for McDonnell Douglas, either. The company had tried and failed with that ploy when it asked the Pentagon for a $1 billion advance. Revenue from new products and programs is always a possible solution for a cash crisis, and McDonnell Douglas entertained some hope that its newest wide-body passenger jet, the MD-11, would rescue the company. But the orders never materialized in sufficient numbers to make the plane a winner for McDonnell Douglas. More efficient, competitive planes from Boeing and Airbus combined with the weak economy to keep the MD-11 in the red.[27]

PAYING THE BILLS SLOWLY The gentle art of borrowing from your suppliers is always available to every business, and McDonnell Douglas, following the receipt of Yockey's advice, pushed this ploy about as far as possible, withholding $400 million that was owed to General Dynamics, General Electric, and Pratt and Whitney.[28] While this definitely improved McDonnell Douglas's cash position, using vendors as a bank of last resort is almost always risky. Taking too long to pay suppliers means taking the chance that they will just cut you off. After all, why should they incur cash flow problems of their own just for the privilege of having you as a customer?

CUTTING CAPITAL SPENDING Yockey strongly suggested halting new construction and renting or leasing needed equipment instead of buying it. He also recommended "postponing elective maintenance." Good ideas for any cash-strapped enterprise.

REDUCING EXPENSES When it came to cutting operating expenses, Yockey had a raft of ideas, many of them affecting John McDonnell

and the folks who ran the company. At a minimum, he suggested halting executive bonuses and all raises, instituting temporary salary cuts, and ordering a hiring freeze. He also thought the company could curtail travel and get rid of some of its fleet of executive aircraft. Advertising and marketing should be cut, as well, Yockey believed. And finally, he offered the idea that McDonnell Douglas might reduce the amount of money it paid to lobbyists to influence the Congress, the White House, and presumably, Yockey himself.

SELLING ASSETS Yockey also urged the company to sell certain divisions and subsidiaries in order to raise cash and reduce debt. And he pressed forward the notion that McDonnell Douglas ought to sell some of its real estate and then lease back the buildings as a way of generating immediate cash.

One indicator of McDonnell Douglas's response to Yockey's list can be found in its head-count records. While the company's employment actually remained around 120,000 through 1990, it began to drop in 1991 and had been cut in half by 1995.[29] Asset sales were numerous. Cash flow improved. But in a very important sense, McDonnell Douglas never really recovered fully, and John McDonnell, son of the company's founder, lived out the subtitle of this chapter: He failed to manage his cash, and soon enough, he wasn't managing anything at all (except the family foundation).

It is worth noting that on the late fall day in Washington in 1991 when the U.S. Congress decided to investigate McDonnell Douglas's cash position, Congressman Slattery was wondering if the Pentagon and the Congress were being lied to. Pursuing this, he asked the Pentagon's procurement chief, Eleanor Spector, a key question: "Are we dealing with a corporation that is fundamentally honest?"

"Yes, we are," Spector replied. But only a moment later, as Slattery bore down on a particular program and asked again if McDonnell Douglas "always told the truth" about it, Spector altered her response a little. "Were they lying or were they lying to themselves is really the question," she said. The evidence is that McDonnell Douglas's managers, like many corporate hierarchies before and since, lied to them-

selves, and this signal mistake led them, in turn, to lie to others, as well. This is extremely dangerous behavior because, as history—including the history of McDonnell Douglas—consistently shows, you can make up any story you want about profits, but you can't make up cash.

The United States simply could not afford to let its biggest military supplier go bankrupt. So thanks largely to the good graces and deep pockets of the Pentagon, McDonnell Douglas survived, at least until 1997, when it was gobbled up by its only remaining domestic competitor in commercial aviation, Boeing. In his farewell speech just before the Boeing deal was approved, John McDonnell seemed to accept that his company was in eclipse and could not have made it on its own. He acknowledged that the Douglas side of his company had lost the edge in commercial aviation when Boeing had launched the commercial jet age in 1957, four decades earlier. As for the McDonnell side—the military side—McDonnell added, "The fact is that we have not won a single competition for design and development of an all-new fighter aircraft since the F-15, more than 25 years ago. That is a disturbing shortcoming in an era of rapid consolidation within the defense industry."[30]

Boeing had a tough time swallowing McDonnell Douglas's problems. The year of the acquisition, its normally healthy 4 percent margins shrank to 1.4 percent amid production problems and fines from the Federal Aviation Administration. Now its CEO, Philip Condit, is turning away from new jets and wants to transform the company into a seller of services.[31] What remains of McDonnell Douglas is its proud history in the early days of aviation and space exploration, and its recent service to the nation as an open class on the necessity of truthful self-assessment and stringent cash management.

Getting Used to It: A Lack of Truth, a Lack of Cash

Before and since McDonnell Douglas, thousands of celebrated corporate cash crashes have been fueled by artificially inflated earnings (i.e., lies), miserable management, atrocious planning, and happen-

stance, all of which the cash-management plank of The Box is designed to avoid. But though the beginning of the twenty-first century has produced a bumper crop of cash disasters far bigger and more dramatic, none teaches any new lessons—largely because there are no new lessons to be learned in this fundamental area of management practice.

The most famous recent debacle, hands down, has been Enron Corp., where lying about profits was so widespread, so blatant, and so egregious that the ultimate cash crash, which forced Enron into bankruptcy in December 2001, is still creating ripples throughout the world's economic establishment. Enron's energy-trading business depended on the company's credibility and its ability to borrow. Both went away quickly when the outfit's self-dealing and debt-concealing ways were finally revealed. With the cash gone, Enron collapsed like the cheap valise it was. Its initial bankruptcy filing listed $13.2 billion in debts and $24.8 billion in assets, but there was a troubling footnote to the debts: "This amount does not reflect off-balance sheet and contingent obligations."[32] Or, in other words, who knows what this company's liabilities really are? Not even the multiple congressional committees and the raft of lawyers and accountants assigned to the Enron mess are likely ever to figure it out.

Maintaining the fiction of Enron as a solvent, growing, and hugely profitable concern required a vast conspiracy of (knowing and unknowing) corporate officers and directors, public accountants, Wall Street research analysts, securities regulators, bankers, lawyers, and politicians. But precisely because the conspiracy was so vast and the criminality so abundant, there's not much for the rest of us to learn about cash management from Enron. It just reinforces the lessons of both Lessin and McDonnell Douglas—don't lie (to yourself, at least) about profits and don't plan on being rescued by new financing, because it might not materialize.

THE THIRD PLANK

1. Profits alone are not enough to preserve a company. Cash must be managed so there's enough on hand to meet a company's bills.
2. Even post-Enron accounting rules will let managers lie to themselves (and others) about profits. A steady focus on cash will help resist the temptation to believe the lies.
3. Cash management is not rocket science. The list of things that can be done is limited. Review this list on a regular basis.
4. The middle of a cash crisis is too late to manage cash.

CHAPTER 4

The Bottom-Line Box: Knowing What Can Be Controlled and What Can't

It is far better (and more certain) to cut expenses than to pray for sales.

The Importance of Being Humble

At the end of the day, there are only two components to any business: revenues and expenses. American business lately has developed the notion of the mythical, all-knowing, all-powerful CEO who can handle anything and is always in control of every aspect of a business. But real-life managers must deal with the humbling fact that revenues cannot be completely controlled; only expenses generally can be. This plank in The Box, then, is about managing expenses as if revenue were about to go out of style (or, in the case of start-ups and new divisions, as if it were not expected to come into style anytime soon).

Revenues are controlled partly by management's efforts, but they are also subject to luck, the will of God, the vagaries of the marketplace (including the competition's crazy discounting policies), the even greater vagaries of the political economy in which we live (including recessions, depressions, wars, and elections), the changing appetites of customers, and a bunch of other wildly uncontrollable elements. Expenses, on the other hand, while subject to variations imposed by outside forces (especially in the case of raw materials and other commodities), are controlled by management to a much greater extent.

Future Revenues Are Docudrama;
Future Expenses Are Reality

In any future-looking business plan, the projected revenues are usually viewed by knowledgeable and disinterested bystanders as more or less completely speculative—a guess, in fact, no matter how good a one. It is certainly true that the longer a company has been on the receiving end of a steadily growing stream of revenue, the more entitled management is to expect the good times to continue to roll. Nevertheless, the correct attitude concerning revenue projections is: "Maybe those revenues will be produced; maybe not. Maybe it will rain tomorrow; maybe it won't." The expenses in the same business plan, on the other hand, will be viewed by the self-same spectators as pretty nearly the gospel truth. Absent some cataclysm, everyone will agree, it is much easier to predict what something will cost than it is to predict how many people will buy something at any given price in any quarter. More to the point, perhaps, it's easier to know how you will spend your own money than it is to know how your customers will spend theirs.

Throughout history, businesses with good, workable profit centers, reasonable cash-management procedures, and steady streams of revenue frequently have gotten themselves into going-out-of-business trouble by ignoring the plank in The Box that says expenses can be controlled and revenue can't. And it is equally true (maybe more true, actually) that start-up ventures with perfectly good plans repeatedly fail because the managers fail to realize this truth: The money being spent on salaries and rent will always get spent right on schedule, but the anticipated revenue from sales may not be as punctual.

Usually, when managers stop displaying sufficient interest in controlling expenses, it is because of a misguided belief that revenues will behave well no matter what. Generally, their failure to understand their own relative powerlessness over revenue becomes manifest in one of three ways: either they allow expenses to increase in anticipation of projected higher revenues (and call it "budgeting for growth"), or they let expenses overall grow faster than revenues (and call it "investing in the future"), or they fail to downsize their opera-

tions when sales fall off (and call it "preserving the business"). Any way it's sliced, these are all just direct routes to losing money and eroding margins, the surest ways on earth to ruin a business, no matter how big or well established it might seem to be.

Screaming Won't Make It So

Richard McGinn was the CEO of Lucent Technologies, a company with a blue-chip pedigree and nearly $29 billion in revenue. McGinn lost his job because he acted as if stridently ordering his sales force to produce more revenue was a workable business plan, when he should have been working to reduce costs.

Lucent, of course, is composed of the former research and equipment-making arms of AT&T, including the world-famous Bell Laboratories. Spun off in late 1996 as an independent public company, in the midst of a global boom in telecommunications (a boom, fueled by the Internet and deregulation, that turned out to be totally unsustainable), Lucent became a Wall Street darling.

McGinn, an AT&T employee since the late seventies, became a hero as his company racked up successive years of double-digit revenue increases, and he may even have believed it was his doing and not the natural by-product of the overheated telecom environment. As the global telecom crash began to unfold in 1999 and 2000, CEO McGinn refused to believe the party was over. Twice during 2000, Lucent had to reduce its financial projections. But instead of turning at last to something within his control, like expenses, McGinn stuck to his simple-minded strategy of just demanding sales.

Then, in mid-August 2000, with the end of Lucent's fiscal year only six weeks away, McGinn's top sales executive, Nina Aversano, told him it wasn't going to work anymore—that orders were drying up, major customers were cutting spending, and even the recently reduced sales projections for the quarter would be missed. McGinn "went ballistic," according to a member of Aversano's team who was on the conference call with the CEO, and sent his sales team into a frenzy of last-minute wheeling and dealing to make the numbers.[1]

The frenzy produced—or appeared to produce—what the boss had demanded: Lucent missed its last quarter sales goal by less than 2 percent, *The Wall Street Journal* reported. But the apparent revenue turned out to be a Potemkin village, more show than substance. As subsequent events demonstrated, Lucent had given lavish credits and discounts to pull sales into the quarter, thus stealing from the future to meet McGinn's demands in the present. *The Wall Street Journal* added, "It booked sales for goods that were shipped merely to distribution channels and not to real customers—'channel stuffing,' as it is called."[2] And it improperly booked some sales that never qualified as revenue.

When Lucent's North American sales chief, Aversano, another long-time AT&T star, added up the effects of all these tricks, she calculated that it meant Lucent would miss its newly issued goals for the following year—2001—by nearly 20 percent. On October 9, 2000, one week into Lucent's new 2001 fiscal year, Aversano told McGinn the bad news and accused him of setting "hopelessly optimistic" sales targets. Then she resigned. About two weeks later, McGinn was fired by the board.

A lot of the rich detail in this corporate debacle is available in the files of New Jersey's Middlesex County Courthouse, because Aversano filed a lawsuit alleging that she was forced to resign for telling the truth about Lucent's misstatements and mismanagement. Lucent and McGinn have denied the charges and are defending the suit. Whatever the truth of who said what to whom and when, the company's 2001 annual report contains more than enough sad detail to fully support the view that McGinn should have been fired much sooner.

As it turned out, Lucent's revenue for the year ending September 30, 2001, dropped 26 percent from the prior year. It was a global downturn that no amount of yelling in sales meetings could have solved. Instead, the management that replaced McGinn had to take drastic action to save the company, including two waves of restructuring involving selling assets, laying off a total of some 39,000 workers, eliminating some product lines, reducing capital spending, and reducing the cash tied up in inventory and receivables. All in all, by

the end of 2001, Lucent was on its way to lowering expenses by a total of some $4 billion a year, reducing working capital needs by some $2 billion, and eliminating nearly $1.2 billion in capital spending.[3]

The Lucent story (and many more like it) demonstrates that a manager's priority is to know what can be controlled and to control it as closely as possible. The corollary is to know what's beyond management control and never to pretend that it isn't. In short, managers can let the global economy alone, since it is quite beyond anyone's control. But management must watch expenses no matter how good revenue may be, or pretty soon, there won't be a business.

A Tale of Two Managements

For deeper insight into the real-life ramifications of this particular business rule, the world owes a debt to two management teams, one in America and one in England. Both approached exactly the same business at about the same time. The strategic goal for both was to make money selling groceries over the Internet. One failed, one succeeded. (See how fast you can tell one from the other.)

The progenitor of the biggest idea in online groceries was Louis H. Borders, one-half of the brother team that had turned a tiny college-town bookstore into an international behemoth rivaled only by Barnes & Noble. Louis and his brother had begun in 1971 with a single store on the quaint main drag of Ann Arbor, Michigan, in the middle of the University of Michigan campus. By 2002, Borders Group had grown to a business with 32,000 full- and part-time employees and stores all over the English-speaking world. Sales were at $3.4 billion, and the business was valued at around $2 billion.[4] The Borders brothers, who had sold out to Kmart in 1992 (which, in turn, sold the company to the public in 1995), were multimillionaires. Just as important, however, was the detail that Louis had made the chain of book and music superstores work by helping to perfect an artificial intelligence software package that could keep track of the vast number of items shelved in a typical superstore—150,000 to 200,000 (as opposed to the 40,000 items in a normal bookstore).[5] So Louis had some credi-

bility in Silicon Valley when he suggested that it would be a swell idea to create a highly automated Web grocery store serving the entire nation (and then the world), offering as many as a million different products.

One of the Silicon Valley outfits Louis Borders won over first was Benchmark Capital, then a relatively new venture group hunting for high-tech investments. It was Benchmark's star partner Bob Kagle, a career investment banker and something of a dot-com legend, who invested early in eBay, turning a few million of his partners' dollars into a few hundred million in one of the Web's very few lasting success stories. (Unlike virtually every other dot-com in history, eBay kept expenses low and margins high, and turned a profit early in its life—just like a real business!) It was Benchmark's David Beirne, a former technology-industry headhunter, who signed the firm up as the earliest backer of Border's e-grocery business.[6] Benchmark was in good (or, at least, good-looking) company in Webvan: Goldman Sachs, the most patrician of the Wall Street investment banks, and CBS were both part of the blue-chip backing.[7] And the blue-chip investors were joined by a more notorious outfit, Softbank America, the U.S. subsidiary of the now-troubled Japanese Internet conglomerate, and by Amazon.com, which seems to have bought into every big loser on the Web sooner or later.[8]

To put the icing on the cake for the initial public offering in late 1999, Louis Borders persuaded none other than George Shaheen, the $5-million-a-year CEO of Andersen Consulting, to leave his prestigious job, outsize salary and all, for the frontier of Web retailing. Shaheen could have stayed with Andersen for about a year more and reaped a $10 million retirement bonus, or he could have hung on for the consulting division's spin-off as Accenture, an event that would have netted him $50 million or more. Instead, he jumped ship, chasing the same rainbow of endless riches that drew so many others to the Web: stock and options potentially worth a billion or more if all the promises came true.[9]

The plan that all these illustrious people and companies were backing was one of the most grandiose and, ultimately, delusional schemes in the largely delusional history of the nineties. It was so

expensive and stood so little chance of success that one well-known analyst, Miles R. Cook, a vice president at Bain Consulting in Atlanta, liked to tell newspaper reporters that Webvan's approach was "profit-proof."[10] What made it profit-proof, of course, was that the business was structured in such a way that it was just too expensive to operate.

What is interesting about Webvan is that Louis Borders was not one of the wackos who said profit was not important. To the contrary, Borders predicted in 1999 that his e-grocery company would make money in a year or less. But Borders based this prediction entirely on his view of where the company's revenues would be within that time—between $5 billion and $10 billion a year. The problem with this thinking is that Borders apparently never understood that Webvan's spending was a whole lot more certain than its prospects for income. And sure enough, while Webvan's money went out the door right on schedule, the revenue was a lot slower coming in.

Webvan's strategy was to create an entirely new kind of grocery infrastructure, spreading itself across the country by building a series of extremely costly high-technology warehouses and equipping them with fleets of refrigerator trucks and company-owned vans to make sure grocery orders arrived fresh and crisp at customers' doorsteps on time, every time. It was a laudable goal. It's just that no one connected with Webvan ever seems to have looked at it objectively and tried to figure out if there might not, in fact, be a much cheaper, less capital-intensive way to take grocery orders on a Web site and deliver the goods to people's houses.

It was David Beirne, the Benchmark investment banker and Webvan's biggest promoter, who reportedly made the deal that got the Internet grocer's massive construction program under way. According to *eBoys*, a book by Randall E. Stross, the same business school professor who wrote *The Microsoft Way*, Beirne ardently wooed and shamelessly flattered Bechtel Corp., the world's largest construction company, to take on the massive job of constructing the Webvan system. At first, Bechtel's senior managers turned down Webvan, explaining that Bechtel didn't do retail. "Guys, don't think of this as retail," Beirne told them. "You will be a major player in electronic commerce," Beirne continued his pitch to Bechtel, according to Stross,

saying, "If this works, we will build over five hundred of these in the next few years in the U.S., plus we go global. This is huge." When he still got a no, Beirne played his last card: "Webvan is every bit as important to Bechtel as the Hoover Dam."[11]

The heroically massive Depression-era water and power project, built by a consortium headed by Bechtel, spans Black Canyon in Nevada with the avowed purpose of putting a "strait-jacket" on the wild Colorado River. The dam's construction, two years ahead of schedule, still resonates inside the company that built it as the deal that made Bechtel's reputation and fortune.[12] With Beirne's comment in mind, Bechtel signed a $1 billion contract with Webvan to build grocery distribution centers in twenty-six U.S. cities over a scant two-year period.[13] The project was never completed, of course, but not because of Bechtel, which was probably the only company big enough to pull it off. Today, in the same official corporate history that boasts of engineering wonders like Hoover Dam and the tunnel under the English Channel, Bechtel still lists Webvan's "automated warehouses" among its proudest accomplishments in a century of global construction.[14]

To make matters even more expensive, Webvan insisted that all its drivers at all its distribution centers had to be highly trained Webvan employees. As the company's 2000 annual report boasted, "Webvan utilizes strict hiring standards in choosing couriers and requires each new employee to complete an intensive training program. The courier training lasts two weeks and includes 36 hours of classroom training, 12 hours of driving training and 28 hours of on the job training. . . . Webvan's couriers receive a competitive compensation package, including cash and stock options, and are encouraged to reinforce Webvan's brand and help to create a lasting one-to-one relationship with Webvan's customers."[15] (Two weeks of training and stock options to deliver groceries?) Following this philosophy, Webvan's employment quickly ballooned to nearly 4,500, including 129 in software development alone and some 3,700 at the distribution centers.[16]

During calendar 2000, its only full year selling groceries on the Web, the company's average daily expenses were $1.8 million—nearly four times higher than its sales of $489,000 on an average day.

This meant Webvan lost more than $1.3 million every day that year—going almost $480 million in the red on operations in 2000.[17]

After Webvan had built one of the world's most cash-eating, expensive operations, it should have surprised no one when, on July 9, 2001, only two years after launching its business, Webvan announced it had run out of cash, was closing its doors and firing its employees, and was filing for bankruptcy. When it threw in the towel, Webvan had the distinction of being the biggest flop in Internet history, a history already rich with big flops. It had burned up almost all of the $1.2 billion raised from public and private sources.[18]

All in all, in directing Webvan's brief life and dismal demise, its famous executives and backers had managed a feat every bit as astounding as the miracle of the loaves and the fishes, except in reverse. Where Jesus, with very limited resources, managed to feed a multitude, Webvan, with vast resources, managed to profligately waste everything and starve everyone in its crowd. In this case, the wages of not controlling expenses was death.

The Triumph of Common Sense over Spending

In the wake of Webvan's farcical collapse, many argued that the cause of death was not Webvan's approach or its grandiosity, but was the sad fact that poor Webvan had gotten itself into a business with no future. Webvan gave it a good try, the argument went, but selling groceries over the Web turns out to be an unworkable business idea.

But if these folks had managed to train their gaze, just for a moment, on the tiny island of England (or the even tinier island of Ireland), they would have seen that, long before Webvan, there had always been a relatively safe, low-employment, low-capital-investment way to sell groceries electronically and deliver them to homes—a way that kept expenses very low so profits could emerge relatively quickly.

The creator of the quiet miracle—a highly successful Internet grocery business—was none other than the United Kingdom's largest grocer and Europe's second-largest retailer, Tesco. With its ordinary brick-and-mortar stores growing sales at double-digit rates, pulling in

some $33 billion (£22.5 billion) in worldwide sales in 2001,[19] Tesco
didn't really need the Internet to help it out.[20]

But that didn't bother Terry Leahy, whose first job at Tesco was
stocking shelves at age seventeen and who, as Sir Terry, is Tesco's
chief executive. Leahy became entranced with the potential of the
Web in 1995, long before Louis Border's elephantine plan emerged
into public view. It was 1997, two years before Webvan's launch,
when Tesco became the first company in the world to sell groceries
online.[21] By 1999, when Webvan finally opened its online store, Tesco
already had nearly 250,000 Internet customers, more than $170 mil-
lion (£123 million) in sales, and could claim to be the world's leading
Internet grocer.[22]

Two years later, just before Webvan shut down, Tesco.com had
more than a million customers placing 70,000 orders a week. And
within a year, in April 2002, Tesco.com could announce that it had
had its first profitable year in the U.K. on some $500 million (£356 mil-
lion) in sales, filling roughly 85,000 orders a week.[23]

The secret of this success is that Tesco, as it does in all its opera-
tions, pursued the lowest-cost, most efficient route it could find to the
Internet. That operating philosophy led the chain to use its existing
stores as the distribution hubs for its Web orders. Instead of beginning
with a brash, high-cost, national rollout, Tesco began by testing its
concept in a few London stores. Instead of high-tech, automated
warehouses for $35 million each, Tesco simply employed a few peo-
ple, mostly retirees at the start, to take a shopping cart and fill the
Web orders in the most sensible way—by wheeling down the aisles of
the store, picking items off the shelves and putting them in the cart,
after which the groceries were bagged and delivered to the surround-
ing neighborhood in a van. As time went on, more of the orders were
filled in the back rooms, saving the cost of restocking shelves. It was
precisely the opposite of Webvan's rocket-science approach.

When Tesco found out the system worked, they expanded it to 100
stores by the end of 1999 and to all of Tesco's 700-plus U.K. stores
within two more years.

The result of Tesco's prudence is a business that actually makes
sense. Expenses, which the company controls, were kept low until

revenues, which the customer controls, could be proven and accurately projected. Remember for a moment that Webvan spent $1.2 billion, managed to produce, at its peak, $178 million in annual sales in a market the size of the United States, lost money at the rate of half-a-billion dollars a year, and went broke. Tesco, on the other hand, estimated in 2001 that it had invested less than $90 million (£60 million) in building its Web grocery—roughly 7.5 percent of the amount burned by Webvan. And Tesco achieved profitability, a goal that eluded Webvan forever, even though the U.K. market is little more than one-fifth the size of the U.S.

By mid-2002, the buzz in the press was that Web grocery stores were the hot new item in cyberspace. In the United States, three different chains were using the Tesco model to sell on the Web.[24] One of the chains, Safeway, converted to Tesco's way of doing things after Tesco paid $22 million for a 35 percent stake in Safeway's online business, GroceryWorks, in June 2001. After that investment, Grocery-Works shuttered its stand-alone warehouses and began using "pickers" to fill orders from the shelves in Safeway stores.[25]

According to *The New York Times*, the analysts in the U.S., still victims of Webvan thinking, somberly declared that "online grocery shopping is likely to be restricted to big metropolitan areas into the near future, at least."[26] But the Dow Jones newswire found a Merrill Lynch analyst who, from his Manhattan desk, clicks onto Tesco.com and orders groceries to be delivered to his second home in Ireland's wild and rural County Galway.[27]

There is no apparent limit to what can be accomplished if expenses are controlled.

You *Can* Save Your Way to Prosperity

The deal that put my career as an entrepreneur into high gear (or, at least, into gear) was the 1986 acquisition of *Chicago* magazine from the city's public television station, WTTW. The magazine, one of the oldest and most established city magazines in America, lost some $700,000 on roughly $11 million in revenue the year that WTTW's board decided to

unload it. My partner, Hillel Levin, and I had just been through a hor-
rendously competitive magazine start-up in Detroit, where it was clear
that revenue couldn't be predicted because our main competitor was
willing to give away virtually everything—especially advertising—to
beat us. So when we came to the Chicago deal, we prudently decided
to assume, for the purposes of business planning, that there was ab-
solutely nothing we could do to improve revenue. The whole game,
we decided, was to control spending. With this maxim in mind, we put
together a simple, step-by-step plan to cut *Chicago*'s expenses by at
least a couple million dollars. It was not a kind plan; it was neither an
inspiring nor a grand plan. But the beauty of it was this: Every element
of it was almost entirely under our control, which meant our plan
could be executed no matter what. We didn't need the permission or
agreement of anyone except ourselves to do what needed to be done to
return *Chicago* to substantial profitability.

The exact details of the plan don't matter. To cut spending, we
looked in all the right places, which is to say, the places a business
spends most of its money. For *Chicago*, that meant people, office space,
printing and paper contracts, and travel and perks. The staff was at
seventy-one, as I recall. We cut it to less than fifty. Net savings: about a
million dollars. Not a bad start. We negotiated long-term contracts
with our major suppliers and shaved another few hundred thousand
off the expenses. Then came the office space.

In keeping with the tastes of the publisher we had deposed, *Chi-
cago* was located in sumptuous offices in an imposing tower on the
lakefront. I remember vividly the first time I claimed the publisher's
office as my own. It was vast and it was on two levels and it was fitted
with hand-hewn rosewood cabinetry and it was furnished with soft,
black leather furniture and it had sweeping views of Lake Michigan
and the fabled Chicago skyline. I immediately called my mother in
Washington, D.C. "Mom," I said, "if you want to see me looking like a
really important guy, you'll have to come here quickly because we're
moving out of this place and my new office will look like a closet." As
it turned out, my mother didn't make it in time. We had already
moved into renovated industrial space opposite the Merchandise
Mart on the Near North Side with half the square footage at about

half the cost per square foot. The furniture was modular. There wasn't an inch of wasted space. Another million in savings.

As it turned out, revenue did improve a little. But mostly on the strength of our cost-cutting, *Chicago* earned $2.4 million the first year we operated it. We had paid about $15 million for *Chicago*. Since strong magazines were trading for ten times operating earnings in those days, we had just increased the value of the property by $8 million to $10 million in less than a year. The lesson of that huge jump in equity value has never been lost on me.

Not every experience I've had in entrepreneur-land has been such a happy one. The worst episode came a few years after the triumph in Chicago when my partners and I lost a Miami-based business to the bank. Looking back on it, I can see that our major mistake was not cutting expenses more ruthlessly. Instead, I devoted almost all my time to working on revenue—building the top line, as they say—and though revenue improved, profits didn't. It never really worked.

I'm not saying that marketing and sales—the essentials of revenue-building—aren't important. Building revenue is clearly the second most important job in business. But controlling expenses is always the first job, because it's a task that management can always control.

As I write these words, I'm working for a very big company—the Interpublic Group of Companies, the world's second-biggest advertising and marketing conglomerate. But my formative experience in business is as I've described it, mostly running small publishing operations, particularly start-ups and turnarounds, usually with revenues well under $100 million.

Running small, new, money-losing enterprises is a very bone-jarring and instructive introduction to business because these enterprises are obviously very fragile. They typically have no reserves, little if any cash flow, and no corporate treasury function linking them to lifelines of cash from stock sales or borrowing. They have no broad bases of customers. They aren't diversified in either their products or their markets. Running these kinds of businesses is like tightrope walking in a high wind without a safety net. Managers tend to lie awake at night wondering how to make payroll. It is absolutely clear that any misstep will most likely be your last. It is clear, in other

words, that such small businesses are relatively easy to kill and that anyone who runs such a company must be very careful about how every nickel is expended, how each minute of time is spent, and how every last corporate resource is invested in chasing goals that no one can guarantee will be achieved.

But on my way from small business to big business, I learned a lesson: Virtually all business is small business. (This can be sung to the tune of "There's No Business Like Show Business," by the way.) The money in most service businesses, even vast enterprises like Interpublic, is made inside relatively tiny operating units and departments. Even in big manufacturing concerns, like auto or aerospace companies, where the scale is necessarily larger, the game is won or lost inside individual factories, marketing departments, and design and engineering departments. Jack Welch, GE's legendary chairman for two decades, once said, "GE is big in its overall size, but small in its execution."[28]

So as the bottom line of The Bottom-Line Box, every line manager should think of the price that small businesses pay when expenses aren't controlled. And then, if you work for a big business, think about the small units that make up your vaster business and remember that the rules about cost control apply everywhere.

HOW TO BUILD THE BOX

THE FOURTH PLANK

1. Hold regular expense control meetings with top managers so everyone can ask, Isn't there a cheaper way to do this? Always assume the answer is yes unless someone can prove otherwise.
2. Big savings come from areas of big spending. Forget the paper clips and pay attention to the areas where your business spends most of its money. Salary and related costs (payroll taxes, benefits, bonuses) are generally at the top.
3. Higher revenue is never certain. Avoid increasing expenses in anticipation of higher sales.
4. When revenue does go up, make certain expenses rise at a slower rate so operating margins improve as sales increase.

The Box Top: Customers Are the Boss

> *Give customers what they want,*
> *not what you want to give them.*

It Pays to Pay Attention to
Customers, not Technology

Proximity Worldwide is the UK-based relationship marketing unit of the global advertising giant BBDO Worldwide, itself a part of Omnicom Group, the globe's third-largest advertising and marketing conglomerate, with just under $7 billion in revenue and half a billion in net earnings in 2001.[1] Proximity, claiming roughly a billion dollars in annual billings, touts itself as a high-tech wonder. Its Web site promotes Proximity's understanding of how the "digital revolution" produces "communication that's personal, interactive and immediate." The company's marketing tag line is "the marriage of marketing and interactive principles to create and nurture brand relationships."[2]

But its CEO, Simon Hall, told an Australian audience in mid-2001 that "the neighborhood butcher's shop and news agency should be the types of businesses large corporations aspire to become in the new customer-centric age." Parachuting in to promote his Australian operation, Hall told a local financial reporter, "This is the battleground in the next 10 years: who offers the *best* customer experience."[3]

It is undoubtedly true that offering the best customer experience will be the main event of the next decade. But this is certain because serving customers has been the "battleground" in commerce for hun-

dreds of years, not because technology has changed anything funda-
mental about the relationship between consumers and sellers.

It has long been an article of faith that the customer, not the CEO,
should be at the top of every organization chart. No business gets
anywhere without knowing, listening to, and talking to its customers.
Any business that leaves off this part of The Box has bought a fast
one-way ticket to oblivion. A thousand years of commercial history
confirms this.

If you listen to most of the business gurus, there's a business revo-
lution every minute, each one driven by technology. Che Guevera's life
begins to sound calm and conservative by comparison. Part of the end-
less hyping of endless change is the barrage of "economies" to which
we are subjected. The "new economy" leads the pack, of course, if only
because it was such a famous and widely credited fiction. The runner-
up in this tedious series of invented economies is something called the
"customer economy." Second only to the new economy in its power to
disappoint and mislead, the customer economy rose to erroneous and
expensive recognition as yet another "brand new" phenomenon—
another sign of relentless technological change in business—in the
very late 1990s. It was as if customers, cash in hand, had just appeared
on the scene as the twentieth century was fading to black. (Prior to
that, apparently, the revenue came from somewhere else.)

One of the great arguments against an overreliance on technology
can be found in the dead center of *Good to Great*, one of the best busi-
ness books of recent times. Author Jim Collins, former academic
turned management consultant, has a section titled "The Technology
Trap," in which he notes with interest "our cultural obsession with
technology-driven change."[4]

As the 1990s dawned, our collective technological fascination
turned its focus on individual customers. Technology—in the form of
something called customer relationship management (CRM)—was
promising to boost sales and profits by transforming the way busi-
ness listens and talks to consumers. These sophisticated hardware
and software systems were supposed to consolidate all data about
customers in one place and then use that information to customize
every interaction with each customer.

CRM is really nothing more than an attempt, so far largely unsuccessful, to automate the secrets of Mr. Jones's corner store down on Main and State circa 1790. Jones made money by knowing each customer ("Mornin', Missus Smith. We just got in the mother-of-pearl buttons you've always wanted") and by treating them like individuals. It now takes a lot of database knowledge, central processing power, and marketing expertise to duplicate Mr. Jones's success on a large scale, but the principles have not changed. And the underlying principles of paying proper attention to customers are not technological. Rather, they involve the challenges of communicating with another human being, a process that is still essentially an art, not a science.

In *Good to Great*, Collins examines eleven companies that suddenly transformed themselves, he says, from merely good companies to truly great ones. After fifteen years or more of very ordinary performance (at or below stock market averages), these companies became extraordinary performers, beating the markets' averages by at least three times over an equally long period. In his book, Collins and a team of researchers set out to determine how these businesses did it. One can argue with Collins's criteria and his whole approach, but one significant finding was that technology was not significant in boosting companies' performance from good to great. "We were quite surprised to find that fully 80 percent of the good-to-great executives we interviewed didn't even mention technology as one of the top five factors in the transition," Collins writes. It wasn't that technology had no role to play in a well-managed company, it was just that human factors were always far more important. You can give two companies the same technology, but you won't see the same results. "Technology by itself is never a primary cause of either greatness or decline," Collins concludes.[5]

Technology produces incredible tools that transform lives, societies, and all of human culture. But until artificial intelligence makes the unimaginable strides necessary to replace the human brain, it's people who make the difference on this planet, not technology. The computer that is enabling me to write this book is a marvel, storing virtually all my notes and giving me instant access to the world's libraries and news archives on the Internet so virtually any question

can be answered instantly at any hour of the day or night. But there is no software available to create the arguments contained in this book or to organize the words into coherent sentences. When it comes to communicating, long experience teaches that technology is a tool that enables solutions; but technology is never the solution. Nevertheless, far too many companies, lost in reverence for the technology, have completely forgotten (or never knew) the human principles of talking to their customers.

It is the accepted wisdom that in order to deliver the appropriate "customer experience," companies must now segment people into ever smaller cohorts according to their demographics and psychographics, zip codes and life stages, lifestyles and income brackets, secret dreams and desires; and must assemble the telltale traces of their behavior in a computerized, relational database so each customer can be tracked and analyzed and addressed one-on-one while being coddled, inspired, and catered to as an individual.

Millions for Software, but Not a Single Kind Word

Put this way, it's (almost) true, of course. (So long as the slicing and dicing of the customer base and the targeting of various subgroups are reasonably related to each group's actual buying behavior.) But it's definitely not new. And it most certainly isn't the result of any sudden, Internet-induced change in the "business model." The customer has been the boss since the first customer was born more than a millennium ago. In fact, all the supposedly hyper-modern ploys of segmenting consumers, creating loyalty programs, and maintaining customer relationships were being developed nearly a thousand years back, as the global economy was blossoming. And these customer-centric tactics were actively in use by sellers in Europe more than five hundred years ago.

Managers can benefit from a knowledge of this history because, to a great extent, the modern emphasis on technology has led many to seriously miss the simple point of a fundamental business principle: Precious few companies have survived without paying attention to

their customers. Customers, as the world's most durable businesses have known for centuries, are absolutely the only source of meaningful information about what current products and services need improvement, what future products and services need invention, and what words and images will best market any product or service so it sells. Despite the self-evident nature of all this, few companies have been able to sustain prolonged attention to their customers since the birth of the modern corporation.

CRM is the most recent example of the seeming inability of global corporate culture to care about customers. This latest management TLA (three-letter acronym) became a widespread disaster at the turn of the twenty-first century. Worldwide, big business was throwing something like $11 billion a year at advanced CRM software and hardware systems and CRM consultants with hefty fees.[6] Most of these billions, however, have failed to produce results.

The purely technological version of CRM, as conceived and foisted upon management throughout the late 1990s, is a perfect example of a wonderful-sounding customer-economy idea that did nothing for customers. Take the case of a very smart client of mine—a company whose stock in trade is high technology. The company's goal is to sell advanced communications technology to large and mid-sized corporations. Like many high-tech firms, success meant making a few multimillion-dollar sales of technical products and services to the leaders of the Fortune 1,000. So my client needed to manage its "relationships" with a couple hundred thousand customers—a relative handful in this day and age.

To get started, this company dutifully spent roughly $10 million on a package of Siebel Systems software, the gold standard of CRM programming, the hardware needed to run it, and an expensive bundle of database services from Dun & Bradstreet, which can sell you lists of American managers sorted by title, industry, main offices and suboffices, zip codes, suit color (just kidding), and a high number of other variables.

Two years into the drill, a major problem with the expensive CRM system was discovered: It could not output even a simple list of the names and addresses of my client's best customers (or its worst ones,

for that matter). The Customer Relationship Management system seemed to have plenty of C—or, at least, customer names and addresses. And it even had some M—the numbers could be managed and manipulated. But there was absolutely no R there at all—it neither embodied nor empowered nor enabled any sort of relationship with anyone.

The fault, strictly speaking, was not in the software, the hardware, or the purchased databases. The problem was that the system wasn't even being used. The sales force wouldn't use it because they saw no benefit in entering their confidential customer information into the system. They figured that giving this information to the company would just make it easier for their bosses to fire them in bad economic times. So the expensive CRM initiative failed to connect internally, ensuring there was no up-to-date information about customers in the system. At the same time, the expensive Dun & Bradstreet lists were languishing; most of the company's marketers and salespeople didn't even know they existed. These lists could have enhanced the company's customer database by adding information about each customer, such as overall size, financial power, subsidiaries, management structure, key contacts, and so on. But since no one maintained the customer database, there was really nothing much to enhance and no reason to learn what the D&B data could do.

Consequently, the company had no record of the things that common sense tells us are most closely related to sales potential. It had no customer history (purchases, inquiries, complaints, and so on); nothing on the size or type of the customer's business (Was it a small industrial firm or a large consultancy?); not even the customer's budget (Did they have thousands to spend or millions or nothing?).

But most critically, there was absolutely no strategy to create or send any particular messages to particular groups of customers based on anything known about them. As alarming as it sounds, there was no way on God's green earth, using this Customer Relationship Management system, to get in touch with any customers. So the CRM system failed on all counts, and this failure could have been foreseen before a single nickel was spent.

My client's experience is no isolated example. Company after

company in the United States and around the world were sold expensive CRM infrastructure that wound up connecting with not one single customer, engendering not one single relationship, and producing not one single dollar of return on investment—no incremental sales, no heightened rate of customer retention, no knowledge or insight into customers' needs and wants. In other words, plenty of pain for no discernible gain. It was widespread results like this that led technology consultants Meridien Research in Massachusetts to predict in 2002 that spending on CRM-related infrastructure would slow "as many institutions examine their ROI from less-than-successful CRM investments."[7] And Peter S. Fader, a marketing professor at the University of Pennsylvania's prestigious Wharton School of Business, said of the CRM fad, "Everyone is sort of flocking to it, but not necessarily getting anything out of it."[8]

In late 2001, *Fast Company*, arguably the best business magazine in America, convened a badly needed roundtable discussion on "The State of the Customer Economy." The chief marketing officer of Reebok International, Angel Martinez, summed it up neatly by saying the typical consumer experience of the new customer economy amounted to being "underwhelmed, overpromised, underdelivered."

Another participant in that same roundtable was Paul Cole, then the global director of CRM practice for Cap Gemini Ernst & Young, one of the world's largest management consulting firms with a specialty practice in IT and the digital world. Cole was exactly right when he said, "The notion that we could automate the whole customer relationship has been oversold by the software industry. The whole CRM thing is a convenient acronym that was created by the software industry to sell applications."[9]

What CRM never addressed or even approached is that the basics of winning and keeping customers involves the entire operation of a business and the complete cycle of a business's contacts and dealings with its customers. The foundation, of course, must be a commitment to providing products and services that actually meet customers' real needs, coupled with a plan to make each contact and every transaction comfortable, easy, and rewarding for each customer. This means following six fundamentals:

1. Every new product or service must begin with an open-ended question: How does this help a real live customer?

2. The choice of what products or services to offer customers must be rooted in the customers' answers about what they want and need, not in the sellers' view of what's best for them.

3. The initial approach to recruit a new customer must be engaging, informative, honest (overpromising will create big trouble down the road), and tailored to the needs and desires of the customer.

4. The shopping experience must be easy and comfortable (which means giving the customer a lot of choices about how to buy).

5. The product or service sold must be as nearly flawless as possible, offering a "defect-free customer experience" (as Horst Schulze, former president of Ritz-Carlton, used to say).[10]

6. The follow-up (like saying "thank you" after the sale and recognizing regular customers when they come back) must be consistent.

Simply put: Find out what customers really want, then give it to them. Make sure they have plenty of choices—in what they buy, where they buy, how they buy, and how they pay for it all. And address them personally, talk to them honestly, and treat them well every step of the way.

Today the right technology is needed to get this job done. Systems need to track what consumers do and say every time they contact a business—at all "touchpoints," as the jargon of relationship marketing puts it. This means putting together a single database that can capture information from a retail transaction in a store or a Web site hit or a phone call or a piece of mail. But technology alone won't do the job. Technology can only organize information and make it accessible. Forming a relationship with a customer requires much more than that.

Catering to customers is hardly modern, and the heart of the mission really has nothing to do with technology. To rediscover and understand the basics of forming and maintaining customer relationships—the critical plank in The Box that tells us the customer is always boss—the best place to start is the thirteenth century, more

than half a millennium ago, when what we call "the customer" first appeared in large numbers in Western commercial history.

The First Thing You Need for Customer Relationships Is a Customer

Ralph Nader, a Harvard-educated lawyer and consumer activist long before he became a political spoiler, probably knows that the first major piece of consumer-protection law was not the so-called Lemon Law he championed in the 1970s (the federal Magnuson-Moss Warranty Act), but a paragraph near the end of the Magna Carta, the great founding document of modern Western law, sealed by King Edward I on March 28, 1297. "One measure of Wine shall be through our Realm, and one measure of Ale, and one measure of Corn," Edward proclaimed, adding a single measure—the yard—for cloth, as well. "And it shall be of Weights as it is of Measures," the king concluded.

Magna Carta's insistence on standard weights and measures reflected a growing need to regulate and foster the consumer trade in all sorts of goods by providing a basis for trust, the one critical element upon which all commerce has always depended (and the central attribute of what we now call brands).

King Edward's concern about commerce and trust reflected the growing volume of trade at ports, market towns, and fairs throughout his realm and, in fact, throughout medieval Europe. As early as 1300, the fairs were being "laid out regularly in 'streets,' some of which were reserved, at a price, for particular trades," writes Dorothy Davis, the British historian of shopping.[11] By 1400, there were some two or three dozen annual fairs throughout England, and scholarly descriptions paint them as nothing less than early, mobile shopping malls that carefully and successfully catered to a wide variety of tastes and budgets with a huge array of local and imported goods.[12]

Even at these early fairs, where much of the trade was what we now call wholesale, it is remarkable that traders and merchants were careful to carry a variety of goods aimed at different audiences. There was very early evidence of well-conceived, fashion-conscious "niche

marketing" at these medieval fairs, which lasted between a few days and a few weeks. Brightly colored silks and velvets, for example, were available for the nobles at high prices. But next to these, there also were the designer knock-offs of the era—coarse, cheap woolens for the common folk, dyed a gaudy red to mimic the rich folks' preference for vivid colors.

It was no later than the 1500s that business began uniformly taking an approach to consumers that continues unabated and largely unchanged today. In the modern jargon, customers were being served some five hundred years ago with a wide choice of goods, price points, methods of payment, and "channels" or points of purchase— all hallmarks of the so-called customer economy of the 2000s. (Continuing the consumer protection legislation begun in the Magna Carta, English consumers also were being protected and directed by a host laws and edicts, handed down by the Tudor monarchy, controlling distribution and pricing.)[13]

Fulfilling their inevitable role as prophets, historians note that one of the greatest challenges facing customer service and sales several hundred years ago was the need to make each customer, regardless of social standing or means, comfortable in the experience of shopping. Thus, in her detailed study of retailing between the sixteenth and nineteenth centuries, historian Nancy Cox devotes an entire chapter to "the relationship between customer and retailer" and the approaches used by each to resolve the tension between them "inherent in a dynamic market."[14] Modern retailers like Benjamin Cole, the seventeeth century London linen draper whose shop catered differently to the nobility, the rich, the middle class, and the working poor, and William Woods, the eighteenth century Cheshire shopkeeper who regularly extended credit to regular customers, are just two examples among many, Cox points out.

Cox notes that centuries ago in Europe, "Customers . . . were categorized, sorted, courted and treated according to their station." If we understand "station" to mean a person's income, education, neighborhood, needs, and aspirations, as it does, then we have discovered true segmentation marketing in medieval England.

Half a millennium ago, the great and grand were served at their

own houses by merchants who arrived with an array of goods selected to please that particular household. At the curb outside their mansions and town homes, the servants of the nobility would buy small items for them—buttons, bows, trinkets—from pushcarts and peddlers. Shops would serve one level of gentry inside the store at glass-fronted display cases and wooden-topped counters, while wealthier regulars would be rewarded for their past purchases by being allowed to pass through a door leading to a private area inside the merchant's living space. Poorer folk, meanwhile, who didn't feel comfortable (and weren't welcome) inside the shop, would stay outside and be served at windows. But there were efforts to make them feel wanted and appreciated, because by the 1700s hardly a shop in England did not carry a few small luxuries like sugar, pepper, thread, and tobacco—all favored by the working poor. And long before the eighteenth century, merchants regularly advanced credit to their regular, poorer customers.

Reaping Riches by Catering to Customers

In this complex world of retail stretching back to the Middle Ages, every customer was accorded precisely the right relationship, the right level of service, the right payment plan, the right environment, the right choice of goods, the right prices, and, we can suppose, the right tone of voice and vocabulary. It was a segmentation marketer's dream come true.[15] It also is an indication that a critical mind, an eye for discerning differences among customer groups, and a plan to exploit those differences for greater profit are, taken together, the most critical part of customer relationship management. Without these ancient assets, a wide-area-network and advanced software will not help set an enterprise on the path to customer-centricity.

Maintaining customer loyalty was critical from the birth of the notion of a customer, it seems, because even if merchant and consumer were friends, "there was the implied threat that customers could choose to go elsewhere," Cox explains.[16] "Already in the sixteenth century," Cox concludes, "shoppers could choose outlets that

best suited their needs or that provided an environment in which they felt comfortable."[17]

So much for the customer revolution of the twenty-first century.

Some of the greatest and longest-lasting successes of modern business can be attributed to a simple, basic understanding of the customer's supremacy in any commercial transaction. From the "creation" of the department store (a sort of medieval fair with a set pricing structure), to the "invention" of mail order (a modern version of the home visits that medieval merchants and peddlers made to the rich), to the construction of the modern consumer products conglomerate, great riches and sustainable businesses have flowed from an understanding of customer relationships and the need to pay careful attention to the wants and desires of one's customers.

The Customers Are Always Right, Even When They Aren't

The great retailing fortunes of America—the urban empires and grand stores of Rowland Macy, Marshall Field, John Wanamaker, and later, the mail order empires of Aaron Montgomery Ward and others who initially served rural America's farm families—were all founded on the notion of customer focus and relentless attention to customers' comfort and needs. It was anchored on an aphorism first uttered by Wanamaker, the legendary Philadelphia clothing seller: "The customer is always right." The statement is undeniably untrue at least some of the time, but it sums up an understanding of the customer's supreme position in business that has never been more succinctly stated. In 1876, just in time for the one hundreth birthday of the American republic, Wanamaker opened a huge "new kind of store" in Philadelphia—the Grand Depot—on the site of the old Pennsylvania Railroad station. With its many specialty stores under one roof, it was his first and most significant contribution to the creation of the modern department store.

At the same moment, Wanamaker's peers were constructing other huge retail enterprises in other major cities, all in the same style as the

Grand Depot. Some of their focus was on cost control. (Wanamaker pointed out that the Grand Depot's scale made it possible to "do a great deal more business with no more expense for rent, taxes, gas," or anything but the salaries of a few additional sales clerks.) Some of their focus was on revenue growth from stocking and selling a greatly expanded variety of goods. (Macy's New York store, in particular, moved into areas that no dry goods store had ever gone into before, including furniture, toys, books, candy, china, glassware and much more.) But most of their collective focus was squarely on the customer—the source, they recognized, of all wealth and commercial happiness.[18]

Intent on expanding their businesses, building on traditions established over a millennium or more, these men relied on a wide variety of customer-focused strategies that remain standard today, more than a century later. They made enforceable pledges not to misrepresent their merchandise and quickly followed the lead of Ward's fledgling mail order concern, which had made its policy "Satisfaction guaranteed or your money back" shortly after it launched its first catalogue in 1872.[19] They replaced the age-old system of haggling over prices with a one-price system for all goods. Then they made sure those prices were low enough to attract return customers. (Ward, of course, was using the power of the U.S. postal system and the railroads to bring low prices and wide choice to America's farmers, who had begun to rebel, sometimes violently, against the inflated prices and limited stock of their local monopoly general stores.)

The urban store owners began turning their huge properties into cathedrals of commerce featuring rotundas, stained-glass skylights, marble arcades, and chandeliers. Macy, anticipating Starbucks cafes in bookstores by a hundred years or so, installed a soda fountain in 1870 and, eight years later, the first lunchroom in a U.S. department store. All this to make the visits of the mostly female customers more pleasant and, thus, longer. Macy added home delivery of his merchandise, so his middle-class customers in New York and New Jersey could enjoy service first offered only to the nobility four centuries earlier and an ocean away.[20]

It wasn't long before Ward's Johnny-come-lately competitor in the mail order business, the Chicago firm launched by Richard Sears,

established another standard component of any smartly managed, customer-focused company—loyalty marketing. At the turn of the twentieth century, building on the ideas of companies that were issuing trading stamps and other premiums to build sales, Sears, Roebuck & Co. developed a program of giving certificates that were redeemable for gifts once a customer's total purchases reached $100. Competitors followed suit.[21]

So it came to be that virtually all the principles and practices of customer-focused management were in place in their modern form more than a century ago—well into the era of the industrial revolution, mass marketing, and mass merchandising; but well before anyone even thought about computers and databases. Some of the customer-centric practices pioneered over the thousand-year evolution of the modern customer have flickered in and out of fashion, as have most of the companies that practiced them. Paying attention to customers and giving them what they want is a critical plank in The Box, but it isn't the whole construct. Thus, Sears and Ward called a mutual temporary halt to their loyalty marketing schemes after only a couple of years. Then, at the end of 2000, Ward called a permanent halt to retailing altogether, closing its last 250 stores and laying off 28,000 workers. At the dawn of the new century—the third it had seen—Ward, by then owned by General Electric, had become a venerable, 128-year-old victim of its CEO's inability to adapt to the new realities of the post-World-War-II world. Sears figured correctly that serving customers meant going where the customers were going, so it spent heavily to secure good locations in the booming suburbs. Ward's sat still, foolishly hoarded cash, and ultimately paid the price.[22] But despite the varied fortunes of the enterprises that first discovered and catered to the supremacy of their customers, the underlying, unchanging, fundamental notion of customer-as-king remains firmly in place.

The world is now filled with examples of businesses that have tried hard, in one way or another, to prosper (or, at least, to restore prosperity) by paying attention to their customers, however belatedly. In late 2001, McDonald's, the world's number one fast-food chain, reacted to sliding earnings and weak same-store sales by announcing a plan to hire 150,000 "mystery shoppers" to pose as hungry cus-

tomers and check out the chain's customer service at some 13,000 U.S. restaurants. A spokesman, Bill Whitman, said at the time, "If we stay focused on the needs of the customers, the sales will take care of themselves."[23] Maybe so; maybe not.

At the time, *The Wall Street Journal* disputed McDonald's chances of turning things around by using mystery shoppers, claiming that the things a mystery shopper can uncover—like unsmiling employees and slow response time—were not the fast-food chain's problem. McDonald's Corp., which typically earns just shy of a couple billion dollars worldwide annually, begged to differ. But maybe McDonald's mystery shoppers *can't* uncover the right answers for McDonald's; maybe McDonald's needs to ask completely different questions.

McDonald's could ask till it's blue in the face, "Which do you prefer: A high-fat hamburger with more bacon and cheese or a high-fat hamburger with jalapeño sauce?" But the answer to that question will never explain why the number of Subway restaurants, with their low-fat sandwiches and no french fries on the menu, surpassed McDonald's high-fat emporiums in 2001.[24] By the same token, using mystery shoppers to force more smiles on more McDonald's employees' faces won't help if the real problem all along has been the menu, the McDonald's image for greasy food, and the chain's inability to change with changing tastes.

In 1933, an author named Leon Epstein published a slim book of encouragement and advice for salesmen entitled *Epigrams on Selling and Advertising*. There is a great deal that is timeless and prophetic about Epstein's book, but McDonald's, along with the rest of us, would do well to pay special attention to epigram number ten in the chapter titled "Selling." Epstein wrote, "To simplify selling, make what the market wants. Avoid trying to force the market to want what you make."[25]

So It Isn't Just Paying Attention to the Customers, as We Now Know from a Thousand Years of History: It's Paying the Right Kind of Attention

Perhaps the greatest example in all time of customer-focus-mania is Procter & Gamble, the perennial king of the consumer products com-

panies. P&G is now recognized as a legendary business. It produces more than 250 brands, most of them, it seems, household names, including Ivory soap ("99-$^{44}/_{100}$% Pure®: It Floats."), Pampers diapers, Tide detergent, Pringles potato chips, Bounty paper towels, Tampax tampons, Joy dishwashing liquid, Charmin toilet paper, and on and on and on and on. Household names or not, P&G's brand names are found in 98 percent of America's households, the company estimates.

Sales worldwide are about $40 billion a year. Against the odds, P&G has remained a juggernaut since the early nineteenth century, always rebounding from slumps, relentlessly growing. Most recently, in the second quarter of its 2002 fiscal year, P&G rebounded from two bad years by finally beating analysts' growth expectations again, despite the miserable economy. It was immediately declared to have "turned the corner" to continued supremacy once more.[26]

Assembled as a two-man partnership in 1837 in the tiny town of Cincinnati, P&G was the first consumer products company to build a research lab. But, perhaps more important, it was one of the first to pioneer consumer research, which ever since has remained a central obsession of P&G and a central pillar of the famed "P&G Way." It all began, according to myth and the media, in 1882, when Harley Procter, son of the company's cofounder William, invited people to talk about their impressions of Ivory soap. Ever since, P&G has consistently gone directly to consumers to check its performance, to see how existing products might be improved, and to ask the customers what new products it should try to invent. Its consumer testing is so relentless that hardly a resident of Cincinnati doesn't participate in multiple studies each year.

P&G now spends about $150 million a year conducting thousands of studies on how consumers' lives and P&G products intertwine or don't. The testing comes in a wide variety of forms—focus groups (panels of roughly a dozen consumers who are led through a discussion while marketers watch behind one-way glass), one-on-one interviews, or research involving slathering creams on consumers or asking them to taste a potato chip.[27]

Searching through the company's corporate Web site can be a fascinating (and somewhat unsettling) study of the random facts about

customers' lives that P&G gathers every day in virtually every major country in the world. In the early 1980s, the company says, P&G research revealed "roughly half the women who used feminine protection pads experienced failures in protection." Another piece of research, released in 2001 in Mumbai, India, found that "Indian mothers feel uneasy about repeatedly giving their children internal consumption medicines (syrups and tablets), as she believes that excess internal medicine does more harm than good for her child's health." This piece of culturally based customer insight was used to market Vicks VapoRub as "safe, external relief" for Indian children with colds or flu. P&G even tests dogs and cats as consumers for its Iams pet food subdsidiary. All in all, the company's Consumer & Market Knowledge department comes into contact with more than seven million customers each year, asking questions relentlessly so the answers will "contribute to the quality of our products today, anticipate future consumer needs, and provide better advertising to communicate our products' benefits."[28]

Over 165 years, a span of time that sees most companies forgotten and crumbled to dust, P&G has remained on top by sticking to an old and revered management discipline in its approach to every aspect of its business. But at the center of it all is a relentless, almost frenetic insistence that every significant product and marketing decision be based on hard data gathered from the customers themselves. This long-term, slavish attention to customers, completely untrendy and completely consistent with the era in which the company was born, is undoubtedly what has kept P&G on top all these decades.

The examples could go on and on. The point is that the principles of customer focus have been in place for a very long time and have been instrumental in the growth of America's greatest businesses. But it is also a sad fact of modern business that almost no one fulfills all the promises inherent in the notion that the customer is the boss. So the idea that a true customer focus is rapidly expanding throughout our corporate enterprises remains today at least part myth and part aspirational goal.

Paul Cole, Cap Gemini's global CRM director, frequently talks about the inability of most firms to get the whole package right, and

he points to the airlines as one perfect example. The frequent flier pro-
grams of most major airlines do a good job of recognizing and reward-
ing good customers with first-class upgrades, shorter lines, and faster
baggage handling. But the airlines still deliver such an exasperatingly
uneven level of customer service in day-to-day flying that the favorite
saying of the frequent flier is, as my father-in-law Edwin Jacob likes to
put it, "The airline you like least is the one you flew last."

The goal of the modern manager, then, must be to pay attention to
customers by actually paying attention to customers. The ultimate goal
here is make every enterprise resemble, as much as possible, a small
fifteenth-century linen shop, or a nineteenth-century department store.

HOW TO BUILD THE BOX

THE FIFTH PLANK

1. The core of pleasing customers is providing a defect-free experi-
 ence. This involves every part of the enterprise.
2. The only way to have a relationship with a customer is to com-
 municate with the customer. This will require having something
 to say.
3. Never assume you know the reason a customer does anything.
 Always ask. Always listen. Always use the resulting information.
4. The best technology is necessary to capture and track what con-
 sumers say and do when they touch a business. But technology
 alone can't do the job, and tracking data, by itself, accomplishes
 nothing.
5. Before spending money on technology, decide what it is you
 want to accomplish for both the customers and the business.
6. When creating a customer relationship plan, ask your manage-
 ment five questions:
 a. Who needs to be talked to and courted?
 b. Intuitively, what different groups do they seem to fall into?
 c. What outcomes are desired?
 d. What messages will be delivered?
 e. How will success be measured?

The Marketing Box: Unifying the Whole Business

> *You should be selling all the time.*

Smart Marketing Unifies Every Part of a Business to Make a Sale

Despite its acknowledged position as the primary business practice, the art and science of marketing is widely and deeply misunderstood. In popular speech, the word *marketing* has become a fancy synonym for advertising. But nothing, of course, could be farther from the truth.

Marketing was first officially defined when the American Marketing Association, newly born in 1937,[1] asserted, "Marketing consists of those activities involved in the flow of goods and services from the point of production to the point of consumption."[2] As broad as this definition may seem, it is too narrowly drawn and represents the kind of truncated thinking that can kill a business. The point of production is too late in the process to start marketing. And the point of consumption is too early in the process to stop it.

Business schools advanced the ball somewhat by instituting the teaching of marketing's Four Ps—product, placement, promotion, price. But even this view has become ossified, failing to comprehend both the quality of production, at one end of the process, or the inner workings of brands and the components of customer loyalty at the other end. What works better is to recast marketing in three broad

areas that encompass all management and make it clear that marketing has no end point. Economists, academics, and marketing professionals have come to see marketing this way—as the single discipline that embraces and unites virtually every aspect of business activity.

Marketing:

1. Guides production by defining what products will be produced—the goods that will be manufactured and the services that will be offered—and how they will be produced to best serve the wants and needs, real or perceived, of real live customers.

2. Governs distribution by determining the most effective ways to price goods and services, place them in front of prospects, sell them to customers, and deliver them into customers' hands.

3. Controls advertising, promotion, and all marketing communications by defining exactly who the target consumer is and what will be communicated to each prospect and customer to attract their attention, stimulate a response, achieve a sale, maintain their loyalty, create a resale, and turn them into advocates of the brand.

Taking the first point first—using marketing to guide production is the heart of the previous chapter. To make a business a success, marketing cannot be a department and it certainly can't be something provided by hiring an ad agency. Believing that marketing and advertising are the same is the equivalent of believing that taking action and *talking* about taking action are the same. Marketing is the entire complex process of putting the customer at the center of a business's concerns and operations.

The management sage and consultant Peter Drucker has written that business's only purpose is "to create a customer," and because of that, "marketing and innovation" are the two basic functions of business.[3] Of those two functions, writes Drucker, marketing "is a central dimension of the entire business. It is the whole business seen from the point of view of its final result, that is, from the customer's point of view."[4] Marketing, in effect, is the process that unites all business activities around the goal of creating a customer and making a sale.

Unless marketing is the guide to production (and the quality of production), a business is doomed to fail. Imagine a product or service that fills neither the needs nor the desires of any living consumer. Now imagine the distribution scheme or promotional effort or ad campaign that would make such a product a commercial hit.

If imagination fails, try this: The upscale Edsel automobile, whose very name became a slang term for "an object no one wants," was produced for only three model years from 1958 to 1960. Then Ford Motor Company admitted defeat and shut down the division. Sometimes described as "a Mercury (or an Oldsmobile) sucking a lemon" because of its weird vertical grill, the Edsel failed despite an expensive campaign to build a strong, independent dealer distribution network and an even more expensive consumer ad campaign created by Foote, Cone and Belding.[5] Or try this: Coca-Cola, feeling the hot breath of Pepsi on its neck, ended the production of Coke in late April 1985 and, with great fanfare, introduced a reformulated cola called New Coke that was sweeter and smoother, and unlike old Coke, did better than Pepsi in blind taste tests. The problem, as it turned out, is that the real world is not a blind taste test. Coke fans did not want *their* Coke changed after a century as an American icon, and they greeted the new cola drink with howls of outrage and disdain. Old Coke was back in production after just seventy-nine days, and New Coke, although it remained available to consumers for some two years, withered and died. Just like any Coca-Cola product, distribution for New Coke was provided by Coca-Cola's extensive sales organization, and advertising was both massive and professional.

Ford and Coke both failed at the first step by failing to see their new products from the customers' point of view. No amount of post-creation marketing can ever make up for such failure. But the obverse is also prevalent—good products and services often fail for lack of appropriate distribution and promotion. The Marketing Science Institute, a corporate-funded think tank in Cambridge, Massachusetts, reports that "at least 60 percent of all new products currently end in failure."[6] And not all of them are bad ideas.

The only way to improve the odds for a new service or product

launch, or to improve the performance of an existing offering, is to reach inside the lives of prospects and customers to increase the opportunities for a sale and to make sure there is a strategy in place to take advantage of every selling opportunity. This is the accumulated marketing wisdom of the ages—and since marketing has been around just as long as customers, the wisdom has been accumulating since the 1200s, maybe longer.

For many centuries, this has been a world where consumers are increasingly distracted by a blinding storm of commercial information and where well-conceived products and services compete vigorously for the hearts, minds, and wallets of the very same intended consumers. All signs point to more of the same in the future. In a world without such information storms and competition, selling might be completely unnecessary. Given reality, however, selling must always be the cumulative end result of marketing. The entire point of this process is to make a sale and then another and another and another. The primary rule of The Marketing Box is that, without a sale at the end of the rainbow, all is lost. So every business had better be selling all the time, or else.

Needless to say, the selling that needs to be done is not simple-minded shouting: "Buy me. I'm cheaper. I'm better." It would be nice to believe that modern markets are too sophisticated for this kind of drivel. The truth, however, is that corporate marketers are still using such tactics with varying degrees of success. But what really is needed is market-driving and market-creating selling—selling focused on customer needs and desires that is constantly finding ways to:

- Attract appropriate prospects and create customers with both rational and emotional appeals.

- Portray products and services within the context of customers' lives, showing how the customers can benefit.

- Place products and services within easy reach of appropriate consumers to multiply buying opportunities.

- Communicate in ways that add value to people's lives and produce a response so more can be learned about the consumers.

- Seize every opportunity to reinforce the rightness of buying the products being marketed, so new customers will actually buy and existing customers will buy again.

Marketing is all about understanding the infinitely various ways in which real people use real products and services, and then employing that knowledge to expand businesses. Because its subject matter is real life, which is complicated, marketing can be complex and far-reaching, unlike most of the other fundamentals of business practice. But understanding how good marketers think—how to approach complicated marketing problems—is not all that complicated itself. As few as three telling examples can point out the path to marketing thinking, which really is nothing more than thinking about people's lives and how those lives intersect with the promises and features of products and services.

Scandinavian Airlines System, for example, shows what can happen when management puts marketing in charge of the entire enterprise; how a whole company can act to multiply selling opportunities and make sure the organization takes advantage of each and every one. A recent marketing war raging in the glamorous, highly competitive sunglasses industry demonstrates that the fundamentals of distribution are often far more important than image or anything else; since people tend to buy what's within reach, it's crucial to be within reach when they're looking to buy. And a gifted group of marketers in Manchester, England, solving the tough problem of recruiting badly needed teachers for Britain's understaffed schools, demonstrate directly how the mind-set of the good marketer always focuses on understanding people's everyday lives and how to reach inside those lives.

Why Fewer Middle Seats Is Better Than State-of-the-Art Jets

As the 1970s gave way to the 1980s, Scandinavian Airlines System fell into trouble. Having bumped along as a profitable airline for seventeen consecutive years, the relatively small company—a consortium of the

national airlines of Denmark, Norway, and Sweden—suddenly accumulated some $25 million in operating losses from late 1979 through the fall of 1981.[7] For a line so small, the losses were massive, and no one in management knew exactly what to do about it. To fix the problem, SAS seized on Jan Carlzon, the young executive who had successfully turned around Linjeflyg, its domestic discount airline in Sweden.

Carlzon, barely forty years old, had put Linjeflyg on solid ground in a traditional way, by slashing fares and filling the deeply discounted seats. It was assumed he would do the same for SAS. But Carlzon quickly concluded that discount fares were not what the ailing airline needed. Instead, he decided to plow more money into reorganizing the entire company around the concept of providing flawless service to his best customers, the business fliers.

In many ways, there was nothing new or noteworthy in Carlzon's announcement that customer service would be his focus. European businesses had been focusing on service for several years. Prominent American consultants like Peter Drucker and Tom Peters, both of whom were retained to advise SAS, also concentrated on customer service. But in a startling move that would demonstrate the real power of marketing, Carlzon's strategy went far beyond the usual slogans and advertising tag lines. Instead of just talking service, Carlzon launched a full-scale reshaping of the way SAS did business—a true marketing revolution.

Carlzon's analysis of his market convinced him that the path to profits began with the frequent business traveler. So Carlzon invested in the pioneering creation of "EuroClass," a first-class service at full coach rates.

Demonstrating dramatically that marketing would permeate every aspect of the business and drive every decision, Carlzon's first marketing call overruled the technology experts at SAS: He canceled the airline's pending order for a dozen new Airbus A-300s.[8] From the company's viewpoint, the planes represented the latest in passenger-jet technology, something every airline believes it must have. But from the customers' viewpoint, the new jets were clearly a mistake. To begin with, they were too big to operate profitably on the short, non-

stop flights preferred by the business fliers. Instead, to fill them up, the A-300s would have to stop at an intermediate hub like Copenhagen, where loads could be consolidated. But stopping was exactly what the customers didn't want to do.

Carlzon opted for aging, smaller DC-9s, the mainstay of the SAS fleet. They could avoid the stops because they could make money with smaller loads. Just as important, where the A-300s have rows of three seats on each side of the center aisle, the DC-9s have one row of two seats and one row of three. This means fewer middle seats. "When was the last time anyone asked for a middle seat before boarding a flight?" Carlzon asked his aircraft experts.[9] It was a shrewd point having nothing to do with aircraft technology and everything to do with marketing.

Carlzon's next steps were more complex and time-consuming, but ultimately more important for SAS. Carlzon took a look at his entire business from the customer's viewpoint and saw that SAS, to a harried flier, was really nothing more than a series of brief interactions between customers and frontline employees. Every year, SAS had some ten million passengers, each of whom had encounters with an average of five SAS workers—baggage handlers, ticket agents, gate personnel, flight attendants, and cockpit crew. Each interaction lasted about fifteen seconds. "Thus, SAS is 'created' in the minds of our customers 50 million times a year, fifteen seconds at a time. These 50 million 'moments of truth' . . . ultimately determine whether SAS will succeed or fail as a company," Carlzon later wrote.[10]

Carlzon had come to the realization that a moment of truth occurred every time his company touched a customer—whenever a question was asked, a ticket purchased, a bag checked, a flight boarded, a flight canceled, a bag lost. Each fifteen-second moment, he saw, was an "opportunity to earn a loyal customer" or to lose one. Each of the 50 million moments represented an opportunity to sell SAS to its customers. And the bulk of those opportunities was in the hands of relatively junior people working the ticket counters, the gates, and the aisles of the airplanes.

Carlzon rightly saw that the dictates of marketing required him to turn his organization upside down. Decision-making power and

responsibility, he decided, had to be placed with the lower-ranking troops, not retained in executive suites or in "rule books and instructions from distant corporate offices." Because if frontline employees "have to go up the organizational chain of command for a decision on an individual problem, then those fifteen golden seconds will elapse without a response, and we will have lost an opportunity," Carlzon concluded.[11] So he decentralized the organization, making the painful changes needed to empower lower-level workers at SAS to make on-the-spot decisions.

All in all, Jan Carlzon offered a comprehensive lesson about how marketing can reshape every aspect of a company. At SAS, marketing changed the routes, the fare structure, the services, the aircraft fleet, and the organization. Carlzon's remaking of SAS shows what can happen when a manager employs the rigorously customer-centered discipline of marketing in running a company to meet customers' needs and desires. The results at SAS are a testament to the power of this kind of thinking.

As SAS put marketing in the driver's seat and took advantage of more selling opportunities, it raised its passenger traffic some 20 percent during a long period of complete stagnation in the European market. It also boosted its average load factor for passenger and freight from under 57 to nearly 64 percent. And as these critical operating numbers went up, so did income. Immediately reversing the losses suffered during its 1980 and 1981 financial years, SAS's airline operations earned nearly $53.5 million in 1982, some $59 million in 1983, and nearly $84 million in 1984. The string of positive earnings reports made SAS one of the industry's most profitable carriers.[12] And based on its financial performance as well as its service leadership, SAS was awarded the 1983 Airline of the Year award by *Air Transport World* magazine, the industry's trade bible.[13]

SAS, like the rest of the airline industry, has had its ups and downs since the 1980s. But Carlzon's willingness to let marketing transform his company has provided a lasting lesson for business. His "moments of truth," described in a book he wrote in 1986, have had a permanent impact on marketing thinking around the world. The critical impor-

tance of such moments for any business still holds true today, of course, only more so. Opportunities to create customers—and to keep them or lose them—have multiplied exponentially thanks to technology. They now occur around the clock and can involve live interactions between consumers and companies or automated interactions using the mail, automated phone systems, and an ever-growing array of Web-enabled devices from computers to PDAs to cell phones.

No matter where or when these moments occur, however, the old rules still apply—if a moment of truth produces no response or a disappointing one, a customer is lost. If the response has no relevance to the customer's life and needs, that's the end. But if an interaction with a company produces a fast, satisfying response for a consumer, then some trust is created.

The point of all this is the need to organize enterprises around the central mission of meeting customers' needs and expectations in ways that create and maintain trust. Trust, as we have seen, has been the basis of all commerce since before the Magna Carta was signed in the thirteenth century. Some seven hundred years later, in 2002, a lack of trust in corporate management was sufficient, all by itself, to undermine the $10 trillion U.S. economy.

Trust is important when things go well—when the plane takes off and lands on time, when the product works, when the stock market is rising. But trust is everything when there's been a problem—when the flight is canceled or the new car doesn't run properly. The crisis created when things go wrong can still produce a loyal customer, but only if there is a basis of trust and if the response to the problem is fast, relevant, and satisfying.

Turning moments of truth to "moments of trust" is one of the most critical goals of marketing, says Pamela Larrick, who is one of the global leaders in relationship marketing, the CEO of MRM Partners Worldwide, the relationship marketing arm of McCann-Erickson WorldGroup (the world's largest marketing agency), and my boss. What SAS teaches is that trust can be turned into profits all day long, but only by an organization in which the mission is shaped by marketing and marketing is everyone's responsibility all the time.

It's Where the Trendy Sunglasses Are,
Not What They Are, That Counts

Looking from the outside at the trendy, fashion-obsessed world of sunglasses, it would seem the competition must be all about image and advertising. Oakley, America's radical-chic shade-maker, invents frames with names like "Mag Switch" and "Scar," fashioned of exotic metal and ceramic materials and sculpted to look like standard-issue gear for trips to the Horsehead Nebula. Competitive Ray-Bans, on the other hand, score big by being the shades of choice for Agents J (Will Smith) and K (Tommy Lee Jones), the men protecting us against incursions from the Horsehead Nebula in successive summer block-buster *Men in Black* movies.

But from the inside, as the classic marketing battle of the international sunglasses wars played itself out in 2001 and 2002, it had nothing to do with the images, the ads, the product placements, or the promotions. It was all about distribution—getting the products within easy reach of the most likely customers—and the marketing-driven vertical integration of a global industry.

The eyewear industry is not to be taken lightly. The leader, Luxottica Group S.p.A., headquartered in northeastern Italy, operates seven plants in Italy and China that manufactured some 31.1 million sunglasses and prescription glasses frames in 2001. Luxottica's products were sold in 115 countries, and sales for the year were $2.7 billion.[14]

Luxottica's life story is a classic tale of marketing through vertical integration—taking complete control of every activity in an industry, from producing the component parts to making the finished products to wholesale distribution and, finally, retail sales to the end consumer. Luxottica began life in 1961 as a supplier of custom tools and parts used in the manufacture of frames for prescription glasses. It produced the first of its own finished eyeglass frames in 1969. Then, hungry for increased control and growth, the frame-maker purchased its wholesale distributor in 1974.

Luxottica steadily expanded its manufacturing and wholesale distribution arms throughout the 1980s, adding licenses to make designer products carrying high-fashion brand names such as Armani, Ungaro,

Ferragamo, Chanel, Brooks Brothers, and more. The multiplication of recognizable brands under its control positioned the company to complete the vertical integration of its prescription eyewear business by taking control of selling directly to consumers. Luxottica's big push into retail sales came in 1995 with the acquisition of LensCrafters, which then had some 600 stores selling prescription glasses to a mass market across North America, then and now the company's single biggest market. As Luxottica explained the move in its annual report, buying LensCrafters served the all-important marketing goals of giving the company both "direct distribution to, and [a] closer relationship with, the end customer." The principle at work was simple: If Luxottica owned the store, it no longer needed to fret about the most important part of its marketing plan—getting shelf space and proper display for its products in the right retail spaces.

Four years after the LensCrafters deal, Luxottica pushed further into the highly lucrative sunglasses business, a segment it had been building since 1990, by acquiring the Eyewear Division of Bausch & Lomb, the 150-year-old Rochester, New York, optical giant. The deal gave the Italians an iconic American brand—Ray-Bans, dating back to the 1930s. More important, buying the Ray-Ban business tilted Luxottica from a company primarily concerned with prescription glasses to one in which sunglasses represented the growing majority of sales. In 1997, Luxottica's business was two-thirds prescription frames and one-third sunglasses. By 2001, it was 57 percent sunglasses.

The number-two player in the industry is a relative latecomer. America's Oakley, Inc., headquartered in Foothill Ranch, California, got into the business roughly two decades later than its Italian rival, and its 2001 sales barely exceeded $429 million, less than one-sixth of Luxottica's. Still, Oakley had some 1,700 full-time employees, was selling its products in seventy countries, and had been growing the top line an average of 22 percent a year for five years, so it was not to be ignored.[15]

Oakley was launched in 1974 but didn't begin to sell sunglasses until a decade later. Its founder, chairman, and CEO, Jim Jannard, is described as a "mad scientist" in corporate literature. Oakley portrays itself as a technology company that "is driven to seek out problems,

create solutions, and wrap those solutions in art."[16] But in 2000, just under 74 percent of Oakley's business was sunglasses,[17] despite all-out attacks on segments including watches, shoes, apparel, and accessories.

Luxottica and Oakley appear to spend roughly the same portions of their income on advertising. Luxottica disclosed that its ad spending in 2001 amounted to roughly $192 million, about 7 percent of sales.[18] Oakley didn't disclose its ad spending, but its costs and margins look very similar to Luxottica's, so it would appear that advertising expense levels are similar. Luxottica tilts toward conventional media; Oakley toward a sports marketing program. Neither buys much (or any) expensive television, but both companies have traditionally spent heavily on point of sale—catalogs, displays, posters, and the like—demonstrating how important it is for both companies to get good visibility for their products in the stores where fashion-fickle young people, their biggest customers, go shopping for the latest eyewear.

So here's what Oakley knew in 2001: It knew that visibility at retail could be the whole game in sunglasses. It knew that Marketing 101 requires watching the competition, so Luxottica's decade-long climb in sunglasses could not have escaped Oakley's notice. And it can be presumed that Oakley also was aware of Luxottica's approach to marketing through vertical integration, a strategy the Italian market leader had been pursuing without letup for four decades. Still, it seems that Luxottica's next big move caught Oakley (and Wall Street) unawares—or, at least, unaware of the consequences—even though it should have been perfectly predictable based on Luxottica's past behavior. More important, its potential consequences should have been apparent to anyone with even the vaguest notion of marketing principles.

Early in 2001, Luxottica announced it had reached an agreement to acquire Sunglass Hut, the world's largest sunglasses retailer. Sunglass Hut's 1,944 outlets, most of them tiny, high-volume shops in U.S. malls and airports, had racked up sales in the preceding year of $688 million. The price for this prize was roughly $653 million.[19] At the time, Oakley's U.S. sales of sunglasses were spread among some 9,000 independent retailers representing about 13,600 locations. But the

sales weren't spread evenly. Sunglass Hut locations in the United States alone accounted for fully 21 percent of Oakley's worldwide sales. Sunglass Hut was Oakley's single biggest customer on the planet. The threat to Oakley of having its best customer taken over by its biggest competitor was material enough and potentially adverse enough to require disclosure to Oakley's shareholders.[20]

On the day the Sunglass Hut deal was announced, Oakley's stock dropped nearly 13 percent. Wall Street analysts, performing with their now famous lack of regard for the facts, reassured everyone that the deal meant nothing. So the stock began to recover and then to climb. Ominously, Oakley disclosed a few months later that its sales to Sunglass Hut, after rising 30 percent in the first quarter, had remained flat in the second quarter. This shock sent the stock down 13 percent again. But the real hit came on August 2, 2001, when Oakley issued a profits warning, saying Sunglass Hut had sharply reduced its orders for Oakley shades and Oakley wouldn't make its numbers for the year. In Milan, Luxottica's investor relations director, Alessandra Senici, told reporters the reason Oakley products were being dropped was a pricing dispute.[21] But describing the change in marketing strategy at Sunglass Hut, she told *The New York Times*, "Our idea is to increase the percentage of sales that will be Luxottica brands." This idea is not exactly rocket science and should have surprised no one. No matter, across the entire breadth of America, from Wall Street to Foothill Ranch, everyone expressed surprise and Oakley stock dropped like a rock, ending the day down 37 percent.[22]

To give Oakley credit, it realized immediately that it had been outflanked, and it fought back bravely in a series of marketing-driven steps aimed at bolstering its distribution and keeping its products in front of consumers. First, it immediately announced a "Premium Retailer" program to solidify its retail network by offering incentives to merchants who would commit to the entire Oakley line. Hungry for new distribution, it cut a deal with Foot Locker to carry Oakley sunglasses in about 350 stores.[23] Taking the cue, at last, from Luxottica, it even bought its own sunglasses retail chain, Arizona-based Iacon. The deal gave Oakley 40 mall stores—nothing like Sunglass Hut's nearly 2,000 stores, but better than the four company-owned

retail outlets that Oakley previously had operated.[24] As if to make sure Luxottica understood whom this flurry of activity was targeting, Oakley rushed into court and secured an emergency injunction preventing the Italians from making blue or green lenses that infringed on Oakley's patents for "Ice" and "Emerald" sunglasses.[25]

After all this drama, Oakley and Luxottica decided to call a truce in December 2001. Oakley signed a new three-year deal with Sunglass Hut in which the retail chain agreed to carry Oakley products. Announcing the contract, Oakley revised its 2002 earnings forecast upward by roughly 10 percent.[26] All seemed to return to normal in the multibillion-dollar sunglasses business. But the long-term consequences of Luxottica's marketing superiority remain quite significant.

The battle between Oakley and Luxottica hinged on the critical marketing disciplines of distribution and retail placement. Being where purchase-minded customers are is clearly a fundamental goal of marketing. It was true in the twelfth century when "chapmen"— traveling peddlers on foot—were the primary means of distributing goods around medieval Europe. Simply put, if your product wasn't in the chapman's rucksack, it was not going to be purchased. It is true today when Sunglass Hut is the foremost channel for delivering trendy shades to young consumers.

Luxottica consistently shaped its entire business strategy on marketing, maximizing the sales opportunities for its products and protecting itself from competitive vulnerability in distribution. Oakley, perhaps distracted by mad science, did not. Even though both companies have been growing at roughly the same rate, the markets have seen the difference and have rewarded Luxottica handsomely. In the five-plus years from 1997 to mid-2002, Oakley's stock price rose a total of 32 percent. In the same period, Luxottica was up 198 percent.

From an Audience of Many to an Audience of One

Forty years ago, a young advertising copywriter put together a letter hoping to find a new, better job. Across the top of the letter, in bold type, he arranged a few words, like this:

| **FREE** | | **SALE** | | **NEW** | |
| **WIN** | | **YOU** | | **LOVE** |

Underneath that eye-catching opening, the body of the letter began, "Some words leap at you. They reach out—seeking attention—squabbling with one another for the public's pocketbook."[27]

The job-seeking copywriter was Stan Rapp, and the letter landed him one of many good positions he would have throughout a long, successful, and extremely influential career. Ultimately, with Tom Collins, he founded Rapp & Collins, which became a global organization and the world's largest direct marketing group. He was founding chairman and CEO of MRM Partners Worldwide, the marketing agency which he helped grow from $200 million to more than $1.5 billion in billings. The six books Rapp co-authored, including the latest, *Max-e-Marketing in the Net Future*, trace the shift from mass marketing to individualized marketing. Rapp is widely credited as one of the foremost visionaries of modern marketing. In a conversation in 2002, he offered a copy of his old job-hunting letter to show that a lot of the fundamentals involved in communicating with consumers remain fundamental. The only word in his list that should be updated, Rapp said, is "love," which has been transformed to "sex" since the fifties.

In a look back at the dim origins of advertising, one key word among those highlighted by Rapp stands out as the bedrock foundation of all marketing communication. Oddly, history's most powerful marketing word is also seemingly the most innocuous, least sexy word on Rapp's list: "You." This word can be found in marketing communications throughout time: Etched on a wall in the ancient Roman city of Pompeii, buried under volcanic ash since the year 79, archeologists long ago uncovered an advertisement that gave travelers on a particular route the location of a tavern owned by an innkeeper named Sarinus. The key line in the ad was "This is to request you to enter."[28] Some 1,400 years later, in fifteenth century England, commercial criers stood in merchants' doorways and, to attract customers, called out repeatedly, "What do you lack, mistress?" or "What do you lack, master?"[29]

Communicating with the right people in the right words—person-

ally and directly addressing the consumers most likely to buy the product or service being described—is marketing's final fundamental. Given a product that meets real needs, an organization that is customer-focused, and distribution that reaches the right consumers, the last step is being able to say, one way or another, "You should buy this because . . ."—making sure that the reason offered is relevant and compelling to the people being addressed.

Here, too, the fundamentals have been under development for a couple thousand years, but the media, driven by technology, have changed drastically. Advertising media have evolved from the pitches of ancient peddlers to the voices of medieval commercial criers to pictorial street signs, which reigned over commercial speech in England from the 1400s to the mid-1700s.[30] What we would call mass media was born in the seventeenth century, when the first newspapers and magazines carried ads. With the nineteenth century came regular mail service, bringing ads in catalogs, fliers, and letters. Radio arrived in 1920, and the first radio ads came three years later;[31] commercial television followed in the 1940s. And the Internet, e-mail, and text messages on mobile phones arrived as the twentieth century gave way to the twenty-first.

These centuries of technological change have not much changed what corporate marketers are telling consumers about products. In the last few decades, however, technology has drastically altered what consumers are telling marketers about themselves and how much of this information businesses can retain. Smart marketing now requires that virtually every contact with a prospect or a customer must produce a response. And the advent of computers and interactive communications makes it possible, at last, to store and retrieve all these responses in an orderly way that vastly increases the marketers' knowledge of each of the people being addressed. As Stan Rapp has been saying for many years, "The straight-line progression is from mass to individualized marketing."[32] Today, as smart marketing guides production, distribution, and communication, it can and should increasingly consider the lives, wants, and needs of individual consumers—not undifferentiated masses, not even well-defined niches, but coherent segments made up of individuals, each of whom

is a known quantity and all of whom share traits, interests, desires, and needs that make them likely to relate to a given set of offerings in the same way.

Colleagues of mine in marketing, working from a beautiful old manor house outside Manchester, England, have produced more than one great example of modern marketing driven by a detailed under-standing of discrete consumer segments. These colleagues work in one of the major offices of MRM Partners Worldwide. I am familiar with their work because I sit on MRM Partners' Worldwide Board as head of the company's global custom publishing division.

In 2001, the Manchester office was asked by the United Kingdom's government-sponsored Teacher Training Agency to help recruit a di-verse and idealistic group of new teachers for the nation's badly short-staffed schools. The writers and media specialists in Manchester first created a powerful line that turns around the idea that teaching is the last resort of people who can't make it in business—that "those who can't, teach." Their line says simply, "Those Who Can, Teach." They created some very effective television spots to get the idea around, and they tagged each spot with a toll-free phone number and a Web ad-dress where people could respond and get more detailed information.

But the most interesting thinking on the project came as the mar-keters considered the major groupings of their best potential targets—students about to graduate, recent grads with unsatisfying jobs, and professionals seeking more meaningful second careers. They then took apart the daily lives of individuals in each of these segments, looking for times and places where the right people could be reached with messages that had the best chance of connecting with them.

"Increasingly, what you have to do is infiltrate people's everyday lives," says Andrew Thomas, Manchester's media chief. "You need people to think about things that aren't on their agendas." The result-ing guerilla tactics—what MRM Partners Manchester calls "ambient media"—were varied, arresting, and extremely successful, always matching messages and media in ways that reinforced one another.[33]

Looking for second careerists tired of the daily commute to a bor-ing job, the marketers attacked commuter buses and trains with sharp British humor. "Can you get hundreds of people into work?" asked a

sign on a bus. "Can you rise to a challenge?" demanded posters alongside up-escalators at train stations. At the end of the commute in London's financial district, sandwich bags at lunch spots were printed with the question, "Can you satisfy an appetite for numbers?" Students were targeted in the pubs they frequented at student unions. Printed coasters for beer glasses read, "Coasters need not apply" and "Fancy something more absorbing?" And in every case, the phone number and Web site address were given so responding was easy and the marketers would know what had worked, what hadn't, and who was answering.[34]

The results were impressive. Inquiries to the Teacher Training Agency phone lines hit 310,262 during the campaign period, a increase of some 186 percent over a two-year period. And average weekly hits on the Web site shot up more than ten times—1,000 percent plus—to more than 150,000.[35] All because a group of smart marketers thought carefully about the real lives of the people they were addressing.

I see this kind of technology-enabled marketing returning us to the personal interaction that was available in commercial transactions in the good old days of the mom-and-pop stores, when consumers were known to businesses. Rapp and some other thoughtful marketers see it as more. "I disagree with the whole contention that we're going back to the mom-and-pop corner store era only now we're electronic and automated. Mom and pop didn't know a tenth as much about their customers as we know. Mom and pop didn't know how much their customers earn . . . what other products they were buying in other stores . . . their financial investment history and, very often, mom and pop didn't even know their names," says Rapp.

Whatever mom and pop knew or didn't know, it is now the job of every marketing-savvy business to know its prospects and customers as individuals—to know their lives well enough to be sure that the products, the distribution, and the messages fit each individual life as perfectly as possible.

HOW TO BUILD THE BOX

THE SIXTH PLANK

1. Selling is defined as doing the right things for customers. To be successful, a company must be selling all the time.
2. Marketing must unify every aspect of a business around one purpose: creating a customer.
 a. Note: "Every" aspect of a business means *every* aspect, not some or most.
3. Every management team must devote time to thinking about its customers' daily lives and how each of those lives intersects with the business's promises and products.
4. Every time a company touches a customer, there is an opportunity to win or lose that customer. These opportunities must be maximized, not avoided.
 a. To win, the company must produce fast, satisfying results every time.
 b. Any other outcome will be a loss.
 c. Sorry, there's no middle ground here—it's either win or lose.
5. Marketing has no end: it begins before a product or service is created, continues as the product is priced and distributed, and doesn't stop when the sale is made.
6. The most important word in marketing is "you." Use it to address customers directly.

The Getting-Bigger-Faster Box: If You Can Buy It, Don't Start It Up

> *Follow the example of virtually every big company in history and buy your way to bigness.*

For Big Business or Small Entrepreneurs, Good Deals Add Up

General Electric, generally the world's most valuable company (with a market capitalization of $300 billion in mid-2002), got that way by buying other companies; for the past few years, it's been buying companies at the average rate of 100 a year.[1] Citigroup, the global financial services conglomerate with $27 billion in worldwide revenue and 192 million customer accounts, got that way after Sanford Weill acquired a nearly bankrupt lending company in Baltimore;[2] a series of subsequent acquisitions built the behemoth that is Citi. Warren Edward Buffett, America's second-richest man, got that way by buying companies—first little pieces of them, then bigger pieces; lately, he's been swallowing enterprises whole.

And these tactics are not the exclusive property of big business or billionaires. Clear Channel Communications, now America's biggest radio broadcaster, started off in 1972 when a young, small-time San Antonio investment banker and his car-dealer buddy acquired a struggling local radio station for $175,000. They borrowed all that money from a bank and spent the next thirty years leveraging their initial purchase into more shrewd media acquisitions.[3] By the fourth quarter of 2002, despite having lost some $5 billion in value in the

steep stock market slide, their acquired empire still had a market capitalization of $23.4 billion—a multiplication in value of more than 133,000 times. Not bad after starting with a company worth less than a nice house.

There are legions of stories about how great wealth has been created and consolidated through strings of smart acquisitions. No formula works all the time, but growing by acquisition, done right, works for everyone from huge conglomerates like General Electric to small, family-oriented entrepreneurs, like the founder of Clear Channel, who is now a genuine Texas billionaire on the strength of his venture's acquisitions. It is one of the best-kept secrets of capitalism that any smart middle manager with experience in an industry, a decent track record, and a business plan can attract investment for an acquisition from banks and leveraged buyout firms. Managers who do this generally get 20 to 25 percent of the equity in the deal even if they put up no money of their own.

Since every company in existence had to be started at some point, every company is arguably a start-up. But once begun, most companies find they can grow far faster and more efficiently, with less risk and more certainty, by buying companies rather than starting them. And many of the most successful entrepreneurs began their ventures with the acquisition of an existing company, not with a start-up. They financed their first deals by borrowing money from friends or friendly banks, or they got the backing of small leveraged buyout firms; then they bought their way to bigness with subsequent acquisitions.

Like most business tactics, mergers and acquisitions have gone in and out of favor with pundits, analysts, and academics. Buying companies, however, has been a mainstay of American business for more than a century, since the end of the Civil War, when rampant mergers gave rise to the rail, oil, and steel trusts whose size and power triggered the first antitrust laws in the 1890s.

As the 1990s boom ended, however, and lots of stocks began falling precipitously, acquisitions not only slowed, they suddenly became as unfashionable as leisure suits. The financial press decided that so-called organic growth was preferable to growth by acquiring.

The Wall Street Journal ran a front-page story in the summer of 2002 saying a study of "serial acquirers" showed their stock values had dropped three times as much as the general market in the scandal-plagued, recessionary climate of that period.[4] Much of the story's rhetoric ("The troubles of the serial acquirers raise new questions about the growth-by-acquisition strategy . . .") made the practice of buying companies sound distasteful.

Heading the list of distasteful acquirers in the summer of 2002 was Tyco International Ltd. Patterning itself after GE's aggressive company-buying strategy, Tyco had grown to a $34-billion-a-year conglomerate by acquiring businesses in electronic component manu-facturing, security and alarm systems, medical products, fiber-optic cable, and most recently, financial services.[5] Not every one of Tyco's hundreds of deals was a good one, but its earnings, at just under $5.5 billion pre-tax for the year ending September 2001, kept pace with its top-line expansion and kept Tyco a fair-haired favorite of Wall Street. By early 2002, its market cap had peaked at roughly $110 billion, a hugely impressive number. Over the ensuing half-year, however, as the stock market took a dive, some 80 percent of Tyco's market value evaporated.[6]

A number of commentators and academics blamed the rapid downhill tumble on Tyco's strategy of aggressive acquiring. But in fact, investors first became uneasy about Tyco when its accounting methods were questioned in the wake of Enron, and the uneasiness accelerated with the announcement of an ill-considered plan to break the company into four pieces. Although the accounting questions largely went away and the break-up was canceled, the uneasiness turned to severe queasiness as stories surfaced about personal finan-cial misbehavior by several Tyco executives, most notably CEO L. Dennis Kozlowski. Then came Kozlowski's sudden resignation, just after it was revealed he may have misappropriated corporate funds for personal reasons and just before his criminal indictment for evading a million dollars in New York State sales tax on some brutally expensive paintings he'd hung in his Manhattan apartment.[7] Finally, in the fall, came formal charges that Kozlowski and two lieutenants had conducted a "criminal enterprise" that looted $170 million from

the company and produced hundreds of millions of additional illicit gain through stock manipulations.[8] All in all, these revelations of criminality, dishonesty, and flagrantly self-enriching behavior were not good events for Tyco. But neither were they the result of Tyco's M&A strategy.

In the past few decades, there has been a great deal of debate about whether acquisitions have created real value for buyers and sellers. Some have contended that mergers are actually a negative financial force, destroying value and hurting the economy. The popular mistrust of growth-by-acquisition strategies that washed over the world in early 2002 was fueled partly by this view and partly by general stock market skittishness. Despite this, however, the most recent and most thorough economic research shows that, over time, acquisitions have added to the economy.

One dense and authoritative research paper, published by Harvard Business School in early 2002, looked at 1,536 mergers from 1970 to 1994 and found that evidence on stock market returns to both buyers and sellers "as well as post-merger operating performance, suggests that mergers on average increase value, and lead to improved profitability in subsequent years."[9]

Another study by the same Harvard research team, published in a journal of the prestigious American Economic Association, looked at more data and added valuable insights.[10] Surveying M&A activity over the past century, the study says that general economic theory provides five reasons to explain why companies buy companies. Restated plainly, the list would look like this:

1. To "create market power" by growing an enterprise to dominate an industry

2. To improve efficiency by creating economies of scale or other synergies that reduce expenses and improve margins

3. To provide diversification that reduces market risks for the acquiring company

4. To impose "market discipline" by getting rid of a target company's less-than-competent managers

5. To feed the egos (and presumably, the pockets) of the less-than-competent managers on the buy side

To complete this list, I would add only one item:

6. To extend a company's core business to new geographic markets, domestic and international: new cities, new states, new countries

Like other studies before it, this one concludes that mergers come in waves, clustered by industry, indicating that a sizable portion of deals in any given decade are driven by changes in the circumstances of an entire industry. It states emphatically that the biggest driver of deals in the nineties was not what we thought it was—not advances in technology, the Internet bubble, or the overheated stock market—but deregulation of the telecommunications, broadcasting, and banking industries. "We can say without exaggeration or hyperbole that in explaining the causes of mergers and acquisitions, the 1990s were the 'decade of deregulation,'" the authors of the study conclude. From 1988 through the 1990s, "deregulated industries account for nearly half of all annual deal volume, on average," the study says.

Prior studies have found, oddly enough, that most of the economic gains generated by M&A activity appear to wind up in the pockets of the sellers, not the buyers. The authors of Harvard's 2001 study agree. "Our analysis of the immediate stock market response to more than 4,000 mergers completed during . . . 1973–1998 concurs with these prior reviews," they declare. They recognize, however, that this finding generates "reason to worry" about the validity of the data. It would be hard to understand, for instance, why anyone would be a buyer if the only winners in deals were the sellers. Assuming a reasonably sane economic world, if this is truly how things work, then one would expect all acquisitions to cease.

In fact, there has been no convincing economic research on this subject and no one really understands, in a big-picture way, how mergers create value. But after pondering the problem, the three Harvard professors who authored the study produced the following piece of common sense, which is worth quoting at length:

Part of the issue here may be that an acquiring firm can seek a merger for a mix of reasons. Many firms mention mergers as their main strategic tool for growth and success, and point to possible economies of scale, synergies, and greater efficiency in managing assets. Alternatively, there is the somewhat contradictory evidence that mergers can be evidence of empire-building behavior by managers. If mergers could be sorted by true underlying motivations, it may be that those which are undertaken for good reasons do benefit acquirers, but in the average statistics, these are canceled out by mergers undertaken for less benign reasons.[11]

Translation: There are good deals and bad deals. The goods ones, done right and for the right reasons, make money for the buyers. The bad ones, which don't adhere to the rules, are losers. This is the essence of all wisdom concerning acquisitions: execution is everything.

A Korean Mogul Plays the Start-up Game and Loses (Billions)

Every once in a great while, a start-up like Microsoft defies the odds and quickly engulfs the world on the force of its original start-up business plan. Bill Gates and Paul Allen started up a partnership in 1975 to create the world's first programming language on a primitive personal computer.[12] Today, Microsoft is the world's second most valuable company on most days (worth roughly $270 billion in mid-2002) and its principal business is still writing software. This has made Bill Gates, famously, America's richest man.

It may sound like a circular argument, but it is important to bear in mind that Microsoft was created because it had to be. There was no way to acquire a software company like Microsoft in 1975 because none existed. In fact, the personal computer—the machine for which Microsoft intended to write software—barely existed in 1975. So Gates and Allen had no choice.

Powered by stories like Gates and Microsoft, the start-up looms much larger in the American imagination than any other method of

generating business activity and creating wealth. The true capitalist dream is to start a one- or two-person company, preferably in a garage or basement, and grow it into a globe-girdling monopoly. This fable mirrors plenty of real-life stories, from Henry Ford's little auto company to Bill Hewlett's and Dave Packard's little electronics firm to Walt Disney's little entertainment company. It was this fable that fueled the technology start-up rage of the 1990s, when any idea, no matter how crazy, could attract millions in capital. Rags to riches is the preferred American dream. It is very gratifying and inspiring to think of people turning nothing into something grand.

But the start-up game is never easy, and as a matter of brutal economic fact, it usually resembles a Las Vegas casino more than a reasoned business investment. For a long time, one widely quoted statistic held that 80 percent of all start-up businesses die before the age of five. More recent research suggests the death rate may be below 50 percent during the first eight years. But that's only if you include start-ups that have changed ownership, which means counting new companies that may have survived only because they were gobbled by larger, more stable firms. Eliminate the companies that changed ownership and the survival rate sinks back to 28 percent.[13] So at best, the odds are equal to flipping a coin; at worst, playing poker would be a better investment. And these long odds are not limited to tiny start-ups with no capital and no experience, as Lee Kun Hee demonstrated.

Lee, chairman of the South Korean giant Samsung Electronics Company Ltd., is one titan of industry who would have done less damage playing poker with his company's money. But Lee was a car buff and loved to run his Porsche around his company-owned racetrack. So in 1994 he announced he was going to start an auto company from scratch at a projected cost of just under $5 billion.[14] He forged ahead despite the entrenched competition, a global excess of auto production capacity, and the objections of his own managers. Leading up to the start of production in March 1998, Samsung Motors did everything a real auto company would do—bought technology from Japan's Nissan, erected a modern plant in South Korea that could churn out 240,000 cars a year, and set up a trendy design studio in Los

Angeles.[15] The only thing it failed to do was sell cars. After moving only 45,000 cars in the face of a steep recession, its losses for 1998 exceeded its revenues. Samsung shuttered its auto factory early in 1999, after less than a year of production, and declared bankruptcy in midyear, owing its creditors some $3.7 billion. Explaining the bankruptcy at the time, Lee said, "At this point, there are no other ways to solve the problems of Samsung Motors." Deeply embarrassed, Lee liquidated a huge portion of his personal fortune to create a $2.4 billion fund to make up vendors' losses and help his displaced employees.[16] It has been estimated that the start-up's total losses ultimately came to $13 billion.[17]

Throughout the period when Lee was playing auto baron, the *real* auto industry was undergoing massive global consolidation, driven by the unchanging economic laws that encourage mergers to eliminate excess capacity in any industry. Germany's DaimlerBenz bought Chrysler in late 1998, and the deal seemed to set the whole industry in play. Soon France's Renault acquired a substantial stake in Nissan, Ford bought Sweden's Volvo, and General Motors snapped up Sweden's other car company, Saab. Shortly after the DaimlerChrysler deal closed, South Korea's Hyundai bought control of Kia, another troubled Korean automaker. And finally, in September 2000, Renault bought 70 percent of Samsung's remains, including Lee's $3 billion factory, for just $512 million,[18] giving the French a cheap entrée to the Korean market.

Whether Samsung would have been able to actually manage an auto company—*any* auto company—will forever be open to question. But it is clear the company would have been far better off if it had done what its experienced competitors did and invested its cash in buying an established auto company rather than trying to start one. Some of the auto mergers of the 1990s, including the Chrysler deal, hit big trouble. But unlike the Samsung Motors start-up, they all still have a shot at producing returns for their shareholders. Even with a minority share of Renault Samsung, Samsung will never see a reasonable return on its money.

Both entrepreneurs and established companies have looked at the odds against start-ups over the years. Most have concluded what Lee Kun Hee proved beyond a doubt: Acquiring on the right terms makes

more sense, in most cases, than trying to start a new business from scratch.

Starting a business means stepping off a cliff into the unknown; with no operating history, forecasts are just guesses, no matter how well educated. Buying a business, on the other hand, means acquiring something that is actually working. At the closing, instead of a hope and a prayer and a business plan, an acquirer is supposed to get all the things that are so hard to create in business:

- A proven approach to making money
- A set of assets whose values can be determined
- An established stream of revenues
- A share of the market
- A list of customers
- Distribution and sales channels
- Experienced managers and workers
- A history of cash flows and profits (or at the very least, a clear path to cutting expenses to produce such profits quickly)

Because established businesses have assets and cash flow, banks will lend money at reasonable rates for acquisitions. This is hugely advantageous. Using borrowed money to finance deals reduces the need for equity investment, so it increases returns on equity. This makes both Wall Street and the acquirers' personal accountants very happy (so long as the debt doesn't rise beyond control). Equally important, since life is short, acquiring is a much quicker route to growing bigger than starting something new, since the profits of an acquisition can be consolidated into the buyer's P&L immediately.

But the most critical disadvantage with start-ups is embodied in the lesson Lee Kun Hee learned: With a start-up, you always have to pay in advance before you see what you're buying. It's no fun to wait two or three years to see whether your start-up will work and then have to walk away from millions or billions of invested dollars when you suddenly learn the hoped-for revenues just aren't going to materialize.

Prospective acquirers, on the other hand, are entitled to thoroughly examine a target business before closing the deal and spending their money. The process, called "due diligence," typically involves accountants and lawyers poring over a target company's books and records, searching diligently for flaws. If the prospective buyer finds that the target business lacks any essential elements for future success—assets, paying customers, profits, good managers, skilled workers, healthy cash flow—it's very easy to just walk away from the deal.

The World's Most Successful Company Buys and Buys and Buys . . .

The question in business, then, is not whether to acquire, but why, when, and how to acquire so the odds in favor of making the merger work are as high as possible. For instruction on these points, there is no better teacher than General Electric. GE is the nearly letter-perfect example of a large company whose core strategy has always included acquiring for growth and diversification. Over more than a century, GE has created an acquisition machine that works fairly consistently to produce favorable outcomes in a wide variety of industries.

GE, which topped *Fortune* magazine's list of America's most admired companies in 2002 (as it has every year since 1998), was born in the merger mania that struck the nascent electrical industry in the late 1800s. Throughout the period following Thomas Edison's invention of the first practical electric light in 1879, dozens of tiny concerns popped up to make and market versions of electric lamps, and they merged in various combinations, seeking size, market share, superior technology, and efficiency. One of the resulting agglomerations of acquired lighting companies was Thomas Edison's legendary Edison General Electric Company, founded in 1878.[19] It was 1892 when Edison's company merged with another major player that happened to have more efficient management, producing a higher return. The merged entity was named the General Electric Company.

Thus, from its prehistory, GE was the result of constant acquisition and consolidation. It was always intended to be a conglomerate, and in

every era, under every one of its nine chairmen (including Jeffrey Immelt, the current occupant of GE's corner office in Fairfield, Connecticut),[20] it has pursued a constant search to acquire other companies.

The early expansion of GE's first core business was fueled by a number of acquisitions during the reign of its first CEO, Charles A. Coffin. The pace of the mergers quickened in 1901 when the National Electric Lamp Association was founded in Cleveland by two entrepreneurs who merged their lamp-manufacturing concerns. Even though they were competing with GE, they believed the bigger company could benefit from helping them and they asked GE for capital from the outset. GE bought 75 percent of National Electric Lamp Association's stock, and the money allowed National to assemble more small lighting companies under its nameplate.[21] GE, meanwhile, got what it wanted: every lamp made by National used GE's proprietary screw-base, helping GE establish its base as the industry standard. In 1911, a federal court saw through the scheme and ordered GE to start operating the business under its own name. National ultimately became the core of the global GE Lighting Division, which is still headquartered on ninety-two acres of countryside eight miles outside of Cleveland, a site picked and developed by the National Electric Lamp Association ("NELA") and known to this day as Nela Park.[22]

The year GE was formed under Charlie Coffin's leadership, it had $20 million in sales. Some ninety years later, when Jack Welch took over as GE's eighth CEO, the company had $25 billion in sales, nearly a 1,250-fold (125,000 percent) increase in revenue. It is impossible to unwind precisely how much of that phenomenal increase—an 8.34 percent compound annual growth rate over nine decades—was due to the constant acquisitions and how much came from so-called organic growth generated inside GE's existing business base. The company has estimated that historically its growth has derived in equal thirds from acquisitions, internal growth, and improved productivity. But it is certain that GE never would have grown as it did without buying larger and larger companies at an ever increasing pace.

Welch's first act as CEO was to reconfigure GE around its best-performing businesses, shucking those that didn't meet his objectives for growth and dominance. Taking the helm in the midst of a reces-

sion, Welch told Wall Street analysts, "In this slower growth environment of the '80s, the winners will be those who insist upon being No. 1 or No. 2 in every business they are in."[23]

During his first five years as CEO, Welch sold off 232 GE businesses for nearly $6 billion, including air-conditioning, housewares, and semiconductors. But in the same period, Welch's GE spent $11 billion acquiring some 338 companies in financial services, broadcasting, and medical equipment, launching GE into a whole new series of industries, concentrating on services to diversify the base of mostly manufacturing companies.[24]

There were dozens of major acquisitions on this list, but in hindsight the most notable was the $1.08 billion purchase in May 1984 of Employers Reinsurance, a major player in the closely held business of providing insurance companies protection against catastrophic losses.[25] The purchase vaulted the division then known as GE Credit (now GE Capital) into high-gear growth. Over the next dozen years, growing internally and gobbling other companies around the world, GE Capital would expand to provide 40 percent of GE's total profits, entering businesses as diverse as aircraft leasing, credit cards, corporate finance, and insurance. Taken on its own, Employers Re, the biggest part of GE Capital, would grow to become GE's third-biggest business worldwide.[26]

Eighteen months after buying Employers Re, Welch agreed to pay $6.28 billion for RCA, which included a large consumer electronics business, defense contracting, and the prize for GE—the NBC television network, five local TV stations, and eight radio stations.[27] Then, capitalizing on the RCA deal, Welch swapped RCA's consumer electronics divisions for $800 million in cash plus the sophisticated medical equipment businesses of France's Thomson, SA. GE got Thomson's big X-ray equipment unit in Baltimore, plus three units in France producing equipment for radiology, ultrasound, and nuclear medicine. The deal added 6,600 employees and roughly $1.1 billion in sales to GE's medical technology businesses, while also giving the growing American conglomerate a foothold in Europe.[28]

So it went for twenty years under Welch, pretty much as it had gone at GE during the eight decades before him.

By the end of Jack Welch's tenure, the pace had escalated to roughly 100 acquisitions annually for GE—two a week—bringing the total number of companies acquired on his watch to an estimated 1,000.[29] In the end, Jack went out the way he had come in—trying to do a deal. His last act as CEO was to stay on past his retirement date, trying to close the massive $45 billion acquisition of Honeywell International. European regulators finally blocked the merger as anticompetitive, and Welch stepped down.

It wasn't that Welch and GE never made mistakes. The $600 million acquisition of the privately held brokerage firm Kidder, Peabody in 1986 was an excellent example of a very bad deal. GE unloaded the scandal-smothered business to PaineWebber in 1994 for preferred stock valued at $670 million—giving GE nearly 25 percent ownership of PaineWebber. GE, which had pumped $800 million into the money-losing Kidder firm, had to record a $500 million loss on its books. And that didn't include the embarrassment suffered by GE for various bond-trading and insider-information scandals that wracked Kidder.[30] Still, even this bad deal ultimately produced nearly $2 billion for GE after the Swiss investment bank UBS acquired PaineWebber in the summer of 2000.[31]

As the growth in the top line, the bottom line, and the all-important market cap line show, most of GE's deals went well, not badly, and allowed Jack Welch to continue the century-old GE tradition of creating more shareholder value than any other company in the world. By the time Welch was finished acquiring for GE, he had grown the value of the company from approximately $12 billion to more than $300 billion. The facts show that General Electric has learned the secret of profiting from acquisitions, having done it over and over until they got it right.

Buying an $8 Billion "Evil Empire," One Deal at a Time

For anyone who may be thinking that this kind of wealth-building is possible only for a century-old behemoth, there are thousands of

examples of small entrepreneurs who built billion-dollar enterprises in a decade or two by acquiring companies. Most of the stellar examples of this sort are privately held corporations that no one has ever heard about. But one publicly held example is Clear Channel, the Texas-based king of radio broadcasting in the U.S.

Clear Channel's founder and chairman, L. Lowry Mays, a Texas petroleum engineer with a Harvard MBA, once told *Forbes* in the early nineties, "I had no intention of getting into the broadcast business." But he and his partner, a car dealer named B. J. McCombs (universally known as "Red"), bought a single radio station in 1972 and just kept on buying. Mays, then only thirty-six years old, managed the company, and McCombs acted as a director and advisor. Mays had bought that first radio station entirely with borrowed money and was adept at using bank debt and equity, following his first public stock offering in 1984, to finance his company's steady expansion. In Clear Channel's first twenty years, Mays cautiously acquired eighteen radio stations and half-a-dozen independent television stations. Together they generated $74 million in 1991 revenue. *Forbes* patronizingly called Clear Channel "a smart little media company."[32]

With growing financial power and management depth, Clear Channel began to steadily ratchet up the pace and size of acquisitions. By the end of 1995, it had doubled its radio holdings and upped its TV stations to ten.[33] By year-end 1996, Clear Channel's deals had brought the company's total to eighty-six radio and eleven TV broadcasters. In the five years since Clear Channel had been proclaimed a smart little company, Mays had raised his revenue a whopping 438 percent to nearly $400 million with pretax earnings of $71.2 million.[34] And he was just getting started.

Clear Channel sailed into the following year with an increased appetite, adding major billboard companies to its shopping list alongside broadcasters, and moving offshore to Mexico and the UK. Total revenue for 1997 nearly doubled over the prior year to $790 million.[35] In that year's annual report, the company stated its strategy simply: "to identify and acquire under-performing stations on favorable terms and to . . . improve the performance of such stations . . . through effective programming, reduction of costs and aggressive promotion,

marketing and sales."[36] This is the strategic bible for any company seeking to consolidate an industry through acquisitions.

By 1999, Clear Channel, with 512 stations, was number one among American radio broadcasters. That was the year it agreed to acquire the nation's number-two radio company, AMFM Inc., for a total of about $23.5 billion. The resulting conglomeration, after selling off some 125 stations to comply with government regulations, would still have 830 radio stations, the company announced.[37]

The deals, of course, kept coming. Even before the mammoth AMFM deal closed, Clear Channel had announced the $3.3 billion acquisition of SFX, a massive live-entertainment enterprise with arenas, amphitheaters, Broadway venues, and agencies representing top sports talent. The deal further broadened Clear Channel's integration of entertainment and advertising, giving it live acts and tours along with the broadcast and billboard assets to promote it all. Clear Channel booked just under $8 billion in sales for 2001, racking up a 1,900 percent increase over the prior five years.[38]

As for L. Lowry Mays, his Clear Channel stock was worth well over $1 billion in the fourth quarter of 2002. And his car-dealer partner, Red McCombs, had stock worth considerably more than half a billion. Mays had installed his two sons, Randall and Mark, as senior managers of the family business and was spending more time on his Texas ranch. Clear Channel's biggest problem was that its rapid, efficient growth in allied, interlocking industries had earned it almost universal fear and envy among competitors and critics of big media. Clear Channel, having grown from a single tiny radio station, was suddenly being referred to in broadcast circles as "the evil empire."

Clear Channel, GE, and countless other successful acquirers have provided businesspeople, academics, and analysts with proof that acquisitions are a critical part of most companies' growth strategies and that M&A can be made to work for a company no matter what the overall statistics might say. The key to doing successful deals, like the key to most business challenges, is knowing how to do them and then executing flawlessly, over and over.

A fascinating study by two consultants at McKinsey & Company confirms this. The consultants looked at 829 acquisitions made by

twenty-one leveraged buyout firms, not corporate acquirers, in the decade from 1985 to 1994. The LBO firms—so-called financial acquirers—have to be good at acquiring because that is all they do. The McKinsey study found that LBO investors are, in fact, very good at what they do and the vast majority of the deals they close produce excellent returns—35 percent per year on average.[39]

Four years after the McKinsey study, a *Harvard Business Review* article revisited the "surprising statistic" revealed by McKinsey. "Why, then, are financial acquirers so successful?" asked the article. "We believe the answer lies in their approach to the acquisition process."[40] It's simple, the article concluded: Most corporate acquirers do poorly at M&A because they never take charge of the process, leaving it to outside investment bankers, consultants, and lawyers. The LBO firms, just like successful corporate acquirers that buy constantly, make M&A a core business activity; they master it and execute it based on a tried-and-true process.

When all is said and done, the evidence shows that there is a timeless set of rules governing successful mergers. We can find these rules by observing GE. We can find them by observing the vast majority of LBO firms. We can find them easily at Clear Channel, whose simply stated strategy hasn't varied over thirty years. We can find these rules in practice at any successful acquirer, public or private, large or small.

Based on the experience of successful acquirers, this is what a brief summary of the rules looks like:

BEGIN WITH A GOOD STRATEGIC REASON FOR BUYING. Mays, for example, demanded companies in broadcasting, advertising, and entertainment where he could cut costs and improve the bottom line. Welch demanded high-growth companies that would place GE first or second in an industry. One GE Capital acquisitions expert once said that to avoid buying without a good strategic reason, always ask this simple question about every deal: "Why am I doing this?"[41]

GET PLUGGED INTO THE DEAL FLOW AND STAY PLUGGED IN. Shopping for companies is like shopping for anything big, complicated, and pricey—in the words of the old Smokey Robinson song, you better shop around. Look at everything. It provides a feel for what's

available, what the prices should be like, how good management operates compared to bad management in the industry being targeted, and how competitors truly stack up against one another. This is not a part-time gig for amateurs. In each significant business unit, GE maintains business development officers whose sole job is to find deals. Cypress Group, a New York LBO firm, once told researchers that it looks at as many as five-hundred deals a year, closely examines some twenty-five, and closes only two or three.[42]

MAKE FRIENDS WITH THE SELLERS. Understand what they want from the deal. This creates a competitive advantage if a bidding war breaks out. It also offers a faster, deeper look into the heart of the matter: Do the sellers seem trustworthy and smart? While being warm and friendly, however, never be reluctant to honestly and bluntly stake out a must-have position. I once began a meeting with a senior executive of a large European media company by suggesting the possibility of buying a portion of one of his divisions to create a joint venture. He said, "That's fine, but we only do JVs that we control." I responded, "I understand that because we, too, only do JVs that we control. So we can forget a JV." Some weeks later, he agreed to an outright sale of the division we had been discussing.

TAKE DUE DILIGENCE SERIOUSLY; MAKE SURE OPERATIONS PEOPLE ARE INVOLVED. Too many companies leave due diligence in the hands of lawyers and accountants, forgetting the critical questions that must be answered about the day-to-day management of the target company. Schedule meetings and lunches and social occasions with the seller's managers. Find out who's good and who's bad, how the sellers really operate, how their operations can be improved, and whether they are capable of change. Find out how key customers will regard the sale. These human factors are most often disregarded and are most often responsible for destroying the value of a merger after the closing, postmortems on countless deals have shown.

REMEMBER, CLOSING THE DEAL ISN'T THE END OF ANYTHING, IT'S THE BEGINNING. Once the deal is done, the real work begins: running the acquired company. Deal-hungry GE Capital, through trial and error

beginning in the mid-1980s, has developed a carefully structured integration process that kicks in during due diligence and continues long after the deal closes. It begins with early discussions during due diligence that focus on what has been learned about the target company and how that knowledge can help manage the target post-closing.

Again, GE's contribution is that this is no job for part-timers or managers distracted by other tasks. For each deal, GE Capital designates an "integration manager" to make sure a detailed post-closing action plan is prepared for immediate execution after the sale is completed. It will never be easier to change things than the moment after the closing, when people are actually expecting change.

This means working out the most minute detail *before* the deal closes. After the closing, it's too late. Know in advance who is being fired and retained, who will lead and who will follow, what facilities will be sold or closed, and every other aspect of operations. Changes in policy, strategy, and attitude have to be communicated immediately. As an account of GE Capital's processes says, "Never tell the acquired staff that it will be business as usual when it never will be again."[43] And customers need to be told and reassured, as well.

Emerging from due diligence, a good M&A team knows everything about the target. If big problems have been uncovered, this is the moment to walk away. If not, the next critical step is to make sure final negotiated terms work, remembering that they must work for both sides. Inexperienced negotiators mistakenly believe they must "come out on top" in the deal. In truth, a successful negotiation means both sides get what they need and both sides fail to get some of what they want.

Deal terms must work financially. The most famous saying in M&A is that the one mistake you never recover from is paying too much. But a purchase contract also must work operationally. Unless the negotiating team includes operations managers as well as lawyers and accountants, it is likely that some points in the deal will interfere with post-closing operations. The operational managers also play the crucial role in endgame negotiations of telling the lawyers what really matters and what doesn't.

No set of rules can ever ensure that every acquisition will work and produce good returns. There's always risk in operating a company. But failing to follow the rules of acquisitions is an almost certain guarantee of failure and losses. And the statistics showing widespread failure in corporate M&A efforts only prove that not enough managers know and practice the rules.

In this case, however, there is no excuse for not getting it right. Many others have been down this path successfully. The answers are out there.

HOW TO BUILD THE BOX

THE SEVENTH PLANK

1. Done right, acquiring is inherently less risky than starting something new. Never start what you can buy.
2. M&A is not a part-time job, a hobby, or a sideline for managers.
3. To get acquisitions right, make M&A a core business activity.
4. Create an acquisition strategy.
5. Be opportunistic, but don't stray too far from the strategy.
6. Learn the M&A practices of the companies that buy over and over again.
7. Designate full-time managers to find and investigate deals.
8. Shop around.
9. Do due diligence diligently, remembering to look closely at the people, not just the buildings, the accounts, and the pending lawsuits.
10. Involve operators, not just lawyers and accountants.
11. Have a painfully detailed integration plan before the deal closes.
12. Never be afraid to walk away from a deal before closing.
13. Never pay too much.
14. Once the deal closes, never hesitate and never look back—execute the post-closing plan without delay.
15. The buyer pays for the closing dinner.

The People Box:
Hire Smart or Manage Hard

> *When it comes to people, you can hire smart*
> *and get out of the way, or you can run yourself*
> *ragged micromanaging.*

Can Your People Make Good Decisions
in a Falling Airplane?

Think of what follows as a management problem confronting the CEO of a multitrillion-dollar corporation that, because of its peculiar line of business, must depend on kids in their twenties to handle the most delicate tasks involving the company's biggest assets and competitors:

A U.S. Navy spy plane with twenty-four crew members was cruising over the South China Sea on April 1, 2001, when a hostile fighter jet begin closing in. The American EP-3 turboprop, so slow-moving and heavy with electronics that naval personnel call it the "flying pig," had no chance of outrunning the Chinese fighter.

Lieutenant John Comerford, the senior evaluator on board, was doing his job—receiving, evaluating, and relaying surveillance reports from the crew—when he became alarmed at what he was hearing about the shadowing fighter. Edging to the hatch for a look outside, Comerford watched the Chinese pilot deliberately fly his jet's wingtip within a scant three feet of the American plane's wingtip. Comerford had never seen such dangerous flying.

The fighter disappeared from Comerford's view momentarily, and

then, with a loud boom, the small jet struck the larger plane's left wing. "The plane rolled to the left, nose down, upside down and I was pinned to the floor of the plane" by forces that were two to three times normal gravity, Comerford recalled later.[1]

Up front, the American pilot in command, Lieutenant Shane Osborne, was pretty sure he and his crew were about to die.[2] But he stuck to his task and, miraculously, pulled out of the free fall at 15,000 feet, after dropping nearly a mile and a half. With the plane level but shaky, Osborne called for bailout procedures.

Back in the confused and crowded cabin, the crew was preparing to bail out as directed. But at the same time, they immediately took the initiative to begin systematically destroying the classified documents and gear for which they were responsible, knowing that part of their mission was to keep the Navy's secrets out of Chinese hands. Up front, working to accomplish the mission of keeping his crew alive, Osborne realized he might be able to make it to the Chinese air base at Lingshui on nearby Hainan Island.

Comerford wielded a fire ax, crushing and smashing equipment and throwing it out an open hatch as his crewmates held on to keep him from flying out of the damaged plane. Minutes later, Osborne managed to set his plane and his people down safely on the runway at Lingshui, where Chinese troops surrounded the disabled aircraft.

Eleven days later, after tense negotiations that captured the world's attention, all American crew members were released. Landing in Hawaii, the crew took a phone call from their boss, a president known for his corporate style of running America. George W. Bush did what Jack Welch or Bill Gates has been known to do in similar circumstances—he praised his employees' work, starting with the senior manager. "You did a heck of a job getting that airplane in," the president told the pilot. And to the entire crew, he said, "We're really proud of you. You represent the best of America."[3]

Michael Useem, a management professor at the Wharton School, appears to concur with this boss's performance evaluation. Useem uses the incident over the South China Sea as an example of how empowered employees can and should take control on the job. "The commander carried total authority on that aircraft, but he had people

on board who were well trained in the art of taking charge and of carrying out their responsibilities and collectively acting as if they were all in command," Useem says.[4]

Since the modern idea of employees and jobs first surfaced some two hundred years ago, a great deal has been written and said about a business's employees—how to select them, how they ought to be treated and managed, and how they ought to perform on the job. But Useem's brief analysis of the EP-3 crew sums up precisely what modern organizations need from employees. As he says, management and nonmanagement employees must "collectively act as if they were all in command" together.

It is particularly telling that the idea of collective command should come from a close look at a military unit. From the viewpoint of the average civilian manager, the military looks like a welcome relief from the increasing democracy of the workplace. At least in the armed forces, we reason, there is an unequivocal chain of command, where everyone still follows orders and where one person—and one person only—is in total charge at any given moment. But as the EP-3 incident illustrates vividly, there is often no time to ask for permission or direction; no opportunity to give or receive orders or instructions; no chance for committee meetings or sign-offs or even water-cooler chitchat. In situations like that, the employees most likely to do the right thing are smart people who have six critical conditions going for them:

1. They should operate under a previously formed consensus.

2. They should work in small units with well-defined goals.

3. They need to have been taught to understand the mission.

4. They must have the incentive to do their jobs well.

5. They need wide freedom in deciding how to perform their duties.

6. They must take collective responsibility for getting the goal accomplished.

None of this would be of much concern to businesspeople, of course, if such collective independent action were required only in the aftermath of midair collisions with hostile fighter jets. But in fact, the times

when business (and the military, for that matter) needs such smart, collective command are far more frequent, occurring hundreds of times a day, every day, in most organizations.

When I was running a fast-growing publishing company in the late 1980s, I happened one day to complain to the chairman of my board about a management employee who wasn't sufficiently self-directed. My chairman, without a moment's hesitation, urged me to fire the guy quickly and find a replacement. Then he shared one of his guiding principles, telling me, "You can either manage hard or hire smart." Since that day, I've heard many people talk about the importance of hiring smart, but no one else has ever explained so succinctly what happens if you fail to hire smart (or fail to give your smart hires the leeway they need to do their jobs).

Managing hard is worse than just a terrible fate and a dreadful waste of time. It is a self-defeating exercise. Managers cannot and should not be everywhere at every moment making decisions for people and supervising every detail. No manager has the time, energy, knowledge, or judgment; no talented worker has the tolerance to be watched and micromanaged. Worse yet, managing hard is managing wrong, pure and simple, because it destroys any possibility of building a constructive relationship between managers and workers.

In two massive Gallup research studies, 80,000 employees and managers were interviewed in depth over a twenty-five-year period. According to Gallup, the studies' "most powerful" discovery was this: "Talented employees need great managers." The single greatest determiner of an employee's longevity and productivity, Gallup found, is the employee's "relationship with his immediate supervisor."[5] So managing hard can be extremely dangerous for a business when the only way to have good employees is to have good managers for them.

Linda Wachner, fired CEO of the once high-flying fashion giant The Warnaco Group, is living proof of these principles. Wachner can be said to have managed hard, which includes, in her case, the habitual virulent abuse of her managers. If joining a good company is like a good marriage, then Wachner's autocratic management style made Warnaco the employment equivalent of a bad date.

The former editor of *DNR*, a men's clothing industry trade magazine, once commissioned a story with the working title "All the Woman's Presidents" to report on the revolving door Wachner's harsh style had created at the top of her Chaps sportswear division. That same editor, Robert Lohrer, wrote in *The Wall Street Journal* that Wachner was "a tenacious but unrealistically demanding manager who bordered on the despotic."[6] *Time* magazine said of her, "You can call Warnaco boss Linda Wachner . . . lots of things, and within New York City's viper-lipped rag trade many do—ruthless, cruel, abrasive, self-serving, vulgar. And then there are the people who don't like her."[7]

One high-ranking former Warnaco executive pointed out recently that the real trouble with Wachner's rule-by-intimidation tactics was that they defeated any long-term building strategy. The executive, who asked not to be identified, said, "Fear only works as a short-term motivator. It doesn't build equity in a long-term strategy. . . . 'Do-this-or-you-will-get-your-head-chopped' doesn't work in the long term. Even people who are succeeding in that environment won't stay. For managers, at some point the pressure of protecting your people will drive you away. And you lose your ability to attract talent. Word about difficult workplaces travels quickly."[8]

Warnaco represented the cream of the fashion crop, manufacturing and distributing clothing under license from Calvin Klein, Polo, Nike, and the like. But despite past success and sales exceeding $2.5 billion, Warnaco saw its 2000 losses top $331 million[9] and its share price dwindle from a high of more than $44 in 1998 to a few pennies a share in 2002. Wachner's management style received its ultimate reward when, burdened by $3 billion in debt from her acquisitions and stock buybacks, Warnaco finally declared bankruptcy in June 2001.[10] Having chased the talent out of her company and having spoiled key relations with vendors and licensors, Wachner was fired by her formerly submissive board following the bankruptcy filing. At last report, she was suing the company for $25.1 million in compensation.[11]

Despite the clear value of treating people well on the job, many other managers, in big and small ways, continually violate basic common sense by treating managers badly or by simply failing to let them

exercise their own judgment and do their own jobs. Harry Cohn, the legendary founder of Columbia Pictures, was once taken to court for verbal abuse by director Charles Vidor.[12] Cohn had a gift for enticing talent to his studio and an even greater gift for cutting the costs of film production. But he also had a vicious tongue and a cruel manner that made him "one of the most despised men in Hollywood," according to a standard reference work of corporate histories. Cohn "cultivated his image as a tyrant, keeping a riding whip near his desk and occasionally cracking it for emphasis and Columbia had the greatest creative turnover of any major studio due largely to Cohn's methods."[13] When the studio head died in 1958, attracting 1,300 people to his funeral, the smart remark around Hollywood was that the people had not come to pay their respects but to make sure Cohn was really dead. More important, Cohn's management style had failed to create any strong successor inside the organization, and for many years after his death, the studio struggled to survive.

In a less dramatic but more common example of a breakdown in people management, a colleague of mine recently promoted a man from heading a successful unit to heading a region. But the colleague then objected to his new regional manager's first decision, the choice of a successor. Why, I wondered, would anyone promote a manager and then fail to show respect for that manager's decisions? Why would anyone want to manage that hard? Executives too often forget that there are many right ways to do anything. Just because it isn't your way doesn't mean it's wrong.

Ideally, every organization needs teams like the crew of the EP-3—people who know what they need to do, feel independently responsible for doing it, and get on with it. And every organization needs senior managers who will get out of the way and let this happen. George Bush can't supervise every U.S. plane in the air (and if he could, it would be a very bad idea); and there's no room in the cramped cabin of an EP-3 spy plane for the members of the National Security Council to hold a meeting.

The primary question, then, is how to find and keep the best people.

Scientific Studies Prove Crystal Balls
Provide Cloudy Answers

Jack Welch, GE's legendary leader for twenty years, liked to say that he didn't manage businesses, he managed people. Smart people, empowered to make decisions, make enterprises happen, while not-so-smart people or people rendered powerless by bureaucracy and micromanagement tend to run companies into the ground. This has always been true, and it is increasingly true in an era when knowledge is becoming more and more critical to job performance.

Peter Drucker, probably the world's most widely respected (and longest-tenured) management guru, once wrote an essay for the *Harvard Business Review* on "How to Make People Decisions." He went on for a thousand words or so and essentially said nothing more helpful than that executives "must take their people decisions seriously and work at them." Drucker estimated that in making hiring and promotion decisions the average manager's "batting average is no better than .333"—they get it right only a third of the time. He branded this a "miserable" average, but gave absolutely no clue regarding the basis for the oddly precise statistic.[14]

Drucker's vagueness represents no special failing on his part. The central problem here is that hiring and promoting are all about predicting the future, which is essentially unknowable, particularly when it comes to human performance. Predicting human performance has always been, at best, a very risky business, exceeded in difficulty only by stock picking and betting on horses. One of the few good sources of wisdom on this point is the world of criminal psychiatry, where an erroneous prediction about human behavior can have consequences somewhat more dire than a typical faulty hiring decision. For reasons having mostly to do with bad guesses about serial killers, forensic psychiatrists have been scrutinized more closely over the years than your average human resources vice president.

But even in the meticulously studied, high-stakes area of extreme mental illness and extreme violent behavior, the answer that comes back is extremely vague. A recent British medical study reviewed twenty-eight other scientific studies around the world that tried to

use mental disorders to predict homicides. The conclusion was not helpful. There may be (emphasis on *may*) some correlation among murder and schizophrenia and profound antisocial attitudes and drugs and alcohol. But the real answer, according to a detailed abstract of the study's findings, is that "prediction of potential for homicide remains elusive. Further research is needed."[15]

Despite the unhelpfully vague results of the research, it is worth noting that when behavioral scientists go looking for clues about someone's future performance, they examine the core of the personality, not a resume or a set of job skills. The object of scrutiny, in other words, is who a person is and how that person thinks about the world, not what a person knows. When behavioral scientists say that past behavior is the only predictor of future behavior, they are looking at behavior that is consistent or inconsistent with someone's central personality traits.

This lesson can and should be applied to business. William C. Taylor, a graduate of MIT's Sloan School of Management and the founding editor of *Fast Company*, once said, "Hire for attitude, not skill."[16] When evaluating a potential hire, it is far more important to examine personal behavior and intrinsic personal qualities, such as intelligence and honesty, than to read a resume listing past jobs. What a person knows can be changed fairly quickly by a training course, a day or a year on the job, a book, or a conversation. Who a person is usually cannot be changed much at all.

Southwest Airlines is one of the world's most successful companies, and it appears to have succeeded largely by understanding the fundamental rule about hiring people for who they are, not what they know. As of 2002, Southwest had made money for twenty-nine consecutive years,[17] an almost unheard-of record in the treacherous airline business. Southwest was the only major U.S. airline to stay profitable in 2001, a year of recession and the September 11 terrorist attacks on America with four hijacked jetliners—a year so tough on the airline industry that the government created a $15 billion bailout program of direct aid and interest-free loans to keep major airlines flying.[18]

Southwest's signal success has been the product of a single-minded focus on finding employees with certain fundamental per-

sonality traits—traits that can ensure Southwest keeps its commitment to make flying "fun" for its customers. These traits include a sense of humor, enthusiasm, flexibility, and patience—nothing that can be taught. "We try to hire people for what they bring individually; we're not looking to make them what they're not," the head of Southwest's recruitment once said. "We want them to let their personalities shine through."[19]

To prove it's serious about fun, Southwest, whose stock symbol is LUV, has been known to send recruiters to national gatherings of cheerleaders. This is not because pom-pom waving is part of a Southwest employee's skill set. It is because the kinds of people who lead cheers are exactly the kinds of people who consistently have earned Southwest the top rank (by a wide margin) as the U.S. airline with the smallest number of consumer complaints per 100,000 boardings.[20]

Scrooge & Marley CEO Improves White-Collar Productivity with Kindness

Hiring fundamentally good people—people who by their very nature are well suited to what will be required of them—is half the battle. The other half, of course, is providing the environment necessary to enable those good people to do what needs to be done. This includes the delicate tasks of providing pleasant places for work, creating units small enough to function cohesively, and making sure that management doesn't get in people's way.

In many ways, it all comes down to treating everyone decently. Randall E. Stross, the academic technology expert and business author, once wrote that "no complex formula is needed to reason that happy employees do tend to be more productive than unhappy ones."[21] Stross was writing about Microsoft, but the idea certainly predates the computer age by quite a bit.

Although exchanging labor for cash payments (along with other kinds of consideration) is several thousand years old, the modern idea of employment for wages, according to most historical reckonings, arose some two hundred years ago in the early nineteenth cen-

tury, as the peasant classes were slowly deprived of their rural subsistence livelihood and shifted to laboring in the rapidly spreading workshops and factories of urban industry. At the same time, a more educated working class arose to do the figure-toting and record-keeping in the emerging offices of the time. The term "working classes" was first coined in England in 1815[22] to describe this new collection of nonfarm laborers. And while these workers were treated abysmally, by all accounts, in all industries, it is still clear that there was widespread recognition of the benefits of treating employees decently and even generously.

Out of the widespread misery of the "Hungry Forties"—the depression of the 1840s in England—came the immensely popular story of Ebenezer Scrooge in *A Christmas Carol*. The story revolved around Scrooge's central sin of heaping abuse on his kindly, troubled clerk, Bob Cratchit, who worked, freezing, "in a dismal little cell . . . copying letters" for the financial firm of Scrooge and Marley. The story was an invention of the era's most loved storyteller, Charles Dickens, himself the son of a debt-ridden, Cratchit-like clerk. But it was no secret to the readers of Dickens's cheap, serialized editions that Scrooge's idea of employee management was a sin. The first redeeming act of the reformed Scrooge, following his reeducation by the spirits of Christmas, was to order a huge turkey for the Cratchit family dinner table and then to reward Bob's lateness on Christmas Day by giving him a huge raise and greatly improved working conditions (including an ample coal supply to keep himself warm at work).

Fifty years later in the New World, as the nineteenth century gave way to the twentieth, Henry Ford was collaborating with the greatest architect of the modern factory, Albert Kahn, to create plants with huge open spaces, naturally lit by enormous windows, and always well ventilated with fresh air. The care that went into designing Ford's factories was exceeded only by the effort he expended to keep them clean and well painted. All this reflected Ford's belief, prevalent at the time, that workers' attitudes toward their tasks could be deeply and positively affected by the quality of their environment.[23]

How Bill Gates Hired His Way to Billions

The birth and growth of Microsoft Corporation forms the primary business legend of the computer age and provides the best all-around contemporary model for smart hiring and people management. Bill Gates, explaining how he built America's second most valuable company and became a billionaire before he was thirty-three, is forever telling interviewers, "I hire smart people that are pretty high bandwidth, and I challenge them to think."[24]

The Microsoft legend begins with *Popular Electronics'* first issue of 1975, featuring on the cover the primitive, kit-built Altair 8800 microcomputer, pride of that era's geek hobbyists. William H. Gates III, a Harvard dropout, and his bearded buddy Paul Allen, read the story and decide to create software for microcomputers. Their first piece of work, a programming language called BASIC, is written and sold to their first customer within a month. By the end of their third year, sales exceed $1 million and the company moves from Albuquerque, New Mexico, to Gates's home town, Bellevue, Washington. In 1981, the IBM PC is introduced, completely dependent on an operating system provided by Microsoft. Windows debuts in 1983. In 1986, Microsoft goes public.[25]

Judged by the standards of the 1990s, it was a painfully slow launch—ten years from start-up to initial public offering. But unlike the dot-coms and many of the tech start-ups that followed, the Microsoft IPO actually worked. A single share of Microsoft stock on its first day closed at $27.50. By the end of 2001, that share had multiplied through splits into 144 shares and had grown in value to $9,540—a return of nearly 35,000 percent. Had you had the foresight to invest $25,000 in Microsoft in 1986, your investment would have been worth some $8.7 million by December 2001.[26]

Today Microsoft is the dominant global software company. Revenue for its 2001 financial year was $25.3 billion and pretax operating profit was $11.7 billion—an amazing operating margin of 46 percent. This incredible margin explains why the corporate balance sheet showed more than $31 billion in cash and investments in 2001.[27] Bill Gates is frequently asked to explain his success and has provided

many answers, some more elusive than others. One of the more forth-coming responses is posted on his Web site. Asked whether hard work or intelligence is the key, he answers, "Hard work, without a doubt. But not just my hard work. What really matters is the hard work of people who come to work with me."[28]

Fueling the phenomenal growth in Microsoft's share value, of course, has been the even more phenomenal growth of Microsoft's workforce. When Gates and Allen began it all in 1975, the payroll at Microsoft totaled three people. As luck would have it, meeting the requirements of their exploding business would require Gates to increase that workforce nearly 16,000 times over the next two and a half decades to the present level of more than 47,000.[29]

The growth was anything but steady. Five years into its life, in 1980, Microsoft's personnel roster had grown to only 40, and it didn't pass 1,000 people until 1986, the year the company went public. But beginning that year, Microsoft's employment went on a five-year growth spurt that saw the workforce explode by 40 to 50 percent each year—more than ten times (1,000 percent) for the period. After that, employment at Microsoft settled down, merely doubling every five years to the current level.

Microsoft's tentacles reach today from corporate and consumer computing to television journalism (MSNBC, its joint venture with GE's NBC), traditional and online publishing (Microsoft Press, the e-zine *Slate*, and much of the content on MSN), Internet access (MSN), interactive games (Xbox), pure research (Microsoft's so-called Bill Labs), and much more. This has meant that Microsoft employs a group of workers as diverse as the world of work, including software engineers, programmers, writers, artists, marketers, accountants, lawyers, animators, musicians, and even theoretical scientists special-izing in obscure areas like "statistical physics," a discipline that is attempting to find rules that explain the way matter seems to behave by looking at its atomic and molecular components.

All of this growth has been possible only because Microsoft's con-sistent strategy has been to make people management its top priority. *The Microsoft Way*, Randall Stross's semi-official corporate biography of Microsoft, is a testament to this emphasis. The entire first section of

the book, "Microsoft Basics," is devoted to the company's approach to hiring, organizing, managing, and retaining talent. As Stross writes, "Helping his managers hire 'smart people' was the single accomplishment that Gates returned to again and again when asked to review the events of a given year. He did not want his company to forget that Microsoft's success in the past, and in the future, was inseparable from its success in hiring and retaining the best brains."[30]

To assemble its vast and diverse workforce and remain faithful to Chairman Bill's pledge to hire smart, Microsoft created an aggressive recruiting office that had grown to some sixty people by the mid-nineties.[31] There was even a "Strike Team in Recruiting" that was manned fourteen hours a day, phoning potential employees.[32] And Gates often made himself available to talk to leading candidates who needed to be sold on a career at Microsoft. To this day, says David Pritchard, senior director of technical recruiting at Microsoft, "We have few things carved in stone except hire very smart people. The only way we can be successful is to hire the very best people in the industry."[33]

Given the explosive growth and all the recruiting, it would be easy to assume that Microsoft paid higher-than-average salaries in a scramble to hire everyone it could get its hands on. But in fact, Microsoft paid lower salaries than its competitors, relying on perks and incentive pay, including stock options, along with the magic of the Microsoft name, to make the difference. Senior management actually made a habit of cutting departmental requests for more people, holding the totals below the levels believed necessary to do the work. This focus on headcount control made it even more important that each person hired be the smartest, best worker possible. Productivity demanded it.

Once Microsoft had hired its smart people, it applied its corporate muscle to the real work of making its investment in employees pay off. Building on the traditions set by pioneers of the workplace environment like architect Albert Kahn, Microsoft started by providing a beautiful place for its people to do their work. In 1986, Microsoft moved its army of software creators out of ordinary office buildings in Seattle and onto a green, tree-shrouded campus in Redmond,

Washington. It furnished the campus with low buildings, constructed to a human scale.

To give its people quiet places to think, Microsoft provided private offices. To emphasize the absence of a corporate hierarchy designed to slow people down, it made virtually all those offices the same size and furnished them identically. To provide a sense of community and to counterbalance the isolation of the private offices, Microsoft built central cafeterias where people could gather and connected everyone to everyone else with e-mail.

To coddle and encourage employees, Microsoft resorted to providing three commodities that essentially cover the most basic human needs in this culture: money, food, and camaraderie.

Money began with signing bonuses, salaries, and annual incentives. But the real financial payoff of being a Microsoft worker was the stock option plan. As early as 1992, according to one report, Microsoft options had made more than 100 employees millionaires.[34] Four years later, another report maintained, that number had ballooned to 3,000 millionaires.[35] Microsoft refuses to participate in the speculation about how many millionaires and multimillionaires it has created, but the numbers are certainly large. As the growth rate of Microsoft stock has leveled off, and particularly as the market tanked in 2001 and 2002, the options have become less compelling for new hires. Still, they send a powerful message to employees about sharing in the company's wealth.

In addition to money, Microsoft provides each employee with a wealth of equipment and perks—everything needed to get the job done and stay awake while doing it. In addition to fancy equipment and software for its developers, there is subsidized food in the cafeterias and free drinks (coffee and soda) all around. "Microsoft spent $8,000 per employee annually on nonmandated benefits," Stross reports.

Finally, on the critically important product development side of the business, Gates made sure that people worked in small teams no matter how big Microsoft grew. He had noticed, according to Stross, that the best software was written by small teams of closely knit, intensely focused, smart people.

None of these tactics, of course, was invented by Microsoft, nor were they first introduced in this century or the last. Much of Microsoft's approach, for example, can be traced directly to a similar but much earlier technology start-up, the Hewlett-Packard Company, launched in 1938, nearly two decades before Bill Gates was born. After its founding, David Hewlett formulated "Four Musts" for his new company, and one of them was that "the company must recognize and respect the personal worth of employees and allow them to share in the success of the company."[36] From the start, HP promoted a management approach of giving its people "as much freedom as possible" in pursuing goals.[37] HP established a profit-sharing program for all employees in the early 1940s that rewarded the lowliest worker and Hewlett similarly. Its stock option plan went into effect as soon as the company went public in the 1950s. Its engineering teams were kept small. And so on.

HP, in turn, probably owes much of its culture to yet another technology predecessor, the phenomenally successful 3M Company, which was formed in 1902. Its first chairman, William McKnight, once wrote, "As our business grows, it becomes increasingly necessary to delegate responsibility and to encourage men and women to exercise their initiative. This requires considerable tolerance. Those men and women to whom we delegate authority and responsibility, if they are good people, are going to want to do their jobs in their own way. . . . Mistakes will be made. But if a person is essentially right, the mistakes he or she makes are not as serious in the long run as the mistakes management will make if it undertakes to tell those in authority exactly how they must do their jobs."[38]

Could the Roman Legions Write Good Software?

Looking across the entire sweep of history, it is difficult to resist some simple comparisons that appear to link many successful organizations. More than two thousand years ago, at its founding, the Roman army consisted entirely of citizen volunteers attracted to the service by good pay, good prospects for advancement, the best equipment,

strong incentives for long service, and the camaraderie of small units joined together in a large enterprise. The soldiers of Rome were kept on track by discipline and a clear mission, and retained for twenty to twenty-five years by rewards of land and cash at retirement. In many ways, the Roman army can be seen as the forerunner of the modern organization. It is easy to feel a distinct lack of sympathy for the Roman vision of conquering the known world and forcing tribute to be paid to Rome. But it is equally difficult to dismiss how effectively the goal was pursued over a millennium and more.[39]

The point is this: When it comes to human nature, there is nothing much new. Many of the benign organizational tactics pioneered in the ancient military have survived in modern times in both the military and business. Looking at the EP-3 crew who performed so brilliantly in a falling airplane over the South China Sea, we see the results of a band of smart people, well trained about their mission, given a $36 million airplane stocked with the world's best equipment, organized into a small unit where personal closeness generates dedication, given more than adequate incentive (defending their country and staying alive) to do their jobs, and trusted to manage themselves when the chips were down. Eliminate the expensive plane and it could be a Roman legion in 100 B.C. Substitute money and stock options for patriotism and survival as the main compensation and it could be Microsoft in 2002.

As Peter Drucker once wrote in a slightly different context, "They're not employees, they're people."[40] Keeping that in mind can confer huge advantages on any organization, no matter what its mission.

HOW TO BUILD THE BOX

THE EIGHTH PLANK

1. Recruit aggressively. Don't wait for the best people to come to you; they won't.
2. Hire primarily for fundamental personality traits—intelligence, curiosity, enthusiasm, honesty. Job knowledge is a secondary factor.
3. Provide strong incentives. Make sure employees share in the success of their unit and the company.
4. Provide a pleasant place to work and the best tools possible.
5. Create small units where camaraderie can flourish, shared responsibility can develop, and bureaucracy cannot take root.
6. Explain the mission, define the goal, get out of the way. Remember: There are always thousands of "right" ways to do any task. Your way is never the only way and rarely the best way.
7. Practice collective command—let people take charge together.

CHAPTER 9

The Treasure Box:
Secure the Real Assets

> *Find your business's real assets*
> *(the ones that generate your profits) and*
> *exploit them for all they're worth.*

From Balance Sheet to Trash Heap
Without Passing Go

It would seem that the real Treasure Box in any business—call it the core business or the real business or the assets that actually produce the profits—should be obvious and easy to find. But that's not always the case. The key assets in most businesses turn out to be unique, abstract stuff that can include a company's structure, expertise, reputation, and relationships. If anything happens to these abstract assets, the hard assets can lose their value rapidly.

History shows clearly that an unchanging business fundamental is the ever-present need to have profit-creating core assets identified, protected, and properly deployed to produce the greatest possible return. But when the core assets are abstractions, both identifying and protecting them can be a difficult task. Fortunately, there are numerous positive models to follow. The venerable Walt Disney Company provides a glittering example of asset identification and protection, having diligently pressed the entire United States government into the service of securing its main assets, all of which are intellectual property rights. Another very different but equally positive model is provided by Prudential Financial, the 127-year-old global insurance

and investing giant. Long before the Wall Street scandals of 2001 and 2002, Pru's managers recognized that their most critical asset was their customer relationships. While the rest of Wall Street kept its head in the sand at infinite risk to its reputation, Pru courageously chose to eliminate the conflicts of interest from its business in order to serve a single set of customers and preserve the all-important asset of those customer relationships.

But negative examples have been even more numerous and powerfully instructive lately. As the new century dawned, both Enron and Arthur Andersen proved that very large and seemingly stable enterprises can be killed more or less instantly by suffering damage to nothing more solid than their reputations. Then these two intertwined disasters combined with an outbreak of other large and small scandals involving lying executives, fictional accounting, and passive directors. The lethal mixture poisoned the general reputation of corporate America to such an extent that the stock markets nose-dived for more than two years and the entire U.S. economy suffered massively. This entire, historic crisis occurred even though the only assets being impaired were abstract ones of reputation and trust. Nothing burned down; no "real" asset was destroyed.

Still, the notion persists that durable, hard assets—items like factories, real estate, equipment, and machinery—are somehow more important than abstract ones and hold some absolute value that will endure no matter what happens to the company that owns the assets. Well, sometimes this is true, but usually it isn't.

One exception—the sector where hard assets are the whole ball game—is natural resources. Saudi Aramco, the state-controlled oil monopoly of the Kingdom of Saudi Arabia, can easily identify its primary profit-producing asset. Holding more than a quarter of the world's proven crude oil reserves,[1] the state-owned oil monopoly of Saudi Arabia needn't care much about other assets, such as its reputation, customer relationships, or employee expertise. Aramco's customers have virtually nowhere else to turn, no matter what they may think of the company or the kingdom, and the massive oil company can easily buy whatever expertise it needs. Its hard assets will remain valuable, presumably, until the wells run dry, which is scheduled to

happen in about a century. Up to that point, no one will have any trouble identifying or exploiting Aramco's core asset.

The same can be said for companies whose main activity is exploiting other natural resources, from copper to diamonds to coal. Or for electrical utilities, where investment in power plants and transmission lines represents both the productive capacity to manufacture the utility's only product and the basis for pricing that product.

But life is not so simple for most other businesses. Particularly in a knowledge-based industry, where the core assets are always abstractions, durable assets can quickly become worthless if they are cut off from money-making ideas or relationships. But the same can hold true in traditional industrial firms. Consider again the fate of Samsung's dismally failed attempt to start an auto company in the 1990s. Samsung's modern, high-capacity auto plant turned out to be essentially valueless without the design expertise to create unique and salable models, the goodwill of a strong dealer organization, and trusting relationships with customers.[2]

No cautionary tale teaches more about the problems with so-called durable assets than the recent history of the telecommunications industry. Beginning in the fall of 2001, two of the world's most respected financial news organizations, New York's *Wall Street Journal* and London's *Financial Times*, found themselves digging through trash heaps to locate the former assets of a multitude of fallen or falling telecommunications companies—from well-known stars like the semimoribund Marconi and the completely moribund Winstar to dozens of lesser-known enterprises.

Financial Times correspondent Dan Roberts, who produced an excellent three-part series on the global telecom collapse, found himself in the summer of 2001 "by the decaying dockyards, in an anonymous industrial park east of London," where large switching cabinets produced by Nortel, Lucent, and Cisco were being stripped of precious metals and disposed of. The refrigerator-sized collections of sophisticated electronics, emblematic of the biggest boom and crash in stock market history, had once carried multimillion-dollar price tags and, listed as multimillion-dollar assets, had occupied prime positions on the balance sheets of massive companies. Now, cut off

from any economically useful role, the high-tech discards were finding their true worth as junk. During the middle of 2001, large telecommunications companies were going bankrupt at the rate of roughly one a week, and the resulting surfeit of unneeded equipment quickly oversaturated the secondhand markets, rendering the electronic components virtually valueless. "It is all part of a $1 trillion bonfire of wealth that has brought the world to the brink of recession," wrote Roberts.[3]

How to Turn a Dollar's Worth of Assets into a Penny's Worth

A half-billion-dollar contributor to the expensive money-pyre lit by the telecommunications collapse, Winstar Communications can serve as an object lesson about the relative valuelessness, in and of themselves, of most seemingly valuable hard assets. Winstar was born in 1988 as a skiwear company and was taken over three years later by a young lawyer named William J. Rouhana Jr., who had no experience in telecommunications. He eventually renamed the company Winstar, and in 1993, turned it into a new kind of wireless broadband provider by purchasing thirty local microwave broadcasting licenses.[4] The initial idea, Rouhana explained as he was launching his network, was to enable businesses to connect directly to long distance phone lines using his high-speed wireless connections, thus bypassing the local phone company and saving money on the local access fees the phone company charged.[5]

As the network grew, Winstar's idea got bigger and simpler. "We provide businesses with broadband services," the company's 1999 annual report stated simply. Winstar was going to provide the legendary "last mile" of connection between global broadband networks and office buildings.

Winstar by then was serving sixty markets in the United States, including the top thirty, and ten markets overseas, providing voice and Internet services. In 1999, Winstar had $445.6 million in revenue, but its losses were more than one and a half times that amount at

nearly $700 million (including dividends that had to be paid to pre-ferred stockholders). Altogether, since launching in 1995, the company had racked up cumulative losses of more than $1.4 billion, roughly twice its cumulative revenue.[6]

Judging from the numbers, the main activity at Winstar was not providing broadband services to businesses, as the annual report asserted. Rather, it appeared to be the building of the "domestic network," as Winstar kept calling it. This was the asset Winstar was creating; the engine it was depending upon to churn out billions in profits in order to create a return for its shareholders.

A tediously loving description of the hardware in its domestic network dominates the very top of Winstar's annual report. As of early 2000, the domestic network, detailed in five breathless bullet points, consisted of "the nation's largest amount of fixed wireless spectrum, covering more than 80% of the U.S. business market," more than 20,000 miles of optical fiber (existing or planned to exist), "access rights to connect more than 8,000" office buildings, and last but not least by any measure, "34 installed Lucent local and long distance voice switches and 135 installed data switches."[7]

At the end of 1999, this elaborate network was being carried on Winstar's balance sheet at approximately the amount it had cost to build, less a little depreciation: $1.8 billion (which included both completed sections and parts still being constructed).[8]

Winstar kept right on building the network and losing vast amounts of money up to and including April 18, 2001, the day it declared bankruptcy. The company's bankruptcy filing showed the money lavished on the network had swollen by more than a billion dollars in one year. Adding another half a billion for Winstar's microwave licenses put the network's total cost (and total asset value on the corporate balance sheet), less depreciation, at just under $3.4 billion.[9] Counting its operating losses and all other costs to build the network, Winstar had blown through roughly $5 billion.

But in the waning days of 2001, IDT, a Newark, New Jersey, company in the prepaid calling card business, bought Winstar's assets out of bankruptcy for a total of $42.5 million in cash and stock.[10] The Winstar network hadn't wound up on a trash heap yet; it still retained

some value as a functioning system. But even as a working network, it could only fetch a bit more than a penny on the dollar. So much for the value of hard assets, especially fiber optics and rooftop antennas and ultra-expensive switches in the midst of a telecom meltdown.

So what were the real assets of Winstar? The unique, irreplaceable, profit-creating assets? It doesn't appear that Winstar had any of those. And it appears that Winstar's managers were blissfully unaware of what they were missing.

Mr. Greenspan Tells Congress About "Capitalized Reputation"

Unfortunately, they weren't the only ones to get this part of business's fundamentals wrong. You would think that if anything could drive home the transitory value of many so-called hard assets, it would have to be the multibillion-dollar Winstar collapse in particular and the multi*trillion*-dollar telecom nightmare in general. But oddly enough, in the spring of 2002, none other than Alan Greenspan, chairman-for-life of the U.S. Federal Reserve Bank Board and the grayest graybeard of modern capitalism, told two committees of Congress exactly the opposite and got away with it completely.

Talking about Enron, then the center of all attention—a case where the core assets were clearly reputation and ideas, not real estate or drill presses—Greenspan told the Congress, "As the recent events surrounding Enron have highlighted, a firm is inherently fragile if its value added emanates more from conceptual as distinct from physical assets. A physical asset, whether an office building or an automotive assembly plant, has the capability of producing goods even if the reputation of the managers of such facilities falls under a cloud. . . . *Trust and reputation can vanish overnight. A factory cannot.*"[11] (The emphasis is mine, but this is also the quote that the newspapers latched onto.)

It's certainly true that real estate usually doesn't vanish (except in Florida, where sinkholes are a problem, and potentially in California, where earthquakes may yet rearrange the economic landscape). Con-

gress may, indeed, need instruction about this fact. But as we have seen time and again throughout history, both ancient and modern, the value of so-called real assets can disappear just as quickly and completely as the value of any abstraction. Separated from profitable customer relationships, Winstar's network—as solid as real estate in many ways—became virtually valueless. Just like office buildings in an overbuilt neighborhood. Or old-fashioned steel plants in Pittsburgh when the cost of labor and modernization have forced steelmaking offshore. Or a modern auto plant in Korea when the global automotive business is burdened with excess capacity.

Still, Greenspan deserves credit for having publicly endorsed an important piece of conceptual bookkeeping. His congressional testimony bestowed an interesting name on an important notion, something that Greenspan, with his gift for making even the simplest economic concepts sound complex and important, called "capitalized reputation."[12] It was, the Fed boss asserted, Enron's principal asset, dwarfing the value to the business of any physical assets. "The physical assets of such a firm comprise a small proportion of its asset base," Greenspan properly concluded.

While the rules of generally accepted accounting principles (universally abbreviated as GAAP), don't tell us how to record capitalized reputation on a balance sheet, or how to depreciate it over time, we now have the chairman of the Federal Reserve Board vouching for it under oath. I would add two more core assets to that one, including capitalized customer relationships and capitalized employee experience. And I believe it's clear that these capitalized concepts have been part of the foundation of business since the beginning of commerce.

A Pediatrician Makes Wall Street Take Its Medicine

There is nothing much to learn from Enron's collapse except the importance of not being a crook. (In 2002, it was being argued widely that Enron proved the need for new laws and regulations to prevent the recurrence of such a disaster. These arguments are analogous to declaring that each homicide committed in America proves the need

for new laws against murder. Sadly, the old laws against both fraud and murder are just fine. It's enforcement that presents the real challenge.) But we have been blessed in recent years—particularly in investment banking, stock brokerage, and accounting businesses—with an embarrassment of horrid, instructive examples of what happens when even big, successful firms neglect the economic centrality of their abstract assets. In the summer of 2001, New York Attorney General Eliot Spitzer launched an investigation into Merrill Lynch, focusing on the analysts who assessed Internet stocks. Spitzer was looking for conflicts of interest that influenced which stocks Wall Street firms recommended to their clients. Spitzer ultimately found the smoking gun he needed in Merrill's e-mail system, uncovering countless messages proving that Merrill had encouraged its employees to lie about certain stocks in order to boost Merrill's profits. These e-mail messages were not good news for Merrill Lynch's capitalized reputation.

Merrill Lynch & Co., Inc., the global holding company for all of Merrill's diverse financial activities, is not a small enterprise. At the end of 2001, America's largest broker and investment banker had more than 57,000 employees and was managing roughly $1.5 trillion in assets for its clients, who ranged from nations to individual investors. Its net revenues for the year—and it was a very bad year that included the September 11 terrorist attack on New York—were $22.9 billion. Not counting a special charge largely incurred for dropping 9,000 employees at the end of the year, Merrill earned $2.4 billion after taxes in 2001. And remember—it was a very bad year. (The year before, Merrill had earned $3.8 billion after tax.)[13]

Among the things that Merrill does to bring in such vast amounts of money, two command our attention. As we all know, the investment banking arm of Merrill gives advice to companies selling stocks and bonds; the stock brokerage arm of Merrill gives investment advice to people who are buying stocks and bonds. The brokerage side is staffed by analysts who are supposed to be tough and independent in rating stocks and bonds, steering clients to good investments and warning them off bad investments without fear or favor. Clear?

Ernest Hemingway once described a kind of common sense that he

called "a built-in, shockproof shit detector." If you read the last paragraph and your detector failed to go off, you should have it checked. Because the truth, of course, is that no company can represent both the buy side and the sell side of a transaction and be true to both clients. Merrill was no exception to this rule, and Merrill's management knew it was no exception. Still, they continued conducting their business as if Merrill's reputation were not a terribly critical asset.

Speaking to the scope of its worldwide investment banking operations, Merrill boasts in its 2001 annual report that it was ranked "number one in global equity and equity-linked origination and number two in global announced mergers and acquisitions" for the year. Its share of the year's M&A work worldwide was 27.4 percent.[14]

But that achievement must now be seen alongside the fact that Merrill, like other big Wall Street firms, routinely skewed its stock ratings to serve some of its investment banking clients. At its most obvious and egregious, this meant Merrill's stock analysts were instructed or encouraged to promote stocks they knew to be losers in order to help Merrill win and retain huge investment banking fees.

Wall Street insiders had known for years about this conflict of interest, but it was the conventional wisdom that this was the only way to make money, and the inherent conflicts were a little neighborhood secret. Then the Internet and telecom bubbles collapsed in 2000, creating trillions of dollars in losses. Finally, large numbers of investors began to get hurt by the bad advice originating from Merrill and its competitors.

Spreading discontent powered a growing debate about reform that thundered along Wall Street in 2000 and early 2001. It was said the investment banking and brokerage sides of the business should be split. It was said that conflicts should be disclosed. The Securities and Exchange Commission announced it was considering new rules. Congress scheduled hearings. Defenders of the system publicly blamed all losses on the bad economy and counseled the losers to take their lumps quietly.

But in the early spring of 2001, a New York pediatrician named Debasis Kanjilal hired a smart lawyer named Jacob Zamansky and

filed an action against his former stock broker, Merrill Lynch, charging that a conflict of interest had motivated Merrill's famous dot-com stock analyst, Henry Blodget, to continue promoting a bad stock long after Blodget had, in fact, lost faith in the stock's future. The stock was InfoSpace. Merrill's investment banking arm had helped the company go public. Kanjilal said he'd lost $500,000 because of Merrill's misleading advice.

While the doctor's arbitration was moving forward very publicly, the forces of American civilization began to gather darkly over Wall Street. Congressional hearings into conflicts of interest affecting stock research were scheduled for mid-June.[15] Trying to head off trouble, the Securities Industry Association, the trade group representing Wall Street's investment houses, stepped forward on June 12 and announced a set of "best practices" for stock analysts.[16] The best practices turned out to be a ringing endorsement of business as usual, but their release fueled the debate, which intensified when Congress actually held its hearings three days later. The Securities and Exchange Commission stepped into the drama on June 28, issuing a highly unusual document it called an "investor alert." The alert said, "Investors should not rely solely on an analyst's recommendation when deciding whether to buy, hold or sell a stock."[17] Not exactly a ringing endorsement of the independence and diligence of the industry's analysts. Then, on July 10, Merrill itself announced that, effective immediately, it was changing its rules to prohibit its analysts from owning the stocks they covered.[18]

A very bad few weeks for Merrill climaxed on July 20 when, after a very public, four-month arbitration with Dr. Kanjilal, Merrill settled the case by paying the pediatrician $400,000. The settlement received widespread television, newspaper, and newswire coverage. At the time, Merrill admitted no wrongdoing, and a spokesman for the firm told news organizations, "We settled to avoid further distraction and expense of protracted litigation."[19]

But the distraction and expense had only begun for Merrill. Inspired by the revelations coming out of the Kanjilal case, New York Attorney General Spitzer began investigating Merrill in June, and

after months of digging, issued a report in April 2002 that read like a magazine exposé of the investment business. Produced in the form of a sworn court deposition from Eric Dinallo, the chief of New York's Investment Protection Bureau, the thirty-eight-page report was based on over 100,000 pages of documents, "including thousands of e-mails," and the sworn testimony of twenty witnesses.[20] Based on this evidence, the state of New York concluded: "Since late 1999, the internet research analysts . . . at Merrill Lynch have published on a regular basis ratings for internet stocks that were misleading." Chief among the reasons they were misleading was that "the ratings in many cases did not reflect the analysts' true opinions of the companies," Dinallo stated. The investigation also had found that "as a matter of undisclosed, internal policy," no analyst at Merrill ever recommended that anyone reduce their holdings in a stock or sell a stock. Only positive recommendations were allowed.

Finally, Dinallo's investigation found, "Merrill Lynch failed to disclose to the public that Merrill Lynch's ratings were tarnished by an undisclosed conflict of interest" and that the research analysts were "often initiating, continuing, and/or manipulating research coverage for the purpose of attracting and keeping investment banking clients, thereby producing misleading ratings that were neither objective nor independent, as they purported to be."[21]

As a result of all this, the attorney general concluded, "In lieu of assigning reduce or sell recommendations to stocks they no longer favored, the internet group instead merely quietly stopped covering the stock, without any announcement or meaningful explanation to the retail public."[22] Thus, as some stocks "plummeted, sometimes all the way to zero, retail customers and the investing public were never advised to sell."[23]

In conducting his investigation, the attorney general's man found the witnesses from Merrill were not very helpful. Dinallo complained mildly that "some of the witnesses examined have displayed an implausible lack of recollection of key conversations and documents."[24] But the e-mails, as it turned out, were more forthcoming.

One stock Dinallo focused on was InfoSpace, the Internet software company that had cost Dr. Kanjilal $500,000. InfoSpace had taken a

phenomenal ride, going public in late 1998 at about $37 and then rising and splitting and rising and splitting and rising, fueled partly by the general hysteria and partly by Merrill's bullish analysis of the stock. At its height in mid-March 2000, an original share was up a split-adjusted 2,100 percent. But by July 2000, the stock was in free fall and by year-end had lost 90 percent of its peak value. (By mid-2002, InfoSpace was hovering around 70 cents a share, 85 percent off its IPO value and more than 99.33 percent off its peak.)[25]

Throughout its steep fall in 2000, however, Merrill rated InfoSpace a "strong buy" and kept the stock on its "Favored 15" list of the hottest Internet stocks. The stock kept its high rating despite disparaging, warning, worrying internal e-mails from senior analyst Blodget. On July 13, 2000, Blodget wrote that "this stock is a powder keg, given how aggressive we were on it earlier this year and given the 'bad smell' comments that so many institutions are bringing up." Then on October 20, he referred to it in another internal e-mail simply as a "piece of junk," while Merrill was still publicly labeling it a strong buy.[26]

The revelations in the attorney general's report went on and on, piling devastating detail upon detail for Merrill to try to explain. At long last, during the annual shareholders meeting in New York on April 26, 2002, Merrill's powerful chairman, David Komansky, found his voice and said he was sorry. "The e-mails that have come to light are very distressing and disappointing to us. They fall far short of our professional standards, and some are inconsistent with our policies. We regret that, and we further regret that the perception of our research integrity has clearly been affected." To show that he *really* meant business, he also fired one of his roughly 850 stock analysts. "We have failed to live up to the high standards that are our tradition, and I want to take this opportunity to publicly apologize to our clients, our shareholders and our employees,"[27] Komansky said.

Predictably, of course, Komansky's apology fell flat. A few days after his speech, *The New York Times* reported, "A rare public apology from the chairman of Merrill Lynch & Company has not managed to defuse the anger of investors large and small over the conflicts of interest that they contend colored the advice of Merrill's stock analysts."[28]

All in all, Merrill management had failed, over a long period of time, to follow the unbreakable rule that says companies must identify, secure, protect, and exploit their core assets. In Merrill's case, the asset most heavily damaged was the company's reputation and its relationships with its retail clients. If anyone wondered whether or not these abstractions were a real, valuable asset for Merrill, they had only to watch the stock market, something that Merrill does well. In the months following the revelations about Merrill's dishonesty, its market capitalization took more than a $10 billion hit—a loss of about 20 percent of the firm's value. In contrast, following September 11, 2001, when Merrill's buildings in the World Financial Center were damaged by the imploding World Trade Center towers, and the company was forced to evacuate temporarily, Merrill's share price was unaffected, rising slightly when the markets reopened.

The client lawsuits, shareholder lawsuits, and other nightmarish spin-offs of all this will surely plague Merrill for some time to come, costing it far more in time, attention, and cash. (One analyst forecast some $2 billion in damage from lawsuits alone. And, in fact, Merrill ultimately agreed to join an Omnibus settlement with state and federal regulators that cost a collection of offending Wall Street firms some $1.6 billion. Merril agreed to pay $200 million of that—half in fines and half to support newly required independant stock research and investor education programs. But none of these payments, of course, ended the threat of civil lawsuits from investors.) By mid-2002, it was being said that the dishonest conduct of Merrill and its peers (compounded by Enron and a raft of revelations about dishonest corporate CEOs) had so undermined faith in America's capital markets that it was deepening the recession and impeding recovery.[29]

It is undoubtedly fitting that this multibillion-dollar debacle was set off by a pediatrician, since Merrill Lynch and the rest of Wall Street had been acting like irresponsible children, leaving fragile family heirlooms out in the rain to rot. Watching the careless way in which Merrill played with its reputation in exchange for some short-term gain, the only plausible conclusion is that the management never understood—or willfully ignored—the true value of that core asset.

It would be natural for many to react to Merrill's sad story with a

that's-the-way-everyone-acts-anyway shrug. But this is not a matter of good behavior versus bad behavior; nor is it a morality play in which it is assumed and hoped that the good are rewarded on earth as well as in heaven. This is something much more hardheaded, involving the discipline that all managers must practice in order to protect their most critical operating assets. So if you were tempted to evaluate Merrill's behavior as anything other than a long-term strategic disaster, consider the story of Prudential Securities and how it faced the same questions as Merrill Lynch, but made precisely the opposite decision.

Did Somebody (Finally) Say "Sell"?

Back in the fall of 2000, long before the Merrill debacle and the plague of investigations on Wall Street, John Strangfeld, a twenty-four-year veteran of Prudential Financial, sat down with his boss, Chairman of the Board Art Ryan. The subject was Strangfeld's impending mission as the new CEO of Prudential Securities. Nearly two years after the meeting, Strangfeld still recalls Ryan's charge to him that day. "Find a way to win," the chairman said. "Don't just be in the game. Find a way to win."[30]

At that moment, Prudential Securities was definitely not winning. "What we looked like strategically was a smaller-scale version of everyone else. And we were embracing all the conventional wisdom that everyone else had," Strangfeld now says.

Prudential Securities, formerly Prudential-Bache, was formed in 1981 when Prudential Insurance acquired the Bache Group brokerage business. In the eighties, the firm's questionable tactics in forming and selling some $8 billion of real estate limited partnerships was the subject of one of Wall Street's biggest scandals. The risky partnerships ultimately lost hundreds of millions for Pru-Bache customers and triggered an avalanche of lawsuits.[31] Pru-Bache eventually settled with regulators and compensated customers through a restitution program, spending some $1.5 billion to put the scandal behind it. So even though all that was relatively ancient history, Prudential Securi-

ties was no stranger to the bad old ways of doing business on Wall Street.

But in the two months following his ascension to the top of Prudential Securities on October 6, 2000, Strangfeld would completely realign the company, making a break with Wall Street's past and turning the conventional wisdom on its head. At the center of the Pru revolution would be the notion, almost unheard-of among Wall Street's major players, that the firm's relationships with its retail customers—institutional and individual investors—was its most important asset.

"It all gets back to that customer relationship," Strangfeld says today.

"The way I was looking at it when I arrived here," Strangfeld recalls, "is that we had some special qualities." These included "a lot of long-standing employees who wanted to win" and "an incredibly large footprint of 5,000 financial advisors and $250 billion in assets." But Strangfeld quickly concluded that "having a strategy that looked like everyone else's was not very convincing" as a way to win.

It didn't help that Pru's investment bank was only the fourteenth-largest on Wall Street and had never worked for the firm. "Furthermore," he adds, "the more you thought about it, the more you realized that most firms are simultaneously trying to profit from serving issuers and investors when the reality is that those two notions are in conflict with one another."

Strangfeld quickly became convinced that Wall Street convention "was a very conflicted business model." He still had to contend with everyone saying, "Yeah, but that's the way it's done." His conclusion, however, was: "Frankly, we're not winning in the way it's done."

So Strangfeld made the radical decision to reject the conventional wisdom and act as if his customers were the most critical asset in Pru's business. "You could," he realized, "make a real virtue—I don't mean spin, but a *genuine* virtue—out of having a business system that knows it only has one master and that's the investor. And success or failure is going to be driven by the ability to fulfill the needs of that investor."

Aligning the business around a single, coherent idea of serving customers clearly defined and differentiated the Prudential Securities

brand for all constituents. "So whether it's talking to your employees or talking to your client or . . . talking to a prospective investor in Pru stock, it's an honest clean story about how we're different. It does differentiate us from what other people do."

Strangfeld's decision had painful consequences. Moving swiftly, he exited from bond underwriting, terminating 450 people in mid-November 2000. The next month he radically curtailed the firm's investment bank, reducing the number of bankers by 160. By January 2001, Prudential Securities was virtually out of the business of representing the sell side of securities transactions.

Strangfeld now says the "beauty" of the decision is that it made all other decisions straightforward by giving the business a single guiding principle. "Number one, it's the right thing to do," he says. But in addition, he explains, "It makes the resource decisions and management decisions really clean, because you're basically saying, 'What's in the best interests of the investor?' And it's the only mantra we have. We're not saying, 'How do we balance this with that?'"

One immediate example of the impact of this realignment is that Pru's research analysts were free to cover companies that interested investors, instead of covering companies that were current or prospective investment banking clients. Even more important, Pru's analysts had no conflicts when it came to telling the truth.

It was early 2001, only two months after Strangfeld initiated the new order at Pru, when Mark Rowen, the Prudential analyst covering Internet stocks, "shocked" Wall Street by advising his clients to sell their shares of Amazon.com. No one was really surprised by the advice, since virtually everyone agreed with Rowen at that point that Amazon was overvalued. (In fact, as Rowen forecast, Amazon would fall from its then-current share price of roughly $14 to a low of about $8 over the ensuing ten months, before heading up again on news of its first-ever profitable quarter.)

So it wasn't Rowen's pessimistic analysis that was stunning, but the fact that he said it out loud. And this wasn't even the first time: Rowen had previously urged clients (accurately) to sell four other dot-com highfliers, including Webvan, the online grocery that we now know declared bankruptcy ten months after Rowen's "sell" rating.[32]

Within a year's time, truth-telling had become a newsworthy trend at Prudential, and it wasn't confined to candidly assessing the turkeys of Silicon Valley. On the first workday of 2002, another Pru analyst, Wayne Hood, shook up the Street by announcing that he saw a potential bankruptcy in the future of the nation's fortieth-biggest company, Kmart. "We would not be surprised if the company were to file Chapter 11 bankruptcy if trends do not improve," Hood said in a research note. Kmart shot back that it had the cash to operate.[33] Then, three weeks later, the $38 billion retailer filed for Chapter 11, having fired its president five days earlier.[34]

As Kmart declared itself broke, Prudential Securities had "sell" ratings outstanding on twenty-four stocks and was beginning to be viewed as virtually the only global financial services company whose written and unwritten policy was to tell the truth about the stocks it researched. The Wall Street Journal's popular "Deals & Dealmakers" column reported, "The strategy was disparaged by some Wall Street rivals as a great way to lose business. To analysts schooled in Wall Street's traditional ways, risking a relationship by turning critical on a company is almost an anathema. Following through with a sell recommendation might be called revolutionary."

By mid-2002, Strangfeld was optimistic about his customer-centered experiment. "Now that we're eighteen to twenty months into it, I can tell you that we have no second thoughts about it at all. And secondly, what I can also say with great confidence is that the risks that we identified going into this thing have not materialized." Those risks included fears that both analysts and financial advisors would defect when the big investment banking fees went away, hurting the quality of research and damaging customer relations; but none of that happened.

Instead, Strangfeld reported that Pru had gained market share with ten of the world's fifteen largest institutional investors, who felt they would benefit from the firm's unbiased research. Strangfeld has "equal conviction" that his business with private investors is growing, but that will take longer to prove. "What we can't remove is the effect of the cycle, and we're in a period where we're at a thirty-year low in investor activity," he said.

On the private client side, Strangfeld is watching fee-based income—money derived from giving advice and managing a portfolio—versus transaction-based income, which is commissions generated from buying or selling a security. In 2000, fees were 18 percent of the total; by 2002, they were 35 percent. Strangfeld is aiming for 50 percent. This is all part of a long-term effort to "change the behavior of the financial advisors," so they are managing their clients' portfolios instead of "flogging the hot idea of the day," Strangfeld said.

The upside of this change in the source of Prudential Securities' income is that the fee-based revenues are far less volatile than brokerage commissions, making it easier for the firm to ride out the next stock market downturn. So the signs are good, but "it's too early to declare victory," he said in the summer of 2002.

Many Wall Street pundits still believe Pru can't make money without investment banking and all the conflicts it entails. They still believe in the old Wall Street ways. The real question, however, appears to be whether any Wall Street firm will be permitted to do business the old way for much longer. History is on Strangfeld's side. Many of the moves he took to serve his customers are now being forced on a reluctant Wall Street by the law.

Thinking about how it all went so wrong on Wall Street, Strangfeld says his major competitors lost sight of the independent interests of their investing customers and began to see them simply as a distribution network for the products the investment bankers needed to sell.

"I think what happened is that a lot of people began thinking about the private client business as distribution, when in fact they should have been thinking about it as relationship management. The more they're thinking about it as distribution, the more they lose sight of the trust in the client relationship and the more they're thinking about how much product they can pump through it," Strangfeld says.

"They're straddling two constituents. One that has the objective of getting the highest possible value for their securities and the other which is trying to get the securities at the lowest possible value." And that, Strangfeld believes, doesn't work for anyone.

In the end, coveting the huge fees of investment banking, Wall

Street seems to have lost sight of the logic of it all: A firm's competitive edge in attracting investment banking assignments stemmed, in part, from its ability to credibly influence the investing public's purchase of securities. But if that credibility goes away, then the firm also loses whatever edge it might have had with investment banking clients. So the trust of the investor is always the key asset—the goose that produces the golden egg of banking fees.

Prudential Financial lost money in 2001—about $227 million—but its financial performance was somewhat hard to assess because the company had just incurred hundreds of millions in one-time costs to end its life as a mutual insurance company, owned by its policyholders, and to launch an initial public offering on December 18, 2001. It is more than merely noteworthy, however, that in the first six months of its life as a publicly traded company, Prudential's market capitalization rose by roughly $2 billion, as its newly printed stock, despite the company's short-term losses, went up about 15 percent. Merrill, nicely profitable, was down about the same percentage for the same period.

The Mouse That Changed the Law (Maybe)

Not every valuable asset is an abstraction, and not every decision to protect an asset is a moral choice. The Walt Disney Company has always been ahead of the pack in understanding the engine that makes its money and moving on all possible fronts all the time to identify, protect, and exploit its core assets, but neither the company nor its longtime CEO, Michael Eisner, has ever been accused of being too nice or too good.

Disney, with $25 billion in revenue and 114,000 employees, owns a lot of assets—about $44 billion worth, according to its public filings—ranging from film libraries to thousands of acres of real estate: theme parks, hotels, and resorts (in four countries); a cruise line; one major television broadcasting network (ABC); several cable TV networks, including 80 percent of ESPN, the country's leading sports broadcaster; a large national radio network; ten local television stations;

fifty-three radio stations; film studios; movie and television production companies; book and magazine publishing companies; and a chain of retail stores.

But at Disney, the ability to make money centers around the relationships that are formed between audiences and an ever-expanding set of characters, beginning with Mickey Mouse and stretching forward to Buzz Lightyear and others yet to come. Disney has been obsessed with these characters and their personalities since the company's inception, and its obsession has shaped the modern entertainment business.

Disney characters take the form of intangible assets, consisting largely of lots and lots and lots of copyrights to characters, stories, movies, books, T-shirts, drawings, paintings, TV programs, and more. Walt Disney, after all, founded the company in 1923 by creating cartoon characters, and both he and his company have always owed literally everything to Walt's first successful character, Mickey Mouse. Without Mickey, Minnie, Donald Duck, Goofy, Pluto, and the whole thousand-character Disney clan, Disney's theme parks in Florida, California, Paris, Tokyo, and soon Hong Kong would be so much overvalued real estate. And it is by operating a unique, seamless marketing machine to constantly exploit the value of these characters and an almost infinite variety of other, similar intellectual properties that Disney continues to make its money and give value to its hard assets.

For Disney, as anyone with a child knows, a good character is many money-making things: a movie (plus sequels), a book, a TV show, a CD, a stuffed toy, a T-shirt, a sweatshirt, a ride at Disney World, an interactive computer game, and on and on. So for Disney shareholders it should have been heartening news when the Disney legal and lobbying machines pulled out the stops on behalf of the Sonny Bono Copyright Term Extension Act (generally abbreviated as "CTEA"), which Congress passed and Bill Clinton signed in 1998. The act essentially extended copyright owners' rights for an additional twenty years. For Disney, this meant, among other things, that Mickey Mouse, created in 1928, would continue to belong exclusively to Disney instead of passing into the public domain in 2003.

Disney worked hard enough on the CTEA to get the lion's share of the public credit for it. In a commentary posted on the popular legal Web site FindLaw, an antitrust expert titled his disapproving article on the law "The Mouse That Ate the Public Domain." The expert, Chris Sprigman, a former Justice Department lawyer, pointed out that Disney had spent millions on campaign contributions around the time it was lobbying for the act.[35] Another prominent expert on intellectual property law has called the CTEA "the Mickey Mouse Protection Act." Perhaps more important to Disney shareholders, lawyers knowledgeable about copyright law say the Disney organization has worked hard on every one of the eleven extensions of copyright protection enacted by the Congress from 1962 to 1998. All in all, these extensions have added thirty-nine years to the maximum term of a copyright.

Edward Samuels, professor at New York Law School and author of *The Illustrated Story of Copyright*, says simply, "Its true that Disney understands what its assets are and it brings lawsuits to protect its rights and lobbies Congress to protect its rights. Of those who are seeking to extend copyright protection, Disney certainly has the deepest pockets."

Samuels believes Disney is getting more credit that any single lobbyist can possibly deserve for passing the CTEA. "People look at the congressional vote and say, 'Disney did it again.' But the reality is that it wasn't a hard sell. You have to have a reasonable pitch to convince Congress, and in this case it was international trade," says Samuels, who believes the statute brings U.S. law in balance with Europe's copyright laws and thus creates balance in the economic value of intellectual property on both sides of the Atlantic.[36]

The opponents of the bill—and they are legion—see it differently, maintaining that Disney and its allies at the big studios and publishing houses want to stifle the free marketplace of ideas for their own gain. The populist view of this issue as an offensive power grab by moneyed interests is well represented in a lawsuit filed by a group of small publishers headed by a New Hampshire man named Eric Eldred, whose critically acclaimed nonprofit Web site makes public

domain literature widely available.[37] Eldred's contention that CTEA is unconstitutional was rejected by the federal District Court and the Court of Appeals. But in a surprising move, the U.S. Supreme Court agreed in early 2002 to hear the case and the oral arguments were completed in October. In January 2003, however, in a less surprising move, the Court sided with Disney, making Mickey and his friends wholly owned assets for another two decades.

Since the suit challenged a federal law, the defendant was the attorney general of the United States, not Disney. But it is certain that Disney aided the fight against Eldred's suit in every way it could. And however you view the underlying political issue, you have to acknowledge that Disney's shareholders, at least, were well served by the company's aggressive war to preserve its core assets. If Merrill Lynch had been as diligent in protecting its reputation as Disney is in protecting its copyrights, there would have been no conflicts of interest between Wall Street investment bankers and investors.

HOW TO BUILD THE BOX

THE NINTH PLANK

1. On an annual basis, review each major segment of your business and identify the ultimate sources of the money that makes the business work. This analysis will point to the key assets that produce your revenues and profits.
2. For most businesses, the critical assets are not physical, they're one of three abstractions:
 a. Capitalized reputation
 b. Capitalized customer relationships
 c. Capitalized human expertise
3. Create a plan to protect key assets from both catastrophic threats and gradual erosion.
4. Setting aside the way your business works currently, ignoring conventional wisdom, ask: How can I best exploit this asset long-term to increase profits?

The Ends-Over-Means Box: Results Are More Important Than Process

*Remember that the end result
is what really matters.*

Before Starting Down a Road,
Make Sure It Leads to Your Destination

On a mild day in Bogotá in August 1998, Andres Pastrana, the new
president of Colombia, marked his inauguration by outlining a peace
process to end four decades of civil war, mass kidnappings, extortion,
assassinations, and other criminal and political atrocities, all of which
had become daily occurrences for his country's forty million people.[1]

The initiation of the "peace process" was welcome news to Pas-
trana's small equatorial country perched at the northwestern fringe of
the South American continent, lapped by both the Pacific and the
Caribbean. Ever since the end of World War II, Colombia had been
wracked by civil conflict and plagued by nightmarish violence among
two left-wing guerrilla forces, a powerful alliance of right-wing para-
military death squads, legions of international drug dealers, and a
corrupt national government. The Colombian people and the United
States government, mindful that most of the cocaine on America's
East Coast originates in Colombia, were eager to see an end to it all.

The peace process that Pastrana put in place was elaborate and
deliberate. It began immediately after Pastrana's landslide election in
June 1998, as the president-elect held unprecedented talks with lead-
ers of the Revolutionary Armed Forces of Colombia, or FARC, the

country's most powerful rebel group. The rebels began negotiations with the seemingly outrageous demand that the government withdraw the Colombian army and police from five cities, essentially ceding some 16,000 square miles to the FARC. Pastrana agreed, creating a sparsely inhabited reservation the size of Switzerland that was alternately referred to as a rebel "safe haven" or a "clearance zone." Limited by the Colombian constitution to a single four-year term, Pastrana was to devote much of his time and energy as president to conducting the peace process with the FARC's leaders.

The peace process brought many headlines, many meetings, many concessions, many hopes, and many predictions. But throughout, it was accompanied by unabated and escalating violence on the part of all the groups involved in Colombia's internecine struggle for power and wealth. Colombia's human rights ombudsman estimated that 1999, the first full year of the peace process, saw a 55 percent increase in massacres and killings, mostly by the right wing, and a record 2,805 kidnappings, mostly by the left.[2] There is no indication that things got any better during 2000 or 2001. The final act of the peace process, in fact, was the FARC's abduction and murder of Consuelo Araujo, Colombia's inspector general, the same popular woman who had served as the culture minister.[3] Following the discovery of Araujo's body in late 2001, President Pastrana announced to the world that, like his people, he had had enough of a peace process that had absolutely no connection to peace. "The process can only be justified," Pastrana wisely concluded in January 2002, "if it yields specific results, tangible actions of peace."[4]

Unable to bear the burden of actually producing results, the so-called peace process quickly withered. Pastrana himself disavowed it in early 2002. Then Colombians overwhelmingly elected a hard-liner who promised to get tougher. The final commentary on the efficacy of Pastrana's peace process came in the last week of his presidency, when virtually the entire population of a jungle village—some 700 men, women, and children—simply vanished, apparently kidnapped or forcibly dispersed by the FARC. Only eight residents of the newly emptied ghost town in south-central Colombia could be located by authorities.[5]

Clearly, Colombia will never achieve peace without following some sort of process to resolve the differences among its warring parties. But just as clearly, as Pastrana finally concluded, the process selected will have to be connected to producing real results, such as disarmament and ending bloodshed. Processes unhinged from results tend to produce no results, as Colombia learned. But such processes are hardly the unique property of troubled South American republics where oil, coffee, and cocaine are the biggest exports. Consider the corporate equivalent of Colombia's problem.

Jeffrey Skilling, the notorious former CEO of Enron Corp., was once a consultant with McKinsey & Company, the global consulting practice that was deeply involved in Enron's management. Skilling wrapped Enron's aggressive corporate culture around a personnel process, imported from McKinsey,[6] called "differentiation and affirmation."[7] Based on the results of a 1997 McKinsey research project, created by a team of McKinsey consultants, the much-talked-about process involves two main activities. "Differentiation" is nothing more sophisticated than splitting employees into groups—A, B, and C workers—where "A players are the best 10 to 20 percent, B players are the middle 60 to 70 percent, and C players are the bottom 10 to 20 percent."[8] What the McKinsey people call "affirmation," however, would more accurately be termed affirmation and disaffirmation, as it involves lavishing outsized portions of bonus money and power on the small cadre of A players, encouraging the B players to hang in there, and moving aside or canning the luckless C players.

With atypical candor, the folks at Enron referred to this process as "rank and yank,"[9] and they played it out in twice-yearly meetings of their Performance Review Committee (known as the PRC), where virtually every significant manager of the company was rated on a six-point scale of individual talent[10] and then richly rewarded or shuffled aside accordingly. The real problem with the process, however, was not so much the ruthless ranking and yanking as the criteria on which the ranking and yanking were based. The PRC theoretically worked by objectively evaluating ten different factors, but every account of how it really worked reveals tales of arbitrary decisions based on who did what to whom, not who did what for Enron's business or shareholders.

Since the rankings of the PRC had to be unanimous, managers became extremely reluctant to disagree with any PRC member. Describing the impact of the process, one former Enron executive told *BusinessWeek*, "You don't object to anything. The whole culture at the vice-president level and above just became a yes-man culture."

The McKinsey consultants who helped create the whole mess offered little guidance about how to separate the As from the Cs. One line from *The War for Talent*, their book about the process, is typically unhelpful: "Whichever approach you use for defining your talent segments, be sure to install a common definition that can be consistently applied."[11] (Thanks for sharing.)

As practiced at Enron, this executive management process heaped riches and promotions on some people whose performance, objectively judged, ranged from the merely ghastly to the felonious.[12] One example of the process at work appears to have been Lou L. Pai, a senior executive in Enron's gas trading business who migrated to electricity trading in 1992.[13] Pai enjoyed great success in dumping Enron stock before its bankruptcy. Ultimately he reaped $353.7 million from his stock sales, far more than any other Enron insider.[14] But he was, by all accounts, a dismal failure at conducting electricity trades for profit.[15]

Pai's first try at power trading involved buying electricity and reselling it to residential customers in newly deregulated markets. In a financial debacle that one of Pai's biggest supporters called a "humiliating setback," he managed to lose $40 million in just three months attempting to market this retail venture in California, signing up only "a tiny handful of customers."[16] The failure appears to stem from a singular lack of attention to business fundamentals—planning, research, and execution.

If his stock options are any indication, however, Pai was rewarded by Enron like an A-plus player. For his dismal performance, he was given the opportunity in 1997 to launch and run Enron Energy Services, a division that was supposed to provide and maintain all the systems and equipment that corporate customers need to turn electrical power into light, heat, and air-conditioning. While Pai headed EES, as it was known, the division signed billions of dollars worth of

contracts and, ultimately, claimed tens of millions of dollars in profits. But as Enron Chairman and CEO Kenneth Lay was informed in an e-mail from a former EES employee in August 2001, "EES had been doing deals for two years and was losing money on almost all the deals they had booked." The ex-employee, Margaret Ceconi, esti-mated the hidden losses at $500 million, but had heard speculation that they might "be closer to $1 billion."[17] Other Enron employees have since joined her in observing that EES's earnings were a mirage.

So precisely what was the PRC measuring in its application of McKinsey's personnel process? The McKinsey consultants who devel-oped the system say it was "talent" being measured. This raises an obvious follow-up question, however, which McKinsey failed to address: Talent for what? Certainly not for making money or adding to shareholder value. As Malcolm Gladwell wrote in a *New Yorker* arti-cle critical of McKinsey's whole approach, "if talent is defined as something separate from an employee's actual performance, what use is it, exactly?"[18]

The truth, of course, is that the personnel process at Enron was as unhinged from reality as President Pastrana's peace process in Colombia. Both processes lacked a firm attachment to results, and consequently, they were far worse than useless. Applying common sense, it is easy to conclude the following: A peace process should not lead to years of increasing bloodshed and the murder of the minister of culture; if it does, you have a strong signal that something might be wrong with the process. By the same token, a personnel process to reward talent should not produce prestigious promotions and hun-dreds of millions of dollars in bonuses for people who fail.

How Does Steve Ballmer Spell "Process"?
R-E-S-U-L-T-S

Management theory holds that it's a good thing to have processes—established ways of doing things. And that is true, as far as it goes. But disaster is waiting for any manager who forgets that the sole point of having a process is to help ensure some degree of manage-

ment control and the replication of good results. If doing something in a particular way makes it manageable and produces a great outcome, it makes sense to enshrine that way of doing things in a process. The next time around, with any luck, doing the same thing in the same way will produce another great outcome. But anything can happen if processes become unstuck from the results they are supposed to produce. When needed results are not well defined, or when an organization fails to exercise control and to measure the actual results, failure is not far off.

None of this is code for "the ends justify the means." They don't, but that's a different argument altogether. The rule under discussion here merely says that results matter more than process; where you end up is more important than how you got there. For any organization—business or government—processes are just a tool to help achieve desired results. Like most business fundamentals, this is not rocket science. But adhering to this fundamental is an essential part of success, while ignoring it leads invariably to disaster.

Look at public and private organizations—businesses, nonprofits, nations—that have either achieved their goals or lost their way. It becomes clear that focusing on results is, essentially, the endless repetition of a five-part process:

1. Determine the goal and define it precisely.
2. Create a plan for achieving it.
3. Create measurements—as objective as possible—that will tell management what progress has been made toward the goal and when the goal is achieved.
4. Capture and report the results regularly so progress can be continually assessed.
5. Once a goal is achieved, start over again at step 1 with new goals.

Microsoft is one of the world's most successful companies, providing uninterrupted growth and performance even in terrible times. Microsoft grew its annual revenues an average of 17 percent per year for the five years ending in June 2002. Revenue in the company's 2002

financial year rose to $28.4 billion, an increase of 12 percent over 2001, despite a worldwide economic downturn that hit technology companies particularly hard. While net income took a hit from Microsoft's heavy investment losses, primarily in cable TV and telecommunications joint ventures, operating earnings managed to inch up by 2 percent to $11.9 billion.[19] All of this while investing heavily to transform Microsoft's business for the Internet and also while spending more on pure research than any other U.S. company.

The man who presided over most of this enviable five-year record is Stephen Ballmer. Having joined Microsoft in 1980 as its first business manager, he became president in 1998 and CEO in 2000, taking over from Bill Gates. So it is noteworthy that when Ballmer is asked about his company's "processes," he seems hardly to know what the question means. Instead of talking about process, Ballmer immediately addresses the results he is trying to produce, musing out loud that what is being sought will differ depending on the time horizon— whether it is five years out or twenty-five years out. His idea of process turns out to be a system that constantly refocuses his managers' attention on the results they should achieve and their accountability for achieving them.

"You reinforce things through the management process," Ballmer said recently, riding in the back of a car through New York City, talking his ideas into a tape recorder.[20] "That's all that you can do. Every time you sit with people you ask them, 'How are you doing? What are your plans?' And six months later: 'Did you accomplish what you said you would? Was it ambitious enough relative to what customer expectations are? Is it ambitious enough relative to the competition?' At the end of the day these are the things that determine success."

Ballmer added, "For the past four years, I've been working on getting a charter of responsibility and accountability—on the technology front and the customer front and the P&L front." Because to fuel Microsoft's relentless performance, Ballmer said, it is critical to have "people understand how they fit in the context of the overall mission—what we expect of them." And with that understanding in place, Ballmer continued, "You arm people with the tools, they get the data, and you let them make the call—and hold them account-

able for the calls that they make through copious and detailed drill-downs."

The difficulty of focusing on results will vary, usually with the size and age of an organization. Generally, the older a company, the more time it has had to ossify and the greater the chance is that its processes have outlived whatever usefulness they once had. Generally, the bigger an organization has grown, the more difficult it is to communicate goals to every level. But it is also true that many very young businesses just never learn to focus on results, getting caught up in other parts of their imagined missions, instead.

Showing Results Is Now the Law of the Land— But Even That May Not Work

General Motors, once the largest and most valuable company in the world, is a prime example of a huge, old business that went into a tailspin for decades because its processes became more important than its results. Founded in 1908, GM grew to the point where it built nearly half of all the vehicles sold in North America, the world's biggest car market. Its size has remained stunning: revenues were $177 billion in 2001, and some 365,000 employees took home GM paychecks.[21] But despite (or partly because of) the big numbers, GM was the acknowledged dog of the global auto industry, with falling earnings, mostly unexciting cars, a hodgepodge of divisions, and consistently deteriorating market share. After peaking in 1978, GM's share of market dropped straight down for twenty-two years, falling well below 29 percent before creeping up just a touch on the strength of interest-free financing ("0 percent," as GM's ads proclaimed) following the terrorist attacks in late 2001. Throughout this two-decade slide, GM maintained strict systems and processes that made sure every General Motors office, no matter where in the world, ran exactly the same way. But this long-term obsession with policies and structures ultimately represented what one management expert called "the failure of GM as an institution."[22]

John Schnapp, a former automotive consultant turned journalist,

offered a diagnosis of GM's illness in the company's hometown newspaper, the *Detroit News*. Schnapp wrote, "A central problem, as one-time GM board member Ross Perot tried unavailingly to persuade former chairman Roger Smith, is the absence of uncompromising results-oriented leadership. General Motors rewards executives who may take seemingly plausible actions but who fail to produce desirable results."[23]

Robert Lutz, the gifted and controversial auto executive who helped Lee Iacocca resurrect Chrysler in the late eighties and early nineties, saw GM's problems coming early. He had begun his highly successful career in 1963, working for GM in Europe. Despite considerable success there, he quit after eight years. Recalling his departure for an interviewer in 1996, the blunt and honest Lutz explained he had left GM because the company "was getting more and more arrogant and hidebound."[24]

Five years after Lutz's candid comments, GM's new chairman, G. Richard Wagoner, showed notable vision and courage when he hired Lutz back as vice-chairman for product development, putting the consummate "car guy" in charge of reviving GM's products. One of Lutz's first official acts was to scrap GM's long-standing cumbersome process for developing new car designs, replacing it with a streamlined system that could get results, including the creation of a rolling model from an idea in just four months.[25] Bob Lutz's hiring, a shock to the insular and tradition-bound auto-industry crowd in Detroit, was one of many signs that Rick Wagoner's GM was finally breaking the mold and facing its numerous institutional problems. GM, having dug deep holes for itself, will be focusing on results for a long time to come before it completely solves its competitive problems. But already it is regaining some of the market position lost in the past.

Results are so obviously more important than processes that getting results has finally become the law of the land in the United States. The American government, after floundering about for 217 years on process alone, finally took a step toward demanding results when Congress passed the Government Performance and Results Act of 1993. The Results Act, as it is called on Capitol Hill (or "GPRA," as the executive branch knows it), was dreamed up by Senate Republicans,

passed in the early days of the Clinton administration, and embraced by then vice president Al Gore as part of his often derided but direly needed drive to "reinvent government."[26] After Bill Clinton's reign, the Results Act was immediately bear-hugged by George W. Bush, who had once proclaimed as governor of Texas, "Government should be results-oriented—guided not by process but guided by performance." The Results Act, in fact, became a cherished management initiative of the Bush administration's attempt to link each government agency's share of the 2003 federal budget to the agency's success in achieving goals.[27]

Familiar only to public-sector experts and true policy wonks, the act maps a plan for radical reform of the United States government's approach to the management of the world's largest administrative organization—some 3,000 political appointees, more than 2 million civil servants and roughly $2.1 trillion in spending. The thrust of the Results Act is that federal bureaucrats and their agencies, having been judged for centuries on processes and "outputs," now need to be judged on their performance.

To most, this probably sounds so simple that it is hard to imagine why even a brief reminder on a Post-it note, let alone an act of Congress, would be required to put such basic management principles into practice. But the very public struggle to implement the Results Act provides insights into the problems every organization, public or private, faces in focusing managers on setting and achieving goals.

The 4,773 words of the Results Act may seem excessive. But peel away the legislative baggage ("Chapter 3 of title 5, United States Code, is amended by adding after section 305 the following new section: Sec. 306. Strategic plans . . ." and so on) and the act makes a more-than-passable management memo. Whether the U.S. government will succeed or fail at this turnaround attempt was still up for grabs almost a decade after the act became a law. But looking inside the U.S. government's attempts to mend its management ways clearly shows the steps that need to be taken to hold managers to achieving results.

The act splits the government's long journey to results-focused management into three stages and eases the bureaucracy through those stages over a ten-year stretch. While the time allowed is cer-

tainly far too long, the steps make perfect sense. In brief, the act directs federal managers to:

- First, create a long-range strategic plan that sets goals for at least five years and gets revised at least every three years.
- Then, draft an annual performance plan that sets out goals for each program or activity "in an objective, quantifiable, and measurable form" and establishes the measurement for each goal. Make sure, the act cautions, that each annual plan is consistent with the long-range strategic plan. (Fortunately, the act also includes an alternative form of handling activities for which it is impossible to set measurable goals.)
- Finally, produce an annual performance report detailing the actual results of each government program and comparing the results to the goals.

Complete performance reports, with three years of comparable results, were supposed to arrive on the desks of Congress and the President for the first time in March 2003. A management expert testifying before Congress in mid-2001 acknowledged that "this measuring process has posed major challenges for many agencies." He predicted "it would probably be fiscal year 2005 before this process has matured to the point where quality outcome information is available across government."[28] In other words, a dozen years from start to finish before the government can see whether the Results Act is producing results in all the affected agencies.

But even the spotty preliminary information has been instructive, showing how critical it is to measure results, how tough it is to get managers to switch their focus from process to outcome, and why people like Steve Ballmer talk so relentlessly about getting results.

At the U.S. Department of Transportation, for example, one goal is to make highways safer. In the old days, public agencies like DOT were routinely judged by their products and processes—how many studies were conducted and issued; how many public hearings were held. But under the Results Act, DOT is supposed to be judged by its measurable success in actually lowering accidents and fatalities.

DOT, in fact, is one of the government's poster agencies for achieving measurable results. After passage of the Results Act, DOT managers set goals for reducing things like the rate of auto fatalities and injuries per million vehicle miles. Both statistics came down between 1993 and 2000, exceeding DOT's goals, and the agency was able to report "that for 77 percent of its performance measures, goals were either met or the numbers were going in the right direction," according to Steven Kelman, a professor at Harvard's John F. Kennedy School of Government and a former Office of Management and Budget official.[29]

Embarrassingly enough, however, the old days never went away at many agencies, and the performance of the Small Business Administration is more typical of the government as a whole than DOT's. A primary SBA goal is to "increase opportunities for small business success," notes a 1999 report from the General Accounting Office (the GAO), Congress's investigative arm. But in assessing its progress toward achieving the goal, the SBA was still using measurements that were all about process and outputs—"an increase in the number of loans made by SBA, the number of clients served, the number of bonds issued, and the amount of dollars invested in small businesses," according to the GAO. "This is important information," the GAO concluded, "but the plan does not show how these measures are related to increasing opportunities for small businesses to be successful—the key result SBA hopes to achieve."[30]

Kelman warns that, like the SBA, much of the federal management corps and even the Congress itself are in dire danger of paying more attention to the arcane processes of the Results Act than to the results themselves. Measuring outcomes, Kelman notes, is all about improving performance. "Extensive psychological research confirms the common-sense observation that giving people a goal improves their performance by serving as a motivator. Performance measures also give employees signals about which tasks . . . the organization wishes them to focus on—what gets measured gets noticed," Kelman writes. "Performance measurement is crucial. Let's not foul it up," he urges.[31]

Ominously, a survey of twenty-eight federal agencies by the GAO underscores Kelman's warning. The GAO survey found that in 2000,

seven years into the transition to performance-based management, a large number of senior federal executives had not convinced their troops that they cared much about results and only a minority of managers were using results data to make decisions. At eleven of the twenty-eight agencies surveyed, the majority of the managers perceived that their bosses did not have a very strong commitment to achieving results. And "at no more than 7 of the 28 agencies did 50 percent or more of the managers respond that they used performance information to a great or very great extent for any of the key management activities we asked about," the GAO noted.[32]

How a Westerner Taught Japan to Forget Tradition and Love Results

It has been the habit of many businesspeople to laugh at government's ability to manage. But given the incredible number of truly stupid things perpetrated on unsuspecting shareholders by private businesspeople in recent years, it would be prudent for private-sector managers to learn whatever they can from wherever they can. In this case, the government's problems in focusing on results, despite strenuous efforts, merely underline the powerful magnetism that process holds for the unwary.

Process is completely an internal artifact of an organization, which makes it familiar, 100 percent controllable, and safe. So focusing on process is very attractive for an organization, since it is a job that can invariably be accomplished. Results, on the other hand, involve interacting with the messy world beyond an organization's walls—delivering products or services, making sales or conducting programs, interacting with customers or constituents. So results are never completely controllable and are always seen as involving risk, which, of course, they do. It is easy to see why even the best managers may tend to drift back to process if left untended. At the very least, it never hurts to constantly refocus a management team on results.

Carlos Ghosn is one international manager who has mastered the massive trick of refocusing a sizable organization, in a relatively short

time, from worshiping process to seeking results. Ghosn's story begins in late 1998, when the nearly bankrupt Nissan Motor Co. Ltd. went looking for a partner. It had earned a profit in only one year of the nineties, was burdened with some $16 billion in debt, and seemed an unlikely prospect for marriage. Ford and DaimlerChrysler both looked at the troubled auto company's dowry, and both said no thanks. That left Renault as the last possible suitor for this unlikely bride. In March 1999, the French automaker acquired a controlling 36.6 percent of Nissan's stock in return for assuming roughly $5.4 billion of the company's massive debt. Renault sent Ghosn to Japan to be Nissan's chief executive.[33]

Ghosn, Brazilian-born with parents of Lebanese descent, had built a strong reputation turning around the U.S. operations of French tire company Michelin before joining Renault in 1996. At the automaker, he cut expenses so enthusiastically that he earned the nickname "Le Cost Killer"—a title he is said to dislike. But the title seemed to make Ghosn the perfect guy for the job of turning around Nissan.

Still, when Ghosn arrived at Nissan, he found that his biggest enemy was not cost, but tradition. "When I arrived at Nissan at the close of the 1990s, established business practices were wreaking huge damage on the company," Ghosn says.[34]

Ghosn faced numerous hurdles as he took over Nissan, and the first was that he definitely was not Japanese. He was once referred to in an Asian newspaper as "a big-shot white corporate guy"[35] and he was greeted with significant hostility when he arrived in Japan to rescue an icon of that country's industrial establishment. But his outsider status also made it easier for him to see that many of the company's tried-and-true business processes were killing it.

To launch his rescue of Nissan, Ghosn adhered to the classic rules of result-focused management, first defining the results he needed to achieve, setting deadlines, and making the goals painfully clear to everyone in the company. "We said that the quality of management is not a fuzzy concept. It can be measured, and we're going to base that measurement on performance," Ghosn told *Fast Company*.[36] Those initial goals, called the Nissan Revival Plan, committed the company to achieving five things by March 2003: cut debt in half, reduce purchas-

ing costs 20 percent, cut the number of suppliers in half, improve operating margins from 1.7 to 4.5 percent, and close five domestic plants.

There were plenty of people who told Ghosn this was not the Japanese way. That management doesn't move fast in Japan; that no one closes plants in Japan. And so on. Ghosn pushed forward, relentlessly working to terminate the devotion to process and substitute a drive for results.

One thing that caught Ghosn's attention immediately was that Nissan had $4 billion in equity investments in its suppliers—an absolutely amazing number given Nissan's chronic losses and even more serious lack of cash. The investments were part of the traditional Japanese keiretsu system, under which firms buy shares in their suppliers to promote, the Japanese believe, loyalty and close cooperation.[37] Part of the system was that Nissan, like other Japanese companies, literally guaranteed its keiretsu partners that it would buy a given component only from them, effectively shielding them from any competition. A complementary piece of the traditional purchasing process in Japan was the structure of the purchasing department, which gave each supplier a shukotan, or relationship manager. The shukotan was supposed to negotiate all prices and terms with his supplier, but exchanges of favors between supplier and shukotan prevented Nissan's people from demanding concessions.[38] In practice, the traditional purchasing process made Nissan's purchasing costs 15 to 25 percent higher than Renault's.[39]

Ghosn saw a way in which he could create enormous value for Nissan—capture cash and permanently reduce operating costs—all by simply doing away with a single long-standing process. Ghosn ordered his top purchasing executive to buy parts and supplies with no regard for who was or wasn't a keiretsu partner and to end the shukotan system. At the same time, he began selling the keiretsu investments to raise needed cash.

The changes in the purchasing process alone reduced Nissan's costs of purchasing by 18 percent, virtually achieving Ghosn's most critical three-year goal in the first full year of his revival plan. As a result, Nissan earned $2.7 billion in the year ending March 2001—its

2000 financial year—the largest annual profit in the company's sixty-eight-year history. Just prior to the end of the following financial year, Ghosn announced that Nissan would meet or beat every goal in his Nissan Revival Plan a year early. Purchasing costs were down by more than the 20 percent demanded in the plan. Debt had been reduced by 54 percent, not just cut in half. The operating margin stood at 6.6 percent, way ahead of the ambitious goal set in 1999.[40] And the number of suppliers had been more than cut in half while the requisite plants were shut down.

For his results, Ghosn has been proclaimed a hero of the international auto business, applauded by allies and competitors alike. In a world where many cross-border mergers and alliances have faltered, like the troubled marriage of Germany's DaimlerBenz and America's Chrysler, Ghosn has made the least likely partnership into the most stunning success. In late 2001, Renault CEO Louis Schweitzer, the man who sent Ghosn to Japan in the first place, added his voice to the chorus by announcing that Ghosn was the logical candidate to be the next head of Renault.

Ghosn, apparently unimpressed by his own good press clippings, has simply devised a new three-year plan for Nissan and is pushing ahead with his focus on results—practicing the craft of management by relentlessly turning everyone's attention to setting and achieving measurable goals. As Ghosn once wrote, "What car buyers want, after all, is performance, performance, performance. They want well-designed, high-quality products at attractive prices, delivered on time. *They don't care how the company does that or who in the company does it.* It's only logical, then, to build a company's reward and incentive systems around performance, irrespective of age, gender, or nationality."[41]

HOW TO BUILD THE BOX

THE TENTH PLANK

1. Set goals that can be measured. Make them ambitious, but achievable.
2. Explain both the results needed and the measurement that will be used to assess progress.
3. Assemble operating plans to achieve the results.
4. Make sure everybody understands how they fit into producing the results.
5. Measure all the time. Then spread the word. Never keep results, good or bad, to yourself. Secrets motivate no one.
6. When a goal is achieved, set a new one.
7. Whenever thinking about a business process or system, always ask: Is this process helping to achieve the desired results? If the answer isn't an unequivocal yes, ditch the process.
8. Pay and promote everyone based on results.
9. Be relentlessly honest, or 1 through 8 will be meaningless (the Enron Lesson).

The Renewable Box: Nothing Lasts Forever

Always be ready to renew your basic business.

Steam Power Is Forever—Isn't It?

By the early 1920s, the mighty Southern Pacific Railroad was a major American business institution, providing the critical link between New Orleans on the Gulf of Mexico and the younger metropolises of the West Coast. As chairman of the sprawling Southern Pacific empire, Julius Kruttschnitt was one of the world's key purchasers of railway equipment, and one of his most trusted vendors was Baldwin Locomotive Works near Philadelphia. Founded in 1883, Baldwin had become the world's largest manufacturer of steam locomotives and a dominant force in railways.[1] So it was not at all surprising that Kruttschnitt decided to write the locomotive-building giant in 1922 about making his company something new and very promising—a diesel-powered locomotive.[2]

Kruttschnitt saw this as a huge opportunity. He had been an engineer before rising through the Southern Pacific ranks,[3] and though he might have loved the rattling, fire-in-the-belly steam locomotives that had transformed the continent, he recognized that putting diesel power on the rails could transform his business, potentially cutting costs and increasing profits. Diesel, it turned out, had triple the thermal energy of steam, and a diesel power plant on wheels was potentially far more efficient than steam. Kruttschnitt was passionate about

these new machines, and he wanted Baldwin to be his partner in exploring the potential of diesel. But Baldwin's answer was dismaying. Sorry, the Baldwin management in effect told the Southern Pacific boss, but we're too busy filling orders for steam locomotives to bother with diesel.[4]

It's all too easy to see why Baldwin told Kruttschnitt to get lost. In 1922, the world-beating American steam-locomotive industry was enjoying one of its best years since World War I ended in late 1918. In the first year after the war, manufacturers had received orders for just 214 locomotives; three years later, however, 2,600 orders poured in.[5] All three of America's major steam-locomotive makers—Baldwin; the Lima-Hamilton Corporation of Lima, Ohio; and the American Locomotive Company, later called Alco Products, with plants in the U.S. and Canada—were enjoying another fat period in an industry that had lived on a feast-or-famine regimen for decades. Steam was king, no matter what anyone might say.

When orders began to wane again in the late 1920s, the managers of these locomotive companies assumed it was just time for another belt-tightening. Despite an abundance of clues, like the letter from Southern Pacific, they remained blind to the fact that their era was dying. "Although their executives remained unaware of the situation, the success of these three companies was fragile,"[6] explains Albert Churella, one historian of this transitional period in the railway industry.

One central reason for the fragility was the increasing difficulty of financing the massive steam machines. In an era when mass-produced automobiles were rolling out of Detroit's production lines, each car exactly the same, steam locomotives were still being custom-built in the nineteenth-century manner. Each railroad company was free to make so many specific design requests that the resulting locomotive was unusable on any other company's line. This made financing the purchases extremely difficult. Banks were understandably reluctant to put up money for one of these technological marvels because it was going to turn into a colossal flowerpot if the railroad that ordered it ran into financial trouble. Since no other line could use

the locomotive, there was no chance of selling it to recover its cost, which might run upwards of $60,000, the equivalent of more than $600,000 today.

The industry was ripe for conversion to easily financed, production-line locomotives. But they weren't going to be using steam because, as Churella points out, that form of motive power was at "a technological dead end."[7] By the 1920s, designers had squeezed about as much efficiency from steam locomotion as they could; the only way to get more power was simply to build bigger and bigger machines, with even more gargantuan appetites for fuel.

Three years after first asking Baldwin Locomotive Works to build him a diesel, Julius Kruttschnitt delivered a paper to the American Society of Mechanical Engineers in which he "predicted that the replacement of steam locomotives by diesels would cut fuel costs by two-thirds."[8] Other railroad executives quickly followed suit. While the dominant steam locomotive companies stuck to steam, new firms came into being to supply the demand for progress. And Kruttschnitt and his colleagues became their customers.

The obvious alternative to steam, especially once the Great Depression took hold in 1929, was to employ a less expensive, fuel-thriftier form of locomotion. Diesel filled the bill, not only because it was inherently more efficient than steam, but also because diesel engines didn't require the transport of carloads of coal and tanker cars of water all over the country. In practice, one tanker car of diesel fuel provided the same motive power as eight hopper cars of coal. And diesel engines didn't need any water for steam production.[9]

General Electric, founded by Thomas Edison in 1880 to develop electric lighting and power generation, actually built the country's first experimental diesel locomotive in 1917.[10] With no steam-engine experience to slow it down, GE made a fast start in diesel. In 1922, the same year the Southern Pacific's chairman was told that Baldwin couldn't bother to build him a diesel, a company called Electro-Motive Engineering was formed in Cleveland to develop and exploit the new diesel technology. With nothing more than drawings and calculations showing what it thought its engines could do, the fledgling

firm sold two locomotives in 1923, and both were in service by 1924. Acquired by General Motors in 1930, the Electro-Motive Division forged ahead with diesel-locomotion work for the ensuing seven decades and is still a leading force in the industry today,[11] alongside its competitor GE.

But the advent of diesel apparently was not so obvious to the steam-power triumvirate, who had long scoffed at diesel's potential on the rails even as the technology to make it work steadily improved. By the time Baldwin, the American Locomotive Company, and Lima-Hamilton began playing catch-up in the thirties and forties, the former titans of the industry suddenly looked like they were madly pumping a hand-car while trying to chase a giant diesel locomotive down the track. Baldwin, the renowned manufacturer of 80,000 steam locomotives,[12] built diesels that were simply unreliable—more laughingstocks than rolling stock. By the 1950s, Baldwin was out of the locomotive business—a business it had once helped define.

Baldwin ended up disappearing into a desperation merger in 1950 with Lima-Hamilton, a coupling that was itself a reaction to being left behind by the diesel revolution. The combined companies survive today as Vishay BLH, a maker of precision weighing equipment, which was once a small sideline business for Baldwin. Now that BLH is a small division of a Fortune 1,000 electronics manufacturer, there's nothing left but a faint reminder of the era when Baldwin made the largest machines that moved on the face of the earth, in a business that seemed indomitable.

Baldwin's failure might have been avoided if its managers had not been so married to the conventions of their industry and so sure that the company's success would be everlasting. What the Baldwin Locomotive Works failed to appreciate is that one of the fundamental functions of running a business is keeping an eye fixed on the future. Not the distant future, and not the science-fiction future; just the immediate future—tomorrow and the next day would do just fine.

To remain a viable force in the locomotive industry, all Baldwin had to do back in 1922 was turn its attention to the needs and desires of an important customer who had made it clear that he, at least, was

deeply interested in diesel power. But Baldwin did not do that, and it paid the price.

Constant Revolution Is the Pathway to Hell

Peter Drucker is the influential management guru who declared that a business has only two "basic functions"—marketing and something that Drucker called "innovation."[13] He makes it very clear that he's not talking about any "flash of genius" as a worthwhile part of business innovation. Flashes of genius "cannot be replicated . . . cannot be taught . . . cannot be learned," Drucker writes. And they are extremely hard to plan.

Leonardo da Vinci was almost certainly the most inventive genius the world has ever known, churning out designs for helicopters, submarines, and countless other inventions that were absolutely dazzling. But these products of da Vinci's inventive genius also were absolutely worthless, given the state of technology in the Renaissance, Drucker points out.

"Purposeful innovation" is what business requires, Drucker says, and it results "from analysis, system, and hard work."[14] Drucker and many others counsel business innovators to follow three straightforward guidelines: Keep it simple; concentrate on the needs of today, not some imagined future; and finally, look for clear opportunities and avoid big risks.

Businesses must be dynamic. Companies have to change. Any company that fails to renew itself ensures its own doom. Inevitably, the world moves on, competitors create better and more relevant products and services, and customers turn away. But that doesn't mean businesses should be restlessly fomenting fundamental change around the clock.

Throughout the last decade, managers have been urged by numerous business gurus to engage in constant revolution and reinvention. These "exhortations that everyone should innovate all the time" have rendered a real disservice to business, says Robert Sutton, a Stanford

University professor and an expert in organizational behavior who has written extensively about innovation. Constant innovation? "That's my idea of hell," says Sutton, who always stresses how unromantic and risky innovation really is. "All the excitement about all things new obscured the fact that most new ideas are bad and most old ideas are good," Sutton once observed.[15]

Renewing and innovating are inherently risky undertakings, involving steps in new directions based on untested ideas. So the key to renewing a business is to make it evolutionary. The need for renewal is not about changing everything—in fact, it's about changing as little as possible. It is about responsiveness, not revolution. Renewal is an essentially conservative cause.

Every business enterprise has to preserve its core mission and values. But at the same time, managers must keep their antennas up to sense any change that could materially affect the business's forward momentum. Success comes to those who "systematically analyze the sources of innovative opportunity, then pinpoint the opportunity and exploit it," Drucker writes.[16] The key, of course, is finding those "sources of innovative opportunity" and paying careful attention to them at all times.

Lessons in locating these sources come from watching long-lived companies that have successfully renewed their businesses over and over again, and from studying once-dominant businesses that have been destroyed by change. What these corporate histories of success and failure demonstrate is that meaningful change, in the vast majority of cases, stems from one or more (usually a combination) of just four main sources:

1. **Technology** Watch for change created by advances in any field of science, bearing in mind that such technologically driven change may have greater indirect than direct effects. For example, improvements in diet and medicine over time have greatly lengthened people's life span in developed nations, creating enormous expansion of services for the aging. Direct impacts, however, are also huge. The transistor, developed by Bell Labs in the late 1940s, changed the face of electronic communications and led to the creation of modern computers.

2. Government policy Monitor change created by constantly shifting government subsidies, taxes, and regulations at the local, state, and federal level. The deregulation of the passenger airline business in 1978 continues to transform that industry, while deregulation of banking, telecommunications, and broadcasting drove the majority of the acquisitions and mergers of the 1990s.

3. Customer needs and lifestyles Changes in the way people live their lives can be responses to change in technology or public policy, or they can drive such changes, or they may have nothing to do with either. Whether customers are initiating change or responding to it, how they live and what they need and want are always at the heart of the matter.

4. Competitors Very often, new competitors or new initiatives by old ones will be the first indication of coming change. Microsoft's aggressive attacks on all competition has epitomized modern "paranoia" about competitors (and produced federal antitrust action). But the truth, of course, is that there can be no such thing as paranoia in business because your competitors really are out to get you.

Once any enterprise gets beyond an initial success, its continued survival will depend on responding to the opportunities afforded by change. So almost any company past the start-up phase can serve to teach the lessons of renewal. The stories of the momentarily dominant steam-locomotive makers show the economically lethal impact of failure to pay sufficient attention to technological change and how it affects customers' needs; it also demonstrates what happens to companies that ignore new competition. But on the positive side of the renewal ledger there are many other stories of businesses turning threatening change into massive opportunity.

Renewal is a constant process that goes on every moment of every business day in every business sector. IBM, for example, has been transforming itself throughout the 1990s from a maker of computer boxes into a provider of computer services and a seller of high-tech parts, such as chips and hard disks. This transformation was based on the view of IBM's longtime chairman Louis Gerstner that computers

themselves were increasingly becoming a commodity with ever shrinking margins, while the increasing complexity of technology was making computer consulting and outsourcing services the high-margin end of the business. IBM's renewal of its business took a big leap in 1999, when Big Blue sold its networking technology to Cisco Systems and got completely out of the networking hardware business—a segment it had once dominated.[17] As part of the deal, IBM got Cisco's agreement to buy some $2 billion in chips over the next five years. IBM also got greatly increased consulting and installation work through Cisco. As a result of IBM's determination to renew its business, services rose from less than 12 percent of IBM's worldwide revenue to some 35 percent over nearly a decade. This represented nearly a fourfold jump, from $7.6 billion in 1993 to $30 billion in 2001.[18]

In similar fashion and for similar reasons—to adapt to changing markets and changing rules—businesses have been renewing themselves throughout history in both logical and totally unexpected ways. So buggy makers like the Fisher family have turned into auto-body manufacturers, the miners at 3M turned themselves into inventors, and one firm of package deliverers, American Express, even turned itself into a financial services giant with its own international currency.

The Logical Leap from Buggies to Cars

If the government's great transportation project of the nineteenth century was supporting railroad expansion across the United States, then its task in the twentieth century was paving America with roads. Opening up the continent to vehicles powered by internal combustion engines had dramatic effects on every aspect of life and business, beginning with the virtual elimination of the horse for transportation and extending to the creation of suburban living. Among the initial effects, road networks increasingly shifted the interstate movement of people and goods from trains to automobiles and trucks. Moving freight on rails survived. But the massive, government-funded road-building programs, accelerating at midcentury, essentially killed the passenger-train business, making it a money-losing ward of the state.

The advent of the automobile, however, created far more opportunities than it killed, and the Fisher family of Norwalk, Ohio, saw the opportunities coming. The Fishers were a carriage-building clan in the late nineteenth century. Lawrence Fisher owned a carriage works along with his brother and brother-in-law, and he taught the trade to his seven sons as soon as they were old enough to swing hammers. Another of Lawrence's brothers, Albert, took his carriage-building know-how from Norwalk to Detroit, where he made a small fortune at the turn of the century with his company, Standard Wagon Works. Albert hired Lawrence's two oldest boys, Fred and Charles, when the young men needed work in 1908, a time when the nascent auto industry, soon to become the nation's and the world's largest and most important business, was about to explode in Detroit.[19]

Though carmakers were tinkering with horseless-carriage designs in cities across the country, it would turn out that Detroit was ideally situated to become the nation's car capital: the Detroit River gave manufacturers ready access both to iron ore in northern Michigan and to the coal and steel mills downriver. The city itself teemed with boatyard workers experienced in dealing with metal ships and engines.[20]

Though the elements of the industry were in place in 1908, carmaking was still tiny, barely on the cusp of turning into a real business. Still, Albert Fisher's Standard Wagon Works already had supplied a few dozen wood-and-metal car bodies for the tiny Ford Motor Company,[21] and Albert, like his nephews, Fred and Charles Fisher, could see the future in supplying automakers.

Albert, however, could see only so far. He agreed to back his two nephews financially in opening the Fisher Body Company, a spin-off of the family's traditional horse-drawn business that would make car bodies exclusively. It quickly became apparent, though, that Fred and Charles had a different vision from Albert's regarding the future of driving. The boys were convinced that automobiles would become widely popular only if they offered the comforts of closed-body design, which protected drivers and passengers from the elements, noise, and dirt. Such an auto body was then reserved exclusively for the most expensive automobiles. Cheaper cars were open to the elements, just like most horse-drawn wagons.

Albert apparently subscribed to the conventional wisdom of the time that most people wouldn't want to be stuck inside a moving box unless it was an extremely luxurious one. Disagreeing with his nephews' view of consumer desires, Albert rebelled and demanded to be bought out of his $30,000 investment in the $50,000 venture. Otherwise, he threatened, he'd sell out to another party. (Albert's financial foresight was as limited as his ability to foretell consumer trends: he had refused Henry Ford's offer to pay him in Ford Motor stock, demanding cash instead.) Fred and Charles found a new backer to replace their disaffected uncle, and Fisher Body survived.[22]

After five years in business, Fisher Body was producing nearly 100,000 car bodies a year for Ford, Studebaker, Cadillac, and many other carmakers. Most of the sales were still for open-body designs, as Uncle Albert might have smugly noted, but that hardly meant the company's technology was still stuck in 1908. Fisher had already developed a new method of executing precision woodworking for mass production, so the wooden parts that still made up a substantial portion of auto bodies were interchangeable and wouldn't have to be hand-fitted, as they were in the carriage trade. Fisher also pioneered a sheet-metal stamping process.

The innovations kept coming: In 1920, Fisher introduced insulation to help maintain a more constant temperature inside the car compartment, and in 1923 the company introduced a lacquer process that replaced the paint-and-varnish standard. The latter had required four weeks to fully paint and trim a car body; the Fisher lacquer method got the job done in six hours,[23] further cutting production costs and making closed-body designs more affordable for the general public.

By then, the Fisher brothers—all seven of them eventually came to work in the family auto-body business—were producing car bodies almost exclusively for General Motors, which had bought a three-fifths interest in Fisher for $27.6 million in 1919. GM bought out the rest of the company in 1926 for $208 million in stock, making Fisher Body a division of General Motors. By then, Fisher was turning out 600 car bodies a day and employed 7,000 workers.[24]

For generations, drivers knew they were getting into a GM car whenever they opened the door and spied a tiny plaque fastened to

the step plate with the motto "Body by Fisher" and an emblem of a fancy coach that hearkened back to the company's roots. Carriage-maker Lawrence Fisher had impressed on his boys the critical business principles of hard work and honesty.[25] But the real genius of the Fisher brothers was their willingness to reimagine the business they were in, first in making the vault from carriage-building to auto bodies, and then in anticipating the technological changes necessary to help convert the automobile from a mechanical novelty owned by a few thousand rich people to a mainstay in the lives of millions.

The Illogical Leap from a Mine Shaft to Diversified Technology

Fisher Body was phased out as a separate division in 1984, but its pioneering dominance of auto-body building continues to benefit GM. Its story, like other tales of successful business renewals, exemplifies the advantages of skillfully balancing single-minded focus on the problems of day-to-day management with the very different task of applying managerial imagination to what will happen tomorrow. It was F. Scott Fitzgerald, the widely acclaimed chronicler of the Jazz Age, who famously said, "The test of a first-rate intellect is the capacity to hold two opposed ideas in the mind at the same time and still retain the ability to function." As an example, Fitzgerald offered that "one should see things as hopeless yet be determined to make them otherwise." While that example certainly applies to any bad day at work, Robert Sutton, the author and academic, has a more widely applicable example of necessarily opposed ideas in business. "The best companies organize themselves around two useful fictions," Sutton told *Fast Company* in 2002. "Routine work is guided by the assumption that everything is a permanent condition. . . . On the other hand, the organizing principle for innovative work is to treat everything like a temporary condition."[26] The mental challenge of both operating and renewing a business each day is to regard all conditions as both permanent and passing.

For 3M Company, belief in innovation and adaptation goes back to

the company's earliest days as the Minnesota Mining and Manufacturing Company. The venture originated in 1902 when five businessmen from Two Harbors, Minnesota, decided to mine a deposit of corundum, which they intended to sell to manufacturers who needed the mineral to make sandpaper and grinding wheels. The only grinding in this plan, though, turned out to involve the teeth of the investors when they discovered that they'd dug up piles of low-grade anorthosite, a rock with little use other than decoration.

After trying without much success to sell their unhappy discovery, the company was on the brink of failure when the founders decided to invert 3M's mission: rather than selling abrasives to other manufacturers, they'd buy abrasive minerals and make the sandpaper themselves. Moving to Duluth and then St. Paul from one-horse Two Harbors, the company struggled for nearly a decade with quality problems and financial worries. During that period, a redheaded, hardworking young man hired as an assistant bookkeeper was rising through the ranks. When he became the sales manager, William McKnight urged his reps to visit shop floors and talk to workers who actually used 3M abrasives—research that would help the company improve its products.

Promoted to general manager in 1914, McKnight allocated $500 for the company's first "laboratory"—a five-by-eleven-foot storage room that he equipped with a sink and glue bath. It was a modest forum for R&D, but after just a few months of experiment and testing, 3M developed a cloth abrasive the company dubbed "Three-M-ite."[27] With its flexibility and superior metal-cutting characteristics, Three-M-ite was a hit with automakers and repair shops and enabled 3M to get out of debt and even pay its first dividend. "There are a lot of people who thought we'd never make it," company president Edgar Ober said at the time.[28] Three-M-ite products are still being sold today.

Renewal of its core business had saved the company, so it's no wonder that experimentation became enshrined as part of the 3M ethos—especially since the endlessly curious and industrious McKnight would play a larger and larger role within the company, eventually becoming its president in 1929 and first chairman of the board twenty years after that. A year before becoming chairman,

McKnight issued a short statement of principles, one of which involved encouraging innovation by discouraging second-guessing. "Management that is destructively critical when mistakes are made kills initiative. And it's essential that we have many people with initiative if we are to continue to grow," McKnight declared.[29]

The ongoing process of reinventing the company's business meant making—and tolerating—plenty of mistakes as 3M attempted to diversify beyond abrasives. A venture into car wax and polish in 1924 turned out to have a less-than-shiny future. But the following year, a young 3M-er named Dick Drew visited an auto paint shop and heard a workman swearing at the jury-rigged and ineffective methods being used on two-tone paint jobs to mask one shade while the other was being painted. Back in his own shop in St. Paul, Drew invented masking tape,[30] followed a few years later by Scotch cellophane tape.

To this day, 3M is studied and probed by management experts and academics trying to understand how it became a virtual innovation machine. At the heart of 3M's success is the fact that, throughout the company's long life, "even the most junior engineer was encouraged, indeed practically commanded, to come to the top-management people with any idea, no matter how wild," Peter Drucker noted nearly thirty years ago. And even if the senior people had no clear idea what the younger employees were proposing, so long as the person with the idea would take responsibility for developing the notion and filing rigorous progress reports, a budget would usually be granted. Drucker, with the concurrence of many others since, concluded, "As a result, the company grew from a small and obscure producer of abrasives into one of America's largest businesses."[31]

The innovations that sprang from 3M's approach didn't have to be targeted at winning a large market; the emphasis was and is on simply coming up with new ideas that—crucially—serve a real human need. 3M has pursued this vision of constant renewal for roughly a hundred years since those disappointed miners in Minnesota wondered what exactly they were going to do next. The result has been a mind-boggling number of new products, from Scotchgard fabric protector to videotape to the first synthetic "Tartan" running track to Post-it notes.

Without its commitment to constant renewal, 3M most likely would have been just a failed mining venture with five disappointed investors. Instead, with its management focused on what customers will need next, 3M in 2001 was a global technology company with revenues of more than $16 billion, nearly 72,000 employees, and a research budget exceeding $1 billion.[32]

A Package Deliverer Decides to Print Money

Originally, American Express was simply a regional package delivery service, the nineteenth-century equivalent of FedEx. It was formed in Buffalo, New York (later moving to New York City), in 1850, and over the next twelve years it spread to ten states in the East and Midwest, creating a network of 890 offices, mostly along 9,200 miles of railroad lines, where customers could send and receive letters, packages, and even envelopes of cash, paying a premium to ensure faster and more reliable service than they'd receive from the U.S. Postal Service.[33]

The express business could be tricky, with unexpected losses liable to come from anywhere. When the steamer *Atlantic* sank between Buffalo and Detroit in 1852, $50,000 in an express safe was lost. The company hired divers and spent four weeks trying to recover the money before giving up. American Express took another $50,000 hit three years later, after a clerk in Dubuque, Iowa, accepted two boxes that were said to contain gold to be shipped to the U.S. Treasury office in New York. When the boxes were delivered to Assistant Treasurer John J. Cives, he popped them open and found he'd taken delivery of a few thousand lead bullets. American Express couldn't prove it had been duped, and forked over a check to cover the shipper's "loss."[34]

A more enduring threat to the company than accidents or scams was the U.S. Postal Service's decision in 1864 to start selling money orders, enabling customers to send money without the worries of putting cash in the mail. American Express watched as the post office ate into one of its major profit centers—the delivery of other people's money—and realized it had to respond. Launched in 1882, the American Express money-order business was an immediate success, selling

11,959 orders in the operation's first six weeks. It continued to flourish as the company began to offer more convenience than the post office could dream of: You could buy American Express's money orders in the company's own far-flung offices, and in railroad stations and drugstores.[35]

Even with one foot in the money-order business, however, American Express was no more a financial services company at that point than the post office is today. But the elements were in place, waiting for the business breakthrough that ultimately transformed American Express's business. The turning point came when American Express president J. C. Fargo (the brother of William Fargo of Wells, Fargo & Company fame, who was one of the original American Express partners) traveled to Europe and came back annoyed at the difficulty of obtaining money when he needed it.

Fargo had been traveling with a letter of credit from his bank, as was the custom. The understanding was that the letter of credit would be honored at European banks, where they'd just advance him the money he requested and note the amount on the letter. "But letters of credit were a nuisance, even for a Fargo," writes one historian of the company. The executive complained that "the moment I got off the beaten path they were no more use to me than so much wet wrapping paper."[36] If the president of American Express couldn't get cash overseas, Fargo said, imagine what ordinary travelers had to go through.

The solution, of course, was the travelers check. They came in denominations of $100, $50, $20, and $10, in a design quite similar to the checks in use today (in the era of rock-solid currencies, the checks featured a scale for calculating exchange rates, which American Express promised to honor no matter when the checks were cashed). Unlike money orders, which had been quickly embraced by the public, the company's innovation got off to a slow start in 1891. Success was impeded by the fact that the checks could only be cashed in American Express offices, and there weren't enough of those overseas yet to make the checks useful.

In that first year, only 248 checks, worth $9,120, were sold. Rather than abandoning the project, however, American Express arranged

for dozens of banks and hotels to cash the checks—enough outlets to fill a fourteen-page listing the company issued in 1892. In that second year of operation, sales jumped to $483,490; by 1909, annual sales reached $23 million[37] (a figure approximately equal to more than $430 million in today's dollars).

Travelers checks were a gold mine. The company banked not just the commissions, but also the money from any checks that customers failed to cash. And if customers took months or years to redeem their checks, as they often did, American Express, in effect, benefited from a free loan in the interim, investing the unspent cash and banking the interest. In recent years, this "float"—the amount of outstanding travelers checks at any given moment—has been roughly $6 billion.[38]

Even though travelers checks were inspired by the travels of J. C. Fargo himself, the American Express president resisted suggestions by his executives that the company capitalize on its growing overseas connections by entering the travel business. Going into the travel business seemed a natural move: booking travel, in addition to bringing in revenues, helped build a customer base for travelers checks. But Fargo, though he pushed for the broad development of the travelers check business, still saw American Express as a successful freight company that also provided financial services. Getting into the travel business itself seemed too great a leap. It wasn't until 1915, after Fargo's retirement the year before, that the company ventured into travel, booking ocean-liner passage and tours abroad, changing currency in American Express offices, and of course, flogging travelers checks. The company quickly became the largest travel agency in the nation.

The introduction of the travelers check, based on Fargo's attempt to address a growing consumer need, was American Express's first major reinvention of its business. The second significant change was spurred not by one of the company's own financial innovations, but in response to a competitor's product. The American Express charge card was a direct response to the introduction of the Diners Club charge card in 1950. Thanks to an increasingly affluent society, better roads, widening air travel service, and a strong dollar, Americans were beginning to travel as never before. Improved telecommunica-

tions also made it possible to track financial transactions around the world. Consumer lifestyles and technological advances had conspired to make charge and credit cards possible and necessary. The Diners cards responded to these changes, filling a new need for a flexible, portable method of payment that didn't involve carrying large amounts of cash or travelers checks.

The American Express president at the time, Ralph Reed, disdained the charge-card business—wasn't Amexco a travel company?—and he thought the cards would undermine travelers checks. But by the late fifties, consumers were clearly moving toward charge cards, pressure was building within the company to jump into the business, and Reed relented. The company introduced its own card in 1958, successfully positioning it as a badge of affluence and accomplishment and spurring what would become another hugely profitable change in the direction of American Express. On the first day the card became available, the company had 300,000 applications in hand, and signed up half a million members within three months.[39]

American Express successfully left behind its roots as a delivery service and today is a worldwide financial services organization with major stakes in charge cards, travel services, private banking, investing, and investment advice. In 2001, the terrorist attacks on New York and the subsequent downturn in corporate and personal travel created a disastrous year for American Express, with earnings less than half that of the prior year. Even so, the company earned $1.3 billion after tax on revenues of $22.6 billion. The fundamentals remained strong—more than fifty-five million American Express charge cards were used to buy nearly $300 billion worth of goods and services, $23.5 billion in travelers checks were sold, and more than 70,000 employees were deployed around the globe.[40]

All in all, not a bad record for a regional delivery company that managed to renew its business a couple of times over a century and a half by paying attention to changing customer needs and changing technology.

HOW TO BUILD THE BOX

THE ELEVENTH PLANK

1. Never be satisfied with your business's products or services. Self-satisfaction is lethal.
2. Every manager needs to hold in balance the conflicting ideas that all business conditions are both permanent and passing; that day-to-day work and innovation are, equally, the most important tasks in business.
3. The only thing more risky than innovation is failing to innovate, so change as little as necessary—but change.
4. Managers should look often for the "sources of innovative opportunity" in at least four places:
 a. Changes in customers' lives
 b. Changes in technology
 c. Changes in government policy and regulation
 d. Changes in the competitive landscape
5. Innovation is not a cult, it's a discipline. Practice it by creating systems for testing new ideas.
6. Punishing failure kills the flow of good ideas in a company. Encourage a high tolerance for experiment and mistakes, but demand accountability for monitoring costs and progress.

The Houdini Box: Always Have an Exit Strategy

Make a plan to get your money out, and keep the plan updated and handy.

Exits Are for Everyone, Not Just the Chosen Few

From baseball to rock 'n' roll, every facet of American popular culture is keenly interested in risk and uncertainty. It was Yogi Berra, of course, who made the most famous contribution to our unwritten encyclopedia of obvious wisdom when he said, "It ain't over till it's over." Country-pop singer Kenny Rogers virtually built a TV and music career by spinning his tale of "The Gambler," a character who offers this classic advice to one down-and-out stranger: "You got to know when to hold 'em, know when to fold 'em . . . You never count your money when you're sittin' at the table . . ." And so on.

Nowhere are these sentiments more appropriate than in business, where risk and uncertainty are always part of the picture no matter how skillfully an enterprise is managed. Since 1783, the end of the Revolutionary War that founded America, the U.S. alone has seen no fewer than nine major panics and depressions—real macroeconomic disasters, not including stock market downturns like the Black Monday crash of October 19, 1987 (when the Dow plummeted 22.6 percent in a day) or the progressive, two-year collapse of 2001 and 2002. And before economic uncertainty arrived in the New World, there were thousands of years of boom and bust in the Old—undulating waves of peaks and valleys that historians have traced throughout recorded history.

The last few years have been no different, proving again that there's disaster waiting around every bend in the economic river. Many businesses will navigate through the trouble that always lies ahead, but some will sink. So it is always important to consult the charts and consider, from moment to moment, whether it makes most sense simply to get out of the river above the falls.

Whether a company is public or private, whether its owners are the big investment funds, the mom-and-pop shareholders of Main Street, some aggressive venture capitalists, or the management team, the preferred exit routes are similar. Businesses can choose among half a dozen basic exit strategies that include, roughly in descending order of likelihood and attractiveness:[1]

1. Selling publicly—selling some or all of the stock in a privately held company to the public through an initial public offering

2. Selling privately—selling all or part of a business to an investor group, the management group, or another business for cash or stock or both

3. Break-up—spinning off a division or some part of a larger company as a separate business and selling it either publicly or privately (really a subset of the first two options)

4. Merger—acquiring or joining with another company, usually a larger one, in a deal that unlocks or preserves value for shareholders

5. Refinancing—borrowing money against the value of a company, using the company itself as the sole collateral, and distributing the borrowed cash to shareholders

6. Write-off—throwing in the towel and walking away from a failing business, creating whatever tax advantages can be had from writing off the losses

The best way to achieve a decent exit, of course, is to plan for it. It's never too early in the life of a business to look at the endgame; the best time to plan on getting out of a business, in fact, is before getting into it. Mapping a good way out means understanding that exit strategies depend heavily on established markets for the business being exited.

If there is a strong history of M&A activity in a given business, if there are widely accepted methods of valuing the business, if banks are in the habit of lending money to such businesses—all these are important signs that favorable exits will be available under most circumstances. If any of these critical signposts are missing, however, investors, owners, and managers have to understand that they may well be unable to find a way out when they most need one.

Whatever the exit strategy, the ironclad rule is that the game isn't over until the bragging and the shares of stock have been turned into cash and at least some significant portion of the risk has been permanently ended or, at the very least, greatly reduced.

Getting out—the last rule of good business practice—is by no means the least important. Failure to secure a profitable exit renders all the other rules of business retroactively meaningless. It is simply impossible to succeed in a business where there is no good way to get the money out of the corporation and into its owners' pockets.

The critical corollary of this rule, of course, is that exits have to be fair to everyone involved. Powerful insiders can't be allowed to exit a business, wholly or partly, and leave everyone else behind. Conduct of this sort, we have seen recently, not only is morally reprehensible, but leads progressively from bad feelings and lawsuits to congressional investigations, criminal prosecutions, stock market crashes, and a general breakdown of our economic system.

Corporations exist to be the vehicles for individuals to engage in communal economic action. This means that the legitimate end of all corporate activity is to enrich the individual members of the ownership community. This is the essence of every CEO's job description and fiduciary responsibility: to look out for the best interests of all the shareholders. Having accomplished that legally required goal, CEOs are bound by ethics, by pragmatism, and in most cases, by contracts to look after the employees and suppliers who are partners in keeping businesses alive.

Giving everybody in the community fair (if not equal) access to the exit is at the heart of management's duties. In good times and bad, at every stage of a business, all owners have to be in roughly the same boat or the system simply breaks down. Without getting tangled up

in the intricacies of capital structures, this doesn't mean, of course, that a company can't legitimately create different classes of owner-ship and treat each class differently. But it all has to be spelled out openly and the rewards have be logically related to the contributions made and the real risks taken by each group of owners.

The most repugnant problem uniting the major corporate scandals of 2001 and 2002 is that rich insiders somehow avoided all the risks that everyone else is required to take in business. Instead, they got their money out and got rich while other owners stayed in and got poor. Laying off risk on the other guy offends the system; exiting through secret doors strikes us all as fundamentally fraudulent. If genuine risk is rewarded with big gains, that's capitalism. But when a corporate officer makes millions while the common shareholders shoulder all the risk for his gain, that's offensive, at the very least, and probably criminal.

This is exactly what happened at Enron, and the ensuing public revulsion was so overwhelming that it triggered the devastating crisis in corporate trust that led inexorably to the stock market debacle of 2002. Enron's all-too-clever CFO, Andy Fastow, pulled out a no-risk $30 million for himself by playing with the now-famous off-balance-sheet partnerships that Enron used to hide losses and debt while fun-neling profits into executives' pockets. Fastow's deputy, confessed felon Michael Kopper, got at least $12 million. "Enron employees involved in the partnerships were enriched, in the aggregate, by tens of millions of dollars they should never have received," reported a special investigating committee of Enron's board of directors.[2] Through stock sales and self-dealing partnerships, Enron's senior executives made their exits, taking hundreds of millions out of the company just prior to its collapse.

What did the shareholders get in return? They took all the risk and lost. When the sleight-of-hand was eliminated from Enron's finan-cials, net earnings were reduced by more than $1 billion, sharehold-ers' equity was reduced by more than $2.1 billion, and corporate debt increased by more than $2.5 billion, according to the same board com-mittee. These startling restatements of profit, debt, and equity for Enron's last five years were announced in October and November

2001. The impact was more than sufficient to drive Enron into bankruptcy less than a month later, effectively reducing shareholders' real equity to zero.[3]

Most good exit strategies are very straightforward sales, involving some variation on this basic theme: A business is developed and then sold, either to the public or to a larger firm in the same business. These kinds of transactions, involving every sector of industry, grace the business pages of newspapers every day.

The Stroh family of Detroit, for example, exited the beer business in the spring of 1999 after 150 years of brewing. Stroh, having failed to compete with the big boys of beer, simply sold its brands and some of its breweries to Pabst and Miller, while shutting down other breweries and writing them off.[4] In an industry where consolidation was the order of the day, the exit was neither difficult nor especially painful.

Using a similar exit strategy in a very different industry, the Thomson family, Canada's richest, marched its publicly traded company out of the business that created the family's multibillion-dollar transatlantic fortune. That business was newspapering, which the family had pursued in North America and the U.K. ever since 1934, when the firm's founder bought his first journal, *The Timmins Press*, in Ontario, Canada.[5] The planned and orderly exit began in 1997[6] and ended four years later with the sale of The Thomson Corporation's last two papers.[7] The company simply made the long-term decision to get out of a couple of its core businesses, newspapers being one, and use the proceeds—nearly $5 billion dollars in all—to expand its interests in information systems, mostly electronic, for businesses and professionals. Getting out of newspapers, like getting out of beer, was easily accomplished because Thomson followed the rules: Newspapers are traded all the time, have established values based on earnings, circulation, and market dominance, and are in a constant state of consolidation. Thomson merely created an exit plan and executed it.

The list of simple, straightforward exits is literally endless. Other exits, however, are neither so numerous nor so simple, involving complex transactions that effectively move companies from high-risk businesses to lower-risk ones, stabilizing the entire enterprise and setting the stage for orderly exits. This is essentially what America

Online managed to do when it swapped its overvalued stock for the real, time-tested assets of Time Warner.

Both simple exits and rocket-science ones deserve attention, if only to fix our collective focus on the point of all business: getting out alive and, hopefully, well.

In Exits, as in Everything Else, Persistence Pays

Wired, the business magazine that gave voice to the Internet era, proved a bumpy ride for its owners and managers despite its astounding initial success. Self-styled as "the journal of record for the future,"[8] *Wired* shows the difficulties involved in foreseeing the future even when you claim that's your core business. More important, as a poster child for the hazards of public exits even in an era of wildly overvalued IPOs, *Wired* illustrates the importance of having a backup plan (or two). For *Wired*'s backers, persistence paid off.

The forerunner of *Wired* began life, oddly enough, in Holland in the summer of 1986 when an American expatriate couple, Louis Rossetto and Jane Metcalfe, joined forces with a Dutch company that was applying brand-new technology—the astounding PC—to do language work and translations. The company wanted a custom-created magazine to raise awareness of its software products and asked Rossetto to launch *Language Technology*. One of the magazine's original editors, Dutch-born Peter Rutten, explains, "It was a very good magazine with a tendency to be a whole lot broader than just language work, covering the whole phenomenon of the PC. The PC was so amazing to people."[9]

Language Technology quickly grew beyond the company's ability or desire to support it, and Rossetto took it to a small Dutch publisher and changed the name to *Electric Word*.[10] Soon, however, Rossetto and Metcalfe were shopping the idea of a magazine about Net business and Net culture to investors in their native United States, clearly the heart of the market for a magazine that aspired to be the voice of the dot-com era.

With strong backers, Rossetto and Metcalfe set up shop in San

Francisco, on the edge of Silicon Valley, and launched *Wired*. Their ambitious vision for their company, Wired Ventures, went far beyond traditional publishing; they intended to build a multimedia empire with magazines, books, Web sites, and TV programming.

Launched in 1993, the magazine grew rapidly and soon attracted a critical new backer—the Newhouse family's Advance Publications, parent of the powerful magazine publisher Condé Nast. Advance came aboard in 1994, the year *Wired* won the highest award in U.S. magazines, the National Magazine Award for General Excellence, along with honors from the advertising industry's two top trade journals—the *Adweek* award for Best Start-up of the Year and the *Advertising Age* award for Best Magazine of 1993.

Taking on investment from Advance's entrepreneurial chairman S. I. Newhouse was a good move for many reasons. Newhouse, an aggressive publisher, could be a valuable source of aid and advice to Wired Ventures' senior management—Rossetto, the CEO, and Metcalfe, the president. But even more important for the other backers, Newhouse represented a potential exit from the print side of the business. Newhouse was already a strategic player in the magazine business in a major way—*GQ, Glamour, Self, Bon Appétit, Gourmet, Vanity Fair, House & Garden*, and so on. So it made sense that his willingness to participate in *Wired* meant he'd be interested in buying the whole magazine one day.

Wired magazine was progressing with phenomenal speed, but Rossetto was pushing the rest of the business even faster, launching new Web sites, expanding to Britain, and burning through cash. In the first half of 1996 alone, the company lost $35 million.[11] Rossetto, a true believer in his magazine's hype about the cyber-revolution in progress, thought the capital markets would see Wired Ventures' mounting losses the same way every other dot-com's losses were being viewed then—as a sign of growth and ambition. He set his sights on the usual 1990s exit for a money-losing company—a highflying Internet IPO.

Wired Ventures proceeded to market with an IPO led by the venerable investment bankers at Goldman Sachs. The exit strategy was familiar enough, but the backers of *Wired* had two problems to con-

tend with: First, Wired Ventures was not the "pure technology play" the public markets then favored, but a traditional publishing venture tied to some Web sites and a search engine. Adding injury to that insult, as *Wired* entered the IPO market, investors suddenly became momentarily reluctant to snap up shares in any money-losing company focused on the Internet. As a result, Wired tried and failed to mount an IPO valuing the company at $450 million. Then, in the fall, Wired tried a cheaper IPO with a $272 million price tag.[12] When that IPO, too, had to be withdrawn for lack of interest, Wired's backers began getting restless.

Badly in need of cash, the company managed to attract some $21.5 million in additional private investment in January 1997, but the deal was sobering because it placed a total value on Wired Ventures of only $125 million.[13] Reacting to investor pressure, despite the objections of founders Rossetto and Metcalfe, Wired cut staff, killed marginal ventures, and reduced its losses to roughly $1 million a month.[14] In the summer of 1997, attempting to show potential buyers the company was solving its problems, Rossetto stepped aside as CEO to make way for more businesslike management.[15] Though he retained the titles of chairman and editor-in-chief, the corporate investors and venture capitalists had taken over the helm and they were steering for the exits.

Retreating to backup exit strategies, Wired decided to break itself up, first shopping its newly profitable magazine. While magazine publishing is a decidedly old-economy activity, it has the decided advantages of stable, well-established values and well-trod exit paths in the marketplace. Magazines at that time were selling regularly for eight to ten times pretax earnings or, alternatively, two times revenues, so long as the magazine had sufficient bulk and promise to offer some certainty of future earnings. With a reputation for innovation, paid circulation of 450,000, five consecutive quarters of profits, and annual revenue projected at $40 million, *Wired* qualified as a very marketable publishing property. The Wired Ventures board began discussions with a likely prospect, Miller Publishing in Los Angeles, owner of the pop-culture music magazines *Spin* and *Vibe*. But Newhouse, the built-in exit in the Wired investor group, made an offer just

over $80 million—right on target at roughly two times revenue—and *Wired* joined his Condé Nast family of magazines in May 1998.[16]

That left Wired Ventures with its online assets and sufficient cash to keep them going, thanks to exiting the magazine business. It took six more months to get the job done, but in October the rest of Wired Ventures was peddled to Lycos, the huge Web portal, for $83 million in stock. Through persistence and planning, the owners of Wired Ventures had managed to exit with roughly $163 million in two transactions. One insider later estimated that Rossetto and Metcalfe got roughly half that amount. It was only a bit more than one-third of what everyone had hoped for some eighteen months earlier, but it was a lot better than what they might have wound up with had the investors not aggressively pursued their exit.

Assuming they were truly prudent sellers and weren't restricted in selling their Lycos shares, we can conclude they all sold their stock immediately. As it turned out, Lycos merged with the Spanish Internet giant Terra in the fall of 2000, just as Terra's value (and the value of the entire tech sector) was beginning a steep downhill tumble. The combined company, Terra Lycos, lost some 96 percent of its market value over the ensuing two and a half years. Had Wired Ventures' investors not run for the exit, that undoubtedly would have been their fate.

Getting Out in the Nick of Time

When the dust finally settles on the nineties and their aftermath, including the great stock market meltdown of the early 2000s, the award for Best Exit of the Era will go, hands down, to America Online and its unassuming, baby-faced young leader, Stephen M. Case. Born in Honolulu, Hawaii, and bent on a career in advertising or marketing, Case used good luck, incredible timing, and a native skill for salesmanship to create the media deal of the century, acquiring Time Warner to form, briefly, the world's biggest information and entertainment business.

For Time Warner shareholders, the deal represents a now legendary piece of management blindness and egomania that cost them

billions of dollars and temporary loss of control over their company. But for AOL's shareholders, the takeover of Time Warner represented a last-minute exit from the crumbling and burning edifice of the high-risk Internet sector—a miracle of timing that almost certainly rescued them from financial oblivion.

Ingeniously engineered as a buy rather than a sale, AOL's escape was the most fortuitous and spectacular of its time. Just consider how Case, his company, and the financial markets arrived at that moment in January 2000 when AOL's takeover of Time Warner was announced, and marvel at how smartly and aggressively Steve got himself and AOL out of the box they were in.

The journey of America Online began in 1983 when Steve Case joined an obscure start-up that had a device to deliver video games to Atari game machines over phone lines. The farsighted vision of the founding entrepreneur, Bill Von Meister, was that games would be only the first of many information and entertainment services to be offered over phone lines. Von Meister's view, which predated the World Wide Web by at least six years, was pure genius, of course, but very early. The company, Control Video, manufactured 125,000 of its boxes and sold less than 2,400 before going belly-up, having spent $12 million in capital while making sales of only $40,000.[17] Still, a nucleus of three people from the failed venture stuck together to start the predecessor of AOL in 1985—James Kimsey as CEO, Marc Seriff as chief technology wizard, and Case, a midlevel marketing guy with some experience at Procter & Gamble and Pizza Hut.[18]

Seriff, who had been working with Von Meister long before Steve Case appeared, used the occasion of his own retirement from AOL in 1996 to tell a large group of AOLers how Case came to be hired in 1983. Seriff began by explaining that Steve Case's older brother Dan had then been the president of the West Coast investment boutique Hambrecht & Quist (now known as JP Morgan H&Q). Dan Case, who died of brain cancer in 2002 when he was only forty-four, was one of the best known and most influential investment bankers of the Internet boom.

Seriff told the crowd that Dan Case had been the lead investor in both Control Video and an earlier Von Meister start-up. "He called us

up one day and said, 'I'd like you to meet my brother. He and his friend have just started a little marketing consulting firm. Hire him,'" Seriff narrated, drawing loud laughter from the AOL troops. "Dan had just given us somewhere in the vicinity of, I think, $2.5 million and was the lead investor in giving us another $5 million or $6 million, so disagreeing with Dan was not a viable option," Seriff continued. "Steve did have impeccable credentials," Seriff deadpanned to more laughter. "He'd spent the last two years traveling from Pizza Hut to Pizza Hut sampling pizza, trying to come up with new flavors for the company."[19]

Kimsey, Seriff, and Case managed to take their little company public in the spring of 1992 and, in fits and starts, began creating the online "community of users" that Case liked to preach about. The company was attacked from all sides: The tech-savvy disdained its simplified approach to the Internet; Paul Allen began accumulating shares in the fledgling public company; its two larger competitors, CompuServe and Prodigy, were doing their best to snuff the life out of AOL; and Bill Gates reportedly threatened to "bury" the company if it didn't sell out to Microsoft.[20]

Gates's offer, delivered in a meeting a little more than a year after AOL went public, ignited a heated debate inside the AOL board of directors about the best time to sell and get out. CEO Kimsey led the exit-now faction, which included one of the venture capitalists behind AOL. Kimsey's group wanted to accept the offer from Gates, who had opened his bid at roughly twice AOL's stock value at the time. "We never knew when the bubble was going to burst and I thought we had to consider what's the best thing for the stockholders," Kimsey told *The Wall Street Journal* years later. "This was a good end game."[21]

But victory went to Steve Case, who led the faction that favored postponing the exit. Today, few even know the name Kimsey. (AOL's cofounder eventually relinquished his titles to Case and left the company's board in 1997. Equipped with the title "chairman emeritus" of America Online, Kimsey focused on philanthropy in his hometown, Washington, D.C.[22] Seriff departed about the same time and went to live quietly in his native Texas.)

Despite numerous technological and competitive problems, AOL's

membership continued to climb. At only 250,000 when Gates made his play for the company in mid-1993, membership reached the half-million mark by the end of that year and hit a million by August 1994. Six months later, membership had doubled again. The value of an AOL share followed right along, approximately doubling in its first year as a publicly traded stock, and then nearly doubling again in six more months.

The vagaries of Wall Street and AOL's own missteps made the climb in value very erratic. AOL was punished in early 1994 when its mass marketing success clogged the system, giving AOL the catchy nickname "America On Hold." Its stock was pummeled again in 1996 when subscribers began leaving in droves for cheaper services, but AOL reversed the exodus by offering unlimited use for a flat monthly fee. Then, as usage soared in response to that offer, busy signals became common, and that August, AOL's network crashed for nineteen hours, producing national headlines.[23] Still, AOL slogged through its problems and vanquished its competitors, earning the title "the cockroach of cyberspace" for its apparent ability to survive any disaster.

From looking at the charts and graphs that portray stock market performance, it is now reasonably clear that the tech-stock bubble began in earnest in October 1998. Prior to that month, the Nasdaq composite index had been bumping along for a couple of decades more or less in tandem with the Dow. But beginning in the late fall of 1998, the Nasdaq became unhinged from both the Dow and reality, taking a dizzying upward course that lasted for roughly seventeen months before beginning to dive in February 2000.[24] During that brief and frenzied time, the Nasdaq composite index, symbol of America's lurid financial affair with Internet technology, scored an increase of nearly 250 percent (producing, in effect, an annualized average return of 176 percent).[25]

AOL, by this time, was trading on the NYSE, but its fortunes were linked to the tech-inspired gyrations of the Nasdaq, where it had started out. As the Nasdaq prepared for blastoff, AOL dominated the Web with nearly 14 million subscribers. It was poised to reap the ultimate payoff merely for having survived to be in the right place at the right time. In the first six months of the tech boom, AOL's stock value leapt by more than 360 percent. Staggered by that surge, the stock

gave up some ground and then clawed back to a new peak as the year ended. AOL closed 1999 at nearly $76 a share, a split-adjusted 377 percent increase over its price at the boom's start.

That per-share price set AOL's market value at roughly $170 billion.[26] For a relatively young company in a relatively new, highly volatile, and price-competitive business, with a history of technical and financial problems, only $4.8 billion in revenue in its most recent fiscal year, and a scant $450 million in operating income, this was a handsome market cap, to say the very least.[27] The market was claiming that AOL was worth roughly 370 times operating earnings, an utterly unsustainable and, frankly, totally unbelievable multiple. But AOL, for that one dizzying moment, stood on the peak of a financial Mount Olympus.

From the beginning of AOL (even before it was AOL), it had been Steve Case who had created the deals that kept the company afloat, beginning with the crucial 1985 deal to create a proprietary online service for Commodore Computer users. Once again in 1999, it was Case to the rescue with a deal. With impeccable timing, Case chose the precise moment of AOL's peak value—the fall of 1999—to approach mighty Time Warner and strike a virtually ironclad deal to buy it.

On January 10, 2000, Time Warner CEO Gerald Levin joined Case in announcing the all-stock deal. Time Warner shareholders would receive 1.5 shares of AOL stock for each Time Warner share. In a very unusual move, however, Levin and Case and their boards agreed that the ratio of the exchange—1.5 AOL shares to 1 Time Warner share—could not and would not be adjusted for changes in AOL's stock value. While Time Warner did get the right to back out of the deal by paying a $5 billion breakup fee, it was virtually assured that the deal would go through.[28]

At AOL's Olympian share price, Time Warner's shareholders would get stock worth about $111 for each of their shares, a nearly 71 percent premium over the predeal value of Time Warner stock. Just before the deal was announced, Time Warner's market capitalization was roughly $80 billion. AOL was offering stock worth about $135 billion. But the value of AOL's stock, of course, had nowhere to go but down, and that is exactly where the value went as the acquisition

awaited shareholder and regulatory approvals. Propelled by the abrupt end of the Internet bubble and AOL's disintegrating prospects for online advertising, the company's stock had dropped some 37 percent by the time the merger was completed a year after it was announced. Locked into the fixed exchange ratio, Time Warner shareholders received AOL stock worth nearly $50 billion less than they had anticipated. The price at completion amounted to only an 8 percent premium over Time Warner's pre-deal share value, a price that any competent investment banker should have advised Time Warner to reject. But it was far too late for that.

AOL's shareholders, on the other hand, had managed to swap the fleeting excess value of their overheated stock for all the assets of one of the world's leading traditional media companies. Although the strange calculus of the stock market bubble gave AOL almost 55 percent of the new company and effective control, the math of the business itself was quite different: AOL was contributing only about 20 percent of the revenue and 30 percent of the operating cash flow to the merger. Time Warner got only 45 percent of the deal, but it was the bigger financial contributor by a factor of three to four times, no matter what the measure.[29]

But calculations of current cash flow and revenues were almost irrelevant to AOL. Most important, what AOL got from the deal was the one-time opportunity to escape a disintegrating sector and transform itself into an entirely different business.

Before the deal, AOL was a very narrowly based business—a pure Internet play, selling consumers monthly subscriptions to its dial-up service and selling online advertising, mostly to dot-com businesses. As such, AOL was completely dependent on continued growth in online users and steady increases in online advertising, both of which were slowing. It also was faced with increasing price competition from other Internet Service Providers (ISPs, as the access providers are called). If access to the Internet was all a customer wanted, it was a commodity that could be purchased from any number of ISPs (MSN, Juno, Earthlink, NetZero, AT&T, Sprint, Wanadoo, etc.), usually for a lot less money than AOL.

In complete contrast, Time Warner's many assets are broadly

based in publishing, movies, music, television, and cable systems. And far from being commodities, the bulk of Time Warner's operations represent the most famous and stable brand names in information, news, and entertainment. Time Warner, born some eight decades ago with the launch of *Time* magazine in 1923, is a huge collection of unique content franchises that defy simple price competition and commoditization. Its numerous key divisions are all powerhouses— HBO, Turner Broadcasting, CNN, Warner Brothers, New Line Cinema, Time, Warner Books. The list of individual Time Warner franchises is nearly endless: Magazines include the U.S.'s top three— *Time, People,* and *Sports Illustrated*—plus more than a hundred others; best-selling books by authors like James Patterson, Jack Welch, David Sedaris, and David Baldacci; groundbreaking TV programs like *The Sopranos;* hit movies like *The Lord of the Rings* trilogy, the Harry Potter series, and the Austin Powers spoofs; platinum-album-producing superstars like Madonna, the Goo Goo Dolls, and R.E.M.

With AOL's stock value set precariously at hundreds of times earnings, it was clear in 2000 that no one was going to provide the online company an exit by buying it; the price was ridiculously high. But the code that Steve Case cracked was this: He could create an exit by swapping his precarious paper value for real, enduring, valuable assets. And that is precisely what he did.

Soon after the merger, it became clear that Time Warner would not get the growth engine it had bargained for. Instead, by mid-2002, AOL's advertising revenue had dropped 40 percent compared to the same period a year earlier and the number of new subscribers being added had been cut in half. AOL was shrinking.

The problems with AOL's core business arrived hand-in-hand with the collapse of the irrational Internet bubble. From the announcement of the Time Warner takeover through the middle of 2002, the value of typical Internet companies tumbled by 80 to 90 percent and more. Yahoo!, once one of AOL's prime competitors, fell just over 90 percent. Earthlink, another large ISP, was down nearly 80 percent.

Most real media companies fared much better. Meredith, another big magazine publisher (*Better Homes & Gardens, Ladies' Home Journal,* etc.) and TV broadcaster (twelve stations reaching 10 percent of the

U.S. audience), even managed to rise fractionally for the period. But AOL's problems dragged down AOL Time Warner like a common dot-com. By mid-2002, the markets had taken away 85 percent of the value ascribed to AOL Time Warner on the day the merger had been announced, even though the Time Warner companies were performing exceptionally well in a poor economy.

The changing fortunes of the components of AOL Time Warner were mirrored in the company's changing leadership. First, Gerry Levin, the former Time Warner leader, was pushed early from the CEO's office. His retirement came after the terrible economics of the deal he had struck forced AOL Time Warner to write down its assets by $54 billion. After cutting through all the accounting arcana, the write-down essentially reflected the fact that the currency he had accepted for Time Warner—AOL's shares—had been unrealistically overvalued.

The company had a choice of two replacements for Levin—its two co–chief operating officers, former AOL president Robert Pittman and former Time Warner president Richard Parsons. Not surprisingly, Parsons, as traditional and old-media as they come, got the CEO's job. As Levin departed, Parsons made it clear that AOL Time Warner under his leadership was going to be a lot like Time Warner and not much like AOL at all. "What the AOL-ers have to understand . . . is that . . . now they're a big—huge, in fact—company with real assets and real businesses," Parsons told one news organization. "They've got something to lose," he counseled, implying, of course, that prior to the merger there had been nothing much there at AOL.[30]

To underscore the ascendancy of Time Warner's enduring assets over AOL's deteriorating value, the company pushed out Case's long-time manager, Pittman. By July 2002, the former AOL president was out of the company altogether in a reorganization that put senior Time Warner executives in the top spots. AOL, briefly in control of the whole empire, had been reduced, in effect, to just another Time Warner division—and the worst performer of the lot.

Pittman's departure and the AOL division's eclipse may have been hastened, it seemed, by the impending launch of an SEC probe into allegations that AOL had used improper accounting to keep its endangered advertising revenue pumped up and looking good just before comple-

tion of the Time Warner takeover. AOL Time Warner denied any wrong-doing, and in fact, the questionable transactions, first revealed in AOL's hometown paper, *The Washington Post*, sounded merely outrageous, not criminal. But in the fourth quarter of 2002, AOL acknowledged having overstated its revenue during the prior two years by $190 million.[31] The downward revision of its financial results was hauntingly familiar to students of AOL—the online company had been fined $3.5 million by the SEC in May 2000 for issuing inaccurate financial statements that ex-aggerated its earnings for two fiscal years in the mid-1990s. According to the SEC, AOL improperly capitalized certain direct marketing costs. "AOL reported profits for six of eight quarters in fiscal years 1995 and 1996, rather than the losses it would have reported had the costs been expensed as incurred," the SEC said. AOL's earnings had been over-stated by a total of $385 million.[32]

But by far the most interesting disappearance from the executive ranks at AOL Time Warner during this tumultuous time was that of Steve Case, himself. The chairman of the firm was a shadow. His work apparently complete with the consummation of the Time Warner takeover, Case just went away. Apart from occasional conference calls with Wall Street analysts, he issued few statements and played no visi-ble role in day-to-day operations. Parsons claimed to talk to Case on the phone twice a day, but there was no physical evidence of the chair-man's involvement in the company. He gave no speeches, made no appearances. In October 2002, his personal home page on AOL had not been updated in more than two years. The lights were on, but there was no one home in the chairman's office. Finally, in early 2003, as the drumbeat for his removal intensified, Case broke his silence. But instead of speaking out for his company, he merely quit, announcing he would officially abandon his creation in May 2003.

Time Warner, in effect, had taken back its company, a couple hun-dred billion dollars poorer but none the worse for wear. Fortunately for everyone involved, Time Warner's assets are enduring, and given rea-sonable management, the value of the company will come back. It may be that no shareholder alive today will ever again see a $300 billion val-uation on the company, but AOL Time Warner will survive and prosper and preserve its value in ways AOL alone could never have done.

Gone for all time is the brief period of AOL's aggressive, new-economy numbers and tactics. Back for the time being are the fundamentals of management as practiced by a long-lived blue-chip company—a "real business," as Parsons called it to distinguish it from AOL.

But the fact remains that AOL's former shareholders owe Steve Case big-time for getting them out while the getting was still good. Whatever value they now hold and may realize in the future flows from the inspired exit that Case managed to engineer—an exit as brilliant and flawed, as initially promising and ultimately disappointing, as bold and as ill-conceived, as the era it ended.

HOW TO BUILD THE BOX

THE TWELFTH PLANK

1. Exit strategies are a mandatory, integral part of every business plan—because failure to get out well renders all previous successes meaningless.
2. Before getting into a business, always ask: "How am I am going get the value out of this?"
3. Look for the four telltale signs of available exits (and be alert for any changes in these signs):
 a. Similar businesses are being bought and sold all the time.
 b. There are widely accepted ways of valuing businesses like this one.
 c. Banks are willing to lend to businesses like this one.
 d. Investors are willing to put money into publicly traded businesses like this one.
4. The object of an exit is to eliminate or greatly reduce risk. This is an important mind-set to maintain when operating any business.
 a. Managers should ask themselves, "How can I reduce the risk of operating this business today?"
5. Selling is a common way to reduce risk or make a complete exit, but buying can also represent an exit. Be alert for both kinds of opportunities.
6. Exits have to get everybody out fairly. When the insiders get rich and leave the rest behind, the system breaks down.

Read This Last

THINK OUTSIDE THE BOX

A fundamental principle in business and in life is that you can't possibly do any constructive out-of-the-box thinking if you don't have a really good box to think outside of. In short, we all have to recognize the apparent paradox that out-of-the-box thinking is inside The Box—or at the very least, it begins there.

I have two great authorities to cite on this somewhat counterintuitive point—Marcel Duchamp, the wild and rebellious French artist, and Robert Sutton, the buttoned-down Stanford University expert on innovation and organizational psychology.

First we hear from Duchamp: In 1917, he purchased a urinal from the Mott Works plumbing supply company in New York, turned it on its back, signed it with the pseudonym "R. Mutt," dated it, and tried to enter it in a famous art show.[1] The exhibit was refused, but in later years the art world proclaimed Duchamp's urinal a classic. Although the original has been lost, a replica now has an honored place in the permanent collection of the world famous Tate Modern Museum in London.

The urinal "sculpture" helped found the Dada Movement, one of modern art's funniest and most profound genres, which used Duchamp-style street theater to raise unsettling questions about the nature of art and reality. But Duchamp's urinal didn't land at the Tate Modern just because it was a wild and crazy out-of-the-box idea. The only reason Duchamp could produce such a work—and the only reason anyone paid attention to him—was because of his deep understanding of the art world's "box." Duchamp had a classical background and could draw and paint gorgeously detailed and realistic figures. It was this background that made his Cubist masterpiece

Nude Descending a Staircase so wonderful. And it was this same background that allowed him to change the world's perception by labeling a urinal "art." Duchamp could think and act out of the box because he knew the art version of The Box inside and out.

Next comes Bob Sutton, the academic who has written with great intelligence about innovation. Sutton tells us the first step in creating anything truly new is knowing as much as possible about all the old stuff—what has worked and what hasn't. When it comes to the perfect execution of the repetitive processes that make up most of day-to-day business, Sutton writes in his book *Weird Ideas That Work*, "Straying from proven ways is rarely a creative act . . . ; rather, it is a sign of poor training, lack of attention, incompetence, substance abuse, or stupidity."

Sutton goes on to point out that "all the excitement about building better products and companies can make us forget that most new ideas are bad and most old ideas are good. After all, that is what Darwinism predicts. The death rate of new products and companies is dramatically higher than old ones. . . . If there was truth in advertising, the slogan 'innovate or die' would be replaced with 'innovate and die.' Tried and true wins out over new and improved most of the time."[2]

In celebrating the power of the tried and true, Sutton wasn't saying that innovation is not critical to a company's survival. His whole book and much of his academic career, in fact, are about how to harness and use innovation. But creativity, as Sutton points out, is largely about seeing old things in new ways. And being creative requires detailed knowledge of old ideas so those ideas can be adapted to new uses and directions.

Sometimes the old thing will be a urinal that you see as a sculpture and that you use to change the way the world sees everything; sometimes it will be a product like the telephone (an adaptation of older technologies) that changes the way the world communicates. The important thing here is that understanding the past is critical to creating the future. Thinking inside The Box in business is the essential first step down the only pathway to thinking outside The Box.

ACKNOWLEDGMENTS

No one produces a book alone. Writing can feel like solitary confinement, but it is a group endeavor in the end. This book is no exception. I have more than a few people to thank.

First, Loretta Barrett, one of the few literary agents who listens to ideas and sounds more like a gifted editor than a multitalented agent. She greatly influenced the proposal that started this process. She also got it sold, which is the proof of her great talent.

Next, my editor at the Free Press, Fred Hills, who is both a fixture and a legend in book publishing, having edited the fiction of Vladimir Nabokov and the nonfiction of David Halberstam, to name just two. It's humbling and exhilarating, needless to say, just to think about it. Fred's impeccable civility, great skill with language and organization, sensitivity, and encyclopedic knowledge inform every page of this book.

Julie Pitta was my patient and diligent research partner, providing insights, telling interviews with a number of business leaders, endless details, and expert advice. John Perra did the research chores on the proposal. Mark Lasswell, an extremely accomplished writer and editor in New York, provided extensive work on Chapter 11.

The editorial professionals at the Free Press are the best. Special thanks are due to Nancy Inglis, whose care with English and finely honed sense of humor got me through many struggles with balky footnotes and even balkier software. The energy and talent of Kelly Gionti, Dolores Dwyer, Tom Lau, and Paul Dippolito also deserve special praise. My thanks go also to Michele Jacob for helping get the word out.

I am indebted to colleagues at McCann-Erickson WorldGroup and

MRM Partners Worldwide. Stan Rapp freely shared his vast marketing knowledge and equally vast store of wisdom. My CEO, Pam Larrick, has been an inspirational teacher, always generous with her time, energy, and insights. Stewart Alter read the manuscript and was always supportive. I want to make it plain that the opinions expressed in this book are mine and in no way reflect those of my colleagues or my employer, MRM; its parent, McCann; or McCann's parent, the Interpublic Group of Companies.

My particular and everlasting gratitude goes to a small circle of friends who challenged me in discussions and helped make this book better. In particular, Bernard Winograd, the smartest business guy I know, was incredibly generous with his time, creative ideas, constructive suggestions, and examples of what works and doesn't work in business. Bernard's wife, Carol, a writer, added her unique perspective to Sunday brunch discussions of the business world. My former partner at The Publishing Agency in New York, Leslie Singer, offered her enthusiasm, which is boundless. I also got great help and encouragement from the people of The Publishing Agency worldwide, including Liza Aelion, Sak van den Boom, Roe Intrieri, Simon Kelly, Jim Small, Marina Specht, Julian Treasure, and Nathaniel Wice.

Finally, my family: My mother, Julia Cohen, always encouraged me to speak my mind, which is how one comes to have the notion that what is on one's mind might be worth the speaking. My brother, Eric Cheyfitz, was the first to take me seriously, which ultimately made it possible for me to take myself seriously. My daughter, Amy Cheyfitz, is an inspiration. And my wife, Ellen Jacob, is a living example of tolerance and support. She listened to endless (undramatic) readings of chapters, read the manuscript countless times, and made numerous critical editing suggestions. She also tolerated me.

Thanks to all,

Kirk Cheyfitz
New York City
2002

NOTES

READ THIS FIRST
Don't Do Anything Stupid

1. "A Tortoise, Many Hares, and a Web of Convergence" by Mark Landler and Geraldine Fabrikant, *The New York Times,* August 4, 2002, Section 3, page 1.
2. Ibid.
3. "Herbert A. Simon—Autobiography," posted on the Nobel Foundation's official Web site, the Nobel e-Museum, at http://www.nobel.se/economics/laureates/1978/simon-autobio.html.
4. *Administrative Behavior* by Herbet A. Simon, 4th ed., Free Press, New York, 1997, pp. vii–viii.

CHAPTER 1
The Basic Box: Some Things Never Change

1. Press release from the Joan Shorenstein Center on the Press, Politics and Public Policy, posted on http://www.ksg.harvard.edu/~presspol/, June 2001.
2. "Do Computers Boost Productivity?" by Andrew Leonard, http://salon.com, April 21, 1998.
3. "The Business Media and the New Economy" by Jeff Madrick, Research Paper R-24, Joan Shorenstein Center on Press, Politics and Public Policy, Harvard University, John F. Kennedy School of Government, December 2001, p. 1.
4. "Lest We Forget: Each Generation Has Its Own 'New Economy'" by Jeff Madrick, "Economic Scene" column, *The New York Times,* May 10, 2001, p. C2.
5. "The Business Media and the New Economy."
6. The so-called broadband glut, the disastrous overbidding for 3G mobile phone licenses, the mounting debts of the telecoms, and the crash of the telecom industry have been widely chronicled in the

press. See, for example, "The Telecoms Crash," a three-part series that ran in the *Financial Times* of London in early September 2001.

7. *Europe and the People Without History* by Eric R. Wolf, University of California Press, Berkeley and Los Angeles, 1982, p. 24.

8. *Europe and the People Without History*, p. 30.

9. *Europe and the People Without History*, p. 22. See also a piece of the work being cited here by Wolf, "The Rise and Future Demise of the World Capitalist System," an essay by Immanuel Wallerstein, which first appeared in 1974 and can be found in *The Essential Wallerstein*, The New Press, New York, 2000, pp. 71–105.

10. Author's interviews with Lawrence Hirschfeld, October 2002.

11. "Late Miocene Hominids from the Middle Awash, Ethiopia" by Yohanes Haile-Selassie, *Nature*, July 12, 2001, pp. 178–181.

12. *Leading the Revolution* by Gary Hamel, Harvard Business School Press, Boston, 2000.

13. *Leading the Revolution*, pp. 212–213.

14. "How Do Fast Companies Work Now?" by Keith H. Hammonds, *Fast Company*, September 2001, p. 136.

15. "Our History," posted in the "Inside Freeserve" section on the Freeserve, PLC website, http://www.aboutfreeserve.com/insidefree serve/ourhistory.html.

16. "America Online Offers Free Internet Use in Britain," by Andrew Ross Sorkin, *The New York Times*, August 25, 1999.

17. "Freeserve's Search for a Likely Partner" by Richard Colwill, *The Times*, London, December 6, 2000.

18. "A Land Where Giants dominate," by Andrew Fisher, *Financial Times*, London, December 6, 2000.

19. "Freeserve Sale Looks a Good Deal for Dixons: But Investors Who Bought at the Peak Are Left out of Pocket," by Thorold Barker, "Companies & Finance UK" section, *Financial Times*, London, December 7, 2000, p. 30.

20. "A Land Where Giants Dominate," by Andrew Fisher, *Financial Times*, London, December 6, 2000.

21. "Ssu-ma Kuang," *The Columbia Encyclopedia*, 6th ed., Columbia University Press, New York, 2002. www.bartleby.com/65/. October 19, 2002

CHAPTER 2
The Jack in The Box: Profits

1. "Net Profits/For a Few, Business is Booming online" by Matthew McAllester, staff writer, *Newsday* (New York, NY). September 1, 1996, Sunday, Nassau edition, p. A59.

2. See also "Making Money on the Net" by Kathy Rebello in San Mateo, with Larry Armstrong in Los Angeles, Amy Cortese in New York, and bureau reports, *BusinessWeek*, September 23, 1996.

3. "Federal Express (B)," a case by Associate Professor Christopher H. Lovelock, Harvard Business School, written 1976, revised June 1, 1982.

4. "The Five Secrets of Entrepreneurial Success," a speech delivered to the Entrepreneurs Conference, February 2, 2001, Casa de Campo, Dominican Republic, by Frederick W. Smith, chairman, president, and chief executive officer, FedEx Corporation. Posted on the FedEx corporate Web site, http://www.fedex.com.

5. "Computed Tomography and Archaeology," a paper delivered to the 84th Scientific Assembly and Annual Meeting, Radiological Society of North America, Chicago, December 1, 1998, by Nachum Appelbaum, Institute of Archaeology, Hebrew University, Mount Scopus, Jerusalem, Israel.

6. "Do Profits Matter?" edited by James Daly and Jeffrey Davis, April 2000, *Business 2.0*.

7. "German Media Firm Bertelsmann to Acquire Online Music Retailer CDnow," by Joelle Tessler, July 21, 2000, Knight-Ridder Tribune Business News, *San Jose Mercury News*.

8. Form SC-TO-T and its attachments, filed with the United States Securities and Exchange Commission on July 26, 2000, describing the offer by BINC Acquisition Corp., a wholly owned subsidiary of Bertelsmann, to purchase CDnow.

9. "The Beat Goes On at CDNow as Most Investors Take a Beating," an interview with Peter Fader, August 16, 2000, published in the online newsletter of the University of Pennsylvania's Wharton School, *Knowledge@Wharton*, on the newsletter's Web site at http://knowledge.wharton.upenn.edu/articles.cfm?catid=7&articleid=226.

10. "As the Brash Stumble, Viacom Finds Itself Leading the Pack" by Mark Landler and Geraldine Fabrikant, *The New York Times*, August 4, 2002, p. 1.

11. "Net Profits: Business Is Booming for Some On-Line Entrepreneurs" by Matthew McAllester, *Newsday* (New York, NY). September 1, 1996, Sunday, Nassau edition, P. A59.

12. Amazon.com five-year financial history filed with the SEC and posted on the company Web site.

13. Amazon.com quarterly income statement for the three months ended 12/31/2001.

14. Interview with author's researcher Julie Pitta in March 2002.

15. Interview with author's researcher Julie Pitta on February 13, 2002.

16. "The Beat Goes On at CDNow as Most Investors Take a Beating."
17. "The Five Secrets of Entrepreneurial Success."
18. "Pets.com's Demise: Too Much Litter, Too Few Funds" by Pui-Wing Tam and Mylene Mangalindan, *The Wall Street Journal*, November 8, 2000, p. B1.
19. "Amazon Invests in Online Pet Store," by Tim Clark, staff writer, CNET News.com, March 29, 1999.
20. Ibid.
21. "PULSE; One Giant Step for a Sock," by Jack Bell, *The New York Times*, July 16, 2000.
22. "Go.com Shapes Alliance with Pets.com" by Greg Sandoval, CNET News.com, January 27, 2000.
23. "Sock Puppet Antics More than Double Pets.com's May Sales" by Jessica Materna, *San Francisco Business Times*, June 16, 2000; "Sock, We're Gonna Make You a Star" by Kiri Blakely, *Forbes*, June 12, 2000.
24. "Sock, We're Gonna Make You a Star" by Kiri Blakely, *Forbes*, June 12, 2000.
25. Pets.com, Inc. Form 10-Q for the period ending September 30, 2000, filed with the United States Securities and Exchange Commission on November 14, 2000.
26. "Do Profits Matter?" edited by James Daly and Jeffrey Davis, April 2000, *Business 2.0*.
27. Pets.com, Inc. Form 8-K, filed with the United States Securities and Exchange Commission on July 27, 2000.
28. IPET Holdings, Inc. Form 10-K for the fiscal year ending December 31, 2000, filed with the United States Securities and Exchange Commission on April 2, 2001.
29. IPET Holdings, Inc. Form 10-K for the fiscal year ending December 31, 2001, filed with the United States Securities and Exchange Commission on March 29, 2002.
30. Interview with the author, April 13, 2002.
31. *Absolutely, Positively Overnight! The Story of Federal Express* by Robert A. Sigafoos, St. Luke's Press, Memphis, Tennessee, of the Mentor paperback edition, 1983, p. 32.
32. "Federal Express Early History," the official history of FedEx posted on the corporate Web site, http://www.fedex.com; "Face Time with Fred Smith" by Charles Fishman, *Fast Company*, June 2001, p. 64.
33. *Absolutely, Positively Overnight! The Story of Federal Express*, p. 41.
34. "Federal Express: Customer Service Department (A)," a case prepared by Penny Pittman Merliss, research assistant, under the direc-

tion of Associate Professor Christopher H. Lovelock, Harvard Business School, 1980.

35. Official history of United Parcel Service, posted on the corporate Web site, http://www.ups.com.
36. "Federal Express (B)."
37. Author's interview of Christopher Lovelock, April 13, 2002.
38. "Federal Express (B)."
39. "Federal Express (B)."
40. *Absolutely, Positively Overnight! The Story of Federal Express,* p. 56.
41. "Federal Express (B)."
42. *Absolutely, Positively Overnight! The Story of Federal Express,* p. 71.
43. "Federal Express (C)," a case by Associate Professor Christopher H. Lovelock, Harvard Business School, 1978.

CHAPTER 3
The Money Box: Cash Is Everything

1. "The Real Legacy of Spring Street Brewing" by Susan Greco, *Inc* magazine, September 1, 1999.
2. "SoundView Tech Group Chairman Lessin to Step Down," Dow Jones News Service, October 23, 2001; company biography of Robert H. Lessin posted on SoundView Technology Group, Inc., corporate Web site, http://www.soundview.com; "SoundView Technology Reports Third Quarter Results," company press release issued over PR Newswire, October 23, 2001.
3. "Unit of One: Dots Dashed" edited by Lucy McCauley and Christine Canabou, *Fast Company,* February 2001, p. 86.
4. "Venture Capital, Previous Offerings," on the SoundView Ventures official Web site, http://www.ventures.soundview.com/become/funds_overview.jsp.
5. Author's interview with Robert H. Lessin, May 8, 2002, New York City.
6. "SoundView Technology Issues First Quarter Guidance," press release issued by SoundView Technology Group, March 11, 2002.
7. Annual financial summaries of SoundView Technology Group (NASDAQ: SNDV), 1998 through 2001.
8. "SEC Interpretation: Management's Discussion and Analysis of Financial Condition and Results of Operations; Certain Investment Company Disclosures," issued by the United States Securities and Exchange Commission, May 19, 1989, 17 CFR Parts 211, 231, 241 and 271, Release Nos. 33–6835; 34–26831; IC-16961; FR-36.

9. *Baltazar and Blimunda* by Jose Saramago, translated by Giovanni Pontiero, Harcourt Brace Jovanovich, San Diego, 1987.

10. "McDonnell Douglas History," on the Boeing Corporation's corporate Web site, http://www.boeing.com.

11. "Major Weapons Programs Oversight," hearing before the House Committee on Energy and Commerce, Oversight and Investigations Subcommittee, October 3, 1991, Serial No. 102–106, opening statement of Chairman John D. Dingell, D-Mich., p. 1.

12. "Major Weapons Programs Oversight," statement of Neil P. Curtin, director of planning and reporting, National Security and International Affairs Division, U.S. General Accounting Office, p. 10.

13. Ibid.

14. "Implementing Acquisition Reform: A Case Study on Joint Direct Attack Munitions (JDAM)" by Cynthia Ingols, D.Ed., and Lisa Brem, Corporate Classrooms, Cambridge, Massachusetts, under contract with the Defense Systems Management College and the Boeing Company, published by the Defense Systems Management College, May 1998, p. 8.

15. "McDonnell Douglas' Make-or-Break Year" by Richard L. Stern and Thomas Bancroft, *Forbes*, January 7, 1991, p. 36.

16. "MD Asks Billion Advance" by John D. Morrocco, *Aviation Week & Space Technology*, July 29, 1991, vol. 135, no. 4; p. 23.

17. "McDonnell Douglas' Make-or-Break Year," p. 36.

18. "McDonnell Douglas Pays a Fine for a 1990 Earnings Report" by Floyd Norris, *The New York Times*, June 25, 1996, Late Edition—Final, p. D10.

19. "MD Asks Billion Advance."

20. Ibid.

21. "Implementing Acquisition Reform: A Case Study on Joint Direct Attack Munitions (JDAM)."

22. *McDonnell Douglas Corporation and General Dynamics Corporation, Plaintiffs, v United States of America, Defendant*, case no. 91–1204C in the United States Court of Federal Claims, judgment for defendant filed August 31, 2001 by Judge Robert H. Hodges Jr.

23. "Major Weapons Programs Oversight," p. 86, where Eleanor Spector, Defense director of procurement, testifies that "we did not see it to the advantage of the Department and the taxpayer to let McDonnell go into a Chapter 11 bankruptcy."

24. "Nomination of Donald J. Yockey to be Under Secretary of Defense for Acquisitions," issued by The White House, March 4, 1991. Source: George Bush Presidential Library, Texas A&M University.

25. "Major Weapons Programs Oversight," p. 89.

26. "Pentagon, McDonnell Douglas Auditors Clash over Firm's Financial Condition" by Patricia A. Gilmartin, *Aviation Week & Space Technology,* October 14, 1991, vol. 135, no. 15; p. 25.

27. Various sources discuss the failure of the MD-11 to meet sales expectations on the MD-11 Resource Web site at http://agrosz.com/md11/index.html; "John McDonnell's Bumpy Ride" by Ralph Vartibedian, *Los Angeles Times Magazine,* December 1, 1991, p. 18.

28. "Major Weapons Programs Oversight," pp. 3 and 92.

29. "Sales and Head Count, 1988–1995," provided by the Boeing Company as Exhbit XIII to "Implementing Acquisition Reform: A Case Study on Joint Direct Attack Munitions (JDAM)."

30. "Towards Pre-eminence," John F. McDonnell's remarks to the McDonnell Douglas shareholders' meeting, July 25, 1997, posted on the Boeing Company Web site, http://www.boeing.com.

31. "Reengineering 101" by Stephane Fitch, *Forbes,* May 13, 2002, p. 82–88.

32. Voluntary Petition, filed in United States Bankruptcy Court, Southern District of New York, by the Enron Corp., December 2, 2001, Exhibit A, p. 1.

CHAPTER 4

**The Bottom-Line Box: Knowing What Can
Be Controlled and What Can't**

1. "Phone Numbers—Behind Lucent's Woes: All-Out Revenue Goal and Pressure to Meet It" by Dennis K. Berman and Rebecca Blumenstein, *The Wall Street Journal,* March 29, 2001, p. A1.

2. Ibid.

3. Lucent Technologies, Inc. Form 10-K (annual report) for the fiscal year ended September 30, 2001, "Our Restructuring Program," pp. 1–3.

4. Borders Group, Inc. Form 10-K (annual report) for the fiscal year ended January 27, 2002.

5. *eBoys: The First Inside Account of Venture Capitalists at Work* by Randall E. Stross, Ballantine, New York, 2001, p. 46.

6. *eBoys: The First Inside Account of Venture Capitalists at Work,* p. 30.

7. "An Ambitious Internet Grocer Is Out of Both Cash and Ideas" by Saul Hansell, *The New York Times,* July 10, 2001.

8. Webvan Group, Inc., Proxy Statement (Schedule 14A Information), May 16, 2001.

9. "eScout Pledge: I, George Shaheen, Promise to . . . Beat the Living Crap out of the Competition" by Stacy Perman, *Business 2.0,* September 2000.

10. "Running Out of Gas" by Vanessa Hua, *San Franciso Chronicle*, April 27, 2001.
11. *eBoys: The First Inside Account of Venture Capitalists at Work*, pp. 282–283.
12. "The Dam," article on Hoover Dam, then called Boulder Dam, in the September 1933 edition of *Fortune* magazine, reproduced on the U.S. Interior Department, Bureau of Reclamation Web site, http://www.hooverdam.usbr.gov/History/articles/fortune1933.htm.
13. "Grocers Count On IT To Keep Cash Registers Ringing" by Christopher T. Heun, *InformationWeek*, December 24, 2001.
14. "History," the official history of Bechtel Group, Inc., on the corporate Web site, http://www.bechtel.com/history.html.
15. Webvan Group, Inc. 10-K (annual report), for the year ending December 31, 2000, dated April 2, 2001, "Delivery Operations," pp. 4–5.
16. Employee count as of December 31, 2000, according to Webvan Group, Inc. 10-K (annual report), for the year ending December 31, 2000, dated April 2, 2001, "Employees," pp. 8–9.
17. Author's calculations based on results reported in Webvan Group, Inc.'s 10-K (annual report), for the year ending December 31, 2000, dated April 2, 2001, "Selected Consolidated Financial Data," pp. 12–13.
18. "An Ambitious Internet Grocer Is Out of Both Cash and Ideas."
19. Tesco Annual Report 2001, "Summary Financial Statement."
20. "Earnings Preview: Tesco FY02 Pft Seen +14% On Intl Sales" by James Hall, Dow Jones Newswires, April 9, 2002.
21. "Tesco Stacks Up Online Sales" by Amy Vickers, *The Guardian*, London, April 10, 2001.
22. "Tesco Aims to be World No 1 for Internet Groceries" by Alistair Osborne, *The Daily Telegraph*, London, December 1, 1999.
23. Tesco press release on europemedia.net, http://www.europemedia.net/shownews.asp?ArticleID=9976.
24. "E-commerce Report: The History of Online Grocery Shopping" by Bob Tedeschi, *The New York Times*, May 6, 2002, p. C7.
25. "Tesco, Entering the U.S.'s Online Market, to Take Stake in Safeway's GroceryWorks" by Steve Stecklow, *The Wall Street Journal*, June 26, 2001, p. A18.
26. "E-commerce Report: The History of Online Grocery Shopping."
27. "Safeway, Albertson's Market Retooled Web Grocery Concept" by Paula L. Stepankowsky, Dow Jones Newswires, April 4, 2002.
28. "Jack on Jack: The HBR Interview" by Harris Collingwood and Diane L. Coutu, *Harvard Business Review*, February 2002.

CHAPTER 5
The Box Top: Customers Are the Boss

1. Omnicom Group, Inc. Form 10-K (annual report) for the year ending December 31, 2001, dated March 28, 2002, "Selected Financial Data," p. 4. Rankings from AdAgeGlobal for 2001.

2. Proximity Worldwide corporate Web site at http://www.proximity-world.com/flash.html.

3. "Big Business Thinking Small" by Rochelle Burbury, *Australian Financial Review,* June 26, 2001, p. 58.

4. *Good to Great: Why Some Companies Make the Leap and Others Don't* by Jim Collins, HarperBusiness, New York, 2001, p. 154.

5. *Good to Great: Why Some Companies Make the Leap and Others Don't,* pp. 155–157.

6. Estimates of hardware, software, and consulting services purchased by some 55,000 enterprises worldwide in 2001, prepared by Meridien Research, a Newton, Massachusetts, technology consultant, and others.

7. "CRM Spending Flattening" by Keith Dawson, CommWeb.com, January 22, 2002.

8. "Making Customer Relationship Management Work," an undated and unsigned article published on *Knowledge@Wharton,* the Wharton School's e-newsletter, at http://knowledge.wharton.upenn.edu/articles.cfm?catid=4&articleid=390.

9. "Fast Talk: The State of the Customer Economy," a discussion in *Fast Company,* September 2001, moderated by Alan Webber, the magazine's founding editor.

10. "The Man Behind the Ritz-Carlton Peers into His Luxury Crystal Ball" by Gene Sloan, *USA Today,* June 8, 2001, p. D11

11. *A History of Shopping* by Dorothy Davis, University of Toronto Press, Canada, and Routledge & Kegan Paul Ltd., Great Britain, 1966. Chapter 2, "Fairs and Their Customers," p. 32.

12. *A History of Shopping,* p. 25.

13. "The Consumer in History" by A. Elizabeth Levett, 1929, Ernest Benn Limited, London, pp. 17–40, reprinted in *Marketing,* Volume 1, edited by Stanley C. Hollander and Kathleen M Rassuli, Edward Elgar Publishing Limited, Aldershot, England, and Vermont, USA, 1993, pp. 492–493.

14. *The Complete Tradesman: A Study of Retailing, 1550–1820* by Nancy Cox, Ashgate Publishing, Aldershot, England, and Burlington, VT, 2000, Chapter 4, p. 116. The chapter is subtitled, " 'For A Tradesman . . . his customers are to be his idols': the relationship between the retailer

and his customers." The part of the subtitle in interior quotes is from Daniel Defoe's *The Complete English Tradesman*, first published in 1745.

15. For a detailed view of commerce in everyday life, see also *Standards of Living in the Later Middle Ages: Social Change in England c. 1200–1520* by Christopher Dyer, Cambridge University Press, Cambridge, England, 1989.

16. *The Complete Tradesman*, pp. 139–140.

17. *The Complete Tradesman*, p. 145.

18. *Counter Cultures: Saleswomen, Managers, and Customers in American Department Stores, 1890–1940* by Susan Porter Benson, University of Illinois Press, Urbana and Chicago, 1986, Chapter 1, "'The New Kind of Store': 1850–90," pp. 12–27.

19. *1872–1972, A Century of Serving Consumers: The Story of Montgomery Ward* by Frank B. Latham, published by Montgomery Ward & Company, Inc., Chicago, 1972.

20. *Counter Cultures: Saleswomen, Managers, and Customers in American Department Stores, 1890–1940*, p. 20.

21. *1872–1972, A Century of Serving Consumers: The Story of Montgomery Ward*, p. 45.

22. "Montgomery Ward to Close Its Doors" by Leslie Kaufman with Claudia H. Deutsch, *The New York Times*, December 29, 2000, page C1.

23. "McDonald's Asks Mystery Shoppers What Ails Sales" by Shirley Leung, *The Wall Street Journal*, December 17, 2001, p. B1.

24. "Fries With That Burger? Fewer Consumers Say 'Yes'" by Jill Carroll and Shirley Leung, *The Wall Street Journal*, February 20, 2002, page B1.

25. *Epigrams on Selling and Advertising* by Leon Epstein, H. Wolff Estate, New York, 1933, p. 10.

26. "Strong 2Q Volume Gain Suggests P&G Turned the Corner" by Cathleen Egan, Dow Jones Newswires, January 31, 2002.

27. "Focus Groupies: P&G Keeps Cincinnati Busy with All Its Studies" by Emily Nelson, *The Wall Street Journal*, January 24, 2002, page A1.

28. Procter & Gamble's corporate Web site, http://www.pg.com/, various pages, February 18, 2002.

CHAPTER 6

The Marketing Box: Unifying the Whole Business

1. "Key Events in AMA History" on the American Marketing Association's official Web site, http://www.ama.org.

2. *Milestones of Marketing* by George Burton Hotchkiss, Macmillan, New York, 1938, p. vii.

3. *Management: Tasks, Responsibilities, Practices* by Peter F. Drucker, Harper & Row, New York, 1973; citing the paperback edition, Harper-Business, 1993, p. 61.

4. *Management: Tasks, Responsibilities, Practices,* p. 63.

5. For a personal reminiscence of the Edsel, see "Reflections of the Edsel Days" by Tom Sneary, a one-time district sales manager for Edsel in Dallas, presented on the Edsel enthusiasts' Web site at http://www.edsel.com.

6. "The Primacy of the Idea Itself as a Predictor of New Product Success," an article in *Insights from MSI,* Summer 1999, reporting on a study by Jacob Goldenberg, Donald Lehmann, and David Mazursky, *MSI Report No. 99–110,* Marketing Science Institute.

7. "Pioneering in People: SAS and British Airways Found that Bringing Personal Satisfaction into Everyday Activity Also Can Produce Success" by Edvaldo Pereira Lima, *Air Transport World,* April 1, 1995, p. 51; and Scandinavian Airlines System Annual Report 1983–84, "Five-Year Summary," p. 30.

8. "Pioneering in People," p. 51.

9. "The Man Who Put the Olive Back in Martinis" by Françoise Hecht, *EuroBusiness,* May 1994, p. 38.

10. *Moments of Truth* by Jan Carlzon, Ballinger Publishing Company, Cambridge, Massachusetts, 1987, p. 3.

11. Ibid.

12. All operating statistics from Scandinavian Airlines System's annual reports for the fiscal year ending September 30, 1980, through the fiscal year ending September 30, 1985. All U.S. dollar figures calculated using the exchange rate for Swedish kroners on September 30 of each year as noted by the footnotes to SAS's financial statements. Industry comparisons from "Flattening the SAS Management Pyramid: How the Scandinavian Airline Plans to Double Profits" by David Brown, *Financial Times,* London, June 6, 1985, Section 2, p. 27.

13. SAS corporate press release carried on the PR Newswire, datelined New York, January 20, 1984; "Flattening the SAS Management Pyramid: How the Scandinavian Airline Plans to Double Profits."

14. Unless otherwise noted, information on Luxottica Group S.p.A. is taken from its Form 20-F (annual report filed by a foreign corporation) for the year ending December 31, 2001, received by the U.S. Securities and Exchange Commission on June 28, 2002.

15. Oakley, Inc., Form 10-K (annual report) for the year ending December 31, 2001, dated March 2, 2002.

16. "Corporate Profile" of Oakley, on the corporate Web site at http://investor.oakley.com/ireye/ir_site.zhtml?ticker=OO&script=2100.

17. Oakley, Inc., Form 10-K (annual report) for the year ending December 31, 2000, dated March 26, 2001, "Notes to Consolidated Financial Statements," Note 11—Segment and Geographic Information, p. 56.

18. Luxottica Group S.p.A. Form 20-F (annual report filed by a foreign corporation) for the year ending December 31, 2001, "Marketing," p. 28.

19. Luxottica Group S.p.A. Form 20-F (annual report filed by a foreign corporation) for the year ending December 31, 2001, "Company History," p. 16.

20. Oakley, Inc., Form 10-K (annual report) for the year ending December 31, 2000, dated March 26, 2001, "Notes to Consolidated Financial Statements," Principal Customers, p. 15; Luxottica Group S.p.A. Form 20-F (annual report filed by a foreign corporation) for the year ending December 31, 2001, "Company History," pp. 15–16.

21. "Oakley Warns of Lower Earnings after Snub by Big Retailer," Associated Press, Los Angeles, August 2, 2001, as presented on the Canadian Internet portal Canoe at http://www.canoe.ca/MoneyEarnings Archive/aug2_oakleywarns-ap.html.

22. "Fear No Evil: Analyzing Stocks with Rose-Colored Shades" by Floyd Norris, *The New York Times* August 3, 2001, p. C1.

23. "Oakley Says Foot Locker to Sell More of Its Glasses" by Delbert Ellerton, *Bloomberg News,* September 25, 2001.

24. "Oakley Completes Acquisition of Mall-Based Sunglass Retailer Iacon Inc.," a joint press release issued by Oakley, Inc., and Iacon, Inc., on the Business Wire, November 1, 2001.

25. "Oakley Obtains Temporary Restraining Order Against Luxottica Group Barring Them from Selling Patent Infringing Emerald and Ice Lenses," an Oakley corporate press release carried on the Business Wire, November 26, 2001.

26. "Oakley Updates 2002 Guidance to Reflect Renewed Sunglass Hut Relationship," an Oakley corporate press release carried on the Business Wire, December 12, 2001.

27. Copy of letter provided to the author by Stan Rapp in July 2002.

28. *The History and Development of Advertising* by Frank Presbrey, Doubleday, Doran & Company, Garden City, New York, 1929, p. 9.

29. Ibid., p. 14.

30. Ibid., pp. 19–25.

31. Ibid., pp. 578–579.

32. Interview with author, July 4, 2002.

33. "Putting Media Where the Customers Are," *Relationship Journal*, MRM Partners Worldwide, Summer 2002, p. 15.

34. "Where the Teachers Are," *Relationship Journal*, MRM Partners Worldwide, Summer 2002, p. 15.

35. "Recruiting Those Who Can" on the Teacher Training Agency Web site at http://www.canteach.gov.uk/community/recruit/index.htm# whenwhere.

CHAPTER 7
The Getting-Bigger-Faster Box:
If You Can Buy It, Don't Start It Up

1. "The GE Machine Is Back" by Luisa Beltran, CNN/Money Web site at http://money.cnn.com/, December 18, 2001.

2. *King of Capital: Sandy Weill and the Making of Citigroup* by Amey Stone and Mike Brewster, John Wiley & Sons, New York, 2002, p. 11.

3. "The Accidental Broadcaster" by Claire Poole, *Forbes*, June 8, 1992, p. 58.

4. "Overbought: Firms That Lived by the Deal in '90s Now Sink by the Dozens" by Robert Frank and Robin Sidel, *The Wall Street Journal*, June 6, 2002, p. A1.

5. Tyco International Ltd. Form 10-K (annual report) for the year ending September 30, 2001.

6. Market capitalization calculations based on historical stock price data on Tyco International Ltd. (TYC) provided on Yahoo! Finance by Commodity Systems, Inc., and on the number of shares outstanding disclosed in the Tyco International Ltd. Form 10-K (annual report) for the year ending September 30, 2001.

7. "Ex-Tyco Chief Is Indicted In Tax Case" by Alex Berenson and Carol Vogel, *The New York Times*, June 5, 2002, page C1.

8. "2 Top Tyco Executives Charged with $600 Million Fraud Scheme" by Andrew Ross Sorkin, *The New York Times*, September 13, 2002, p. A1.

9. "Investigating the Economic Role of Mergers" by Gregor Andrade and Erik Stafford, Harvard Business School, February 2002.

10. "New Evidence and Perspectives on Mergers" by Gregor Andrade, Mark Mitchell, and Erik Stafford, *Journal of Economic Perspectives*, Spring 2001, vol. 15, no. 2, p. 103.

11. "New Evidence and Perspectives on Mergers," p. 118.

12. "Microsoft Corporate Profile and Organizational Structure Overview" as presented on the Microsoft corporate Web site at http://www.microsoft.com/presspass/corpprofile.asp.

13. "The Incredible Shrinking Failure Rate" by Martha E. Mangelsdorf, *Inc* magazine, October 1, 1993, as presented on the *Inc* Web site at http://inc.com/incmagazine. The article is based on research published in *Entrepreneurship and Dynamic Capitalism: The Economics of New Firm Formation and Growth* by Bruce Kirchoff, Praeger Publishing Co., 1994. Kirchhoff is a professor at New Jersey Institute of Technology.

14. "Full Speed Ahead: A World-Wide Glut Doesn't Sway Samsung from Auto Business" by Michael Schuman and Valerie Reitman, *The Wall Street Journal*, August 25, 1997, p. A1.

15. "Samsung's Myth of Invincibility Crashes" by Sohn Young Ju, *Business Korea*, August 1999, vol. 16, no. 8, pp. 20–23.

16. "Korea's Samsung to Seek Protection from Creditors for Firm's Auto Business" by Michael Schuman, *The Wall Street Journal*, July 1, 1999, p. A19.

17. "Why Companies Fail" by Ram Charan and Jerry Useem, *Fortune*, May 27, 2002, p. 56.

18. "A French Recipe to Savor" by Moon Ihlwan in Seoul, with Chester Dawson in Tokyo, *BusinessWeek International* editions, October 7, 2002, p. 28.

19. *Built to Last* by James C. Collins and Jerry I. Porras, HarperBusiness, New York, paperback edition, 1994, Appendix 2, p. 261.

20. "Our History—Leaders through the Years," on the General Electric corporate Web site at http://www.ge.com/news/exec_lead.html.

21. "Burton G. Tremaine (1863–1948)," "Franklin S. Terry (1862–1926)," brief biographies presented on the Web site of Union College, Schenectady, New York, at http://engineering.union.edu/community/project95/HOH/Biography/terr.trem.html.

22. "The History of Nela Park," the GE Lighting North America company profile on the corporate Web site at http://www.gelighting.com/na/pressroom/pr_history_nela.html.

23. "GE Goes Light-years beyond the Light Bulb" by Mark Clayton, *The Christian Science Monitor*, March 23, 1987, "Business Monday," p. 18.

24. *Get Better or Get Beaten* by Robert Slater, McGraw-Hill, New York, 2001, Foreword, p. ix; "GE Goes Light-years beyond the Light Bulb."

25. "G.E. Credit: A Buyout Pioneer" by Thomas J. Lueck, *The New York Times*, June 15, 1984, p. D1.

26. "Too Big for Its Booties: General Electric's Baby, GE Capital, Will Soon Make More Money than the Rest of the Group Put Together" by Richard Waters, *Financial Times*, London, October 9, 1997, p. 17.

27. "At NBC Network, Mood Is Relaxed" by Geraldine Fabrikant, *The New York Times*, December 12, 1985, p. D5.

28. "GE to Sell Consumer Lines to Thomson, Get Medical," *Electronic News*, July 27, 1987, vol. 33, p. 4.

29. "How Jack Welch Runs GE: A Close-up Look at How America's #1 Manager Runs GE" by John A. Byrne, *BusinessWeek*, June 8, 1998; "The Right Way—and Some Wrong Ways—to Make an Acquisition," written by the Wharton School newsletter *Knowledge@Wharton* for GE Capital and presented on the corporate Web site of GE Capital Commercial Equipment Financing at http://www.ge-cef.com.

30. "It's Official: GE Selling Kidder to PaineWebber Securities" by James F. Peltz, *Los Angeles Times*, October 18, 1994, p. D1.

31. "GE's Investment in Kidder Finally Pays Off" by Tim Arango, TheStreet.com/NYTimes.com, July 12, 2000, as filed on the Web site TheStreet.com at http://www.thestreet.com/brknews/brokerages/997551.html.

32. "The Accidental Broadcaster" by Claire Poole, *Forbes*, June 8, 1992, "Up & Comers" section, p. 58.

33. Clear Channel Communications Form 10-K (annual report) for the period ending December 31, 1995.

34. Clear Channel Communications Form 10-K (annual report) for the period ending December 31, 1996.

35. Clear Channel Communications Form 10-K (annual report) for the period ending December 31, 1997.

36. Ibid.

37. "The Leader in U.S. Radio to Buy No. 2" by Bill Carter, *The New York Times*, October 5, 1999, p. C1.

38. Clear Channel Communications Form 10-K (annual report) for the period ending December 31, 2001; "Clear Channel in $3 Billion Deal to Acquire SFX Entertainment" by Stuart Elliott, *The New York Times*, March 1, 2000, p. C1.

39. "Growth through Acquisitions: A Fresh Look" by Patricia L. Anslinger and Thomas E. Copeland, *The McKinsey Quarterly*, 1996, no. 2, pp. 96–109. First published in the *Harvard Business Review*, January-February 1996.

40. "The Fine Art of Friendly Acquisition" by Robert J. Aiello and Michael D. Watkins, *Harvard Business Review*, November-December 2000, pp. 101–107.

41. John Lanier quoted in "The Right Way—and Some Wrong Ways—to Make an Acquisition."

42. "The Fine Art of Friendly Acquisition," p. 102.

43. "Making the Deal Real: How GE Capital Integrates Acquisitions" by Ronald N. Ashkenas, Lawrence J. DeMonaco, and Suzanne C. Francis, *Harvard Business Review*, January-February 1998, pp. 6–15.

Chapter 8
The People Box: Hire Smart or Manage Hard

1. "Three Feet Tip-to-Tip" by Lieutenant Commander George S. Capen, U.S. Navy, *Shipmate*, the alumni magazine of the U.S. Naval Academy, June 2001, p. 8.

2. "Navy Pilot on Collision: 'I Wouldn't Change a Thing,'" April 17, 2001, CNN.com/WORLD, at http://asia.cnn.com/2001/WORLD/asiapcf/east/04/16/us.china/.

3. From a White House transcript of a press briefing on the return of the crew of the EP-3 from China: "Remarks by Senior Administration Official to Travel Pool," Aboard Air Force One, En Route to Fort Hood, Texas, April 12, 2001, 5:30 P.M. EDT, The White House, Office of the Press Secretary (Waco, Texas).

4. "Leading Up: The Art of Managing Your Boss," an interview with Michael Useem by *Knowledge@Wharton*, the newsletter of the Wharton School at the University of Pennsylvania, undated, posted on the Wharton School Web site at http://knowledge.wharton.upenn.edu/articles.cfm?catid=2&articleid=350.

5. *First Break All the Rules* by Macus Buckingham and Curt Coffman, Simon & Schuster, New York, 1999, pp. 11–12.

6. "Manager's Journal: The CEO Was Only Part of Warnaco's Troubles" by Robert Lohrer, *The Wall Street Journal*, June 18, 2001, p. A18.

7. "Washed Up at Warnaco?" by Daniel Eisenberg with reporting by Carole Buia in New York, *Time*, June 25, 2001, p. 36

8. Interview with Julie Pitta, author's researcher, June 2002.

9. Warnaco Group, Inc. Form 10-K (annual report) for the year ending December 31, 2000, dated April 16, 2001.

10. "Saddled by Debt, Clothing Maker Warnaco Seeks Bankruptcy Protection" by Teri Agins and Erin White, *The Wall Street Journal*, June 12, 2001, p. B1.

11. "Warnaco Creditors Fight Claim by Former Chairwoman," Bloomberg News, *The New York Times*, May 9, 2002, p. C4.

12. *The Merchant Prince of Poverty Row* by Bernard F. Dick, University Press of Kentucky, Lexington, Kentucky, 1993.

13. *International Directory of Company Histories*, St. James Press, Chicago and London, 1990, vol. 2, pp. 135–136.

14. "How to Make People Decisions" by Peter F. Drucker, *Harvard Business Review*, July–August 1985, pp. 4–7.

15. "Mental Disorder and Homicide: A Review of Epidemiological Research" by M. Woodward, J. Nursten, P. Williams, D. Badger, *Epidemiologia e psichiatria sociale*, July–September 2000, vol. 9, no. 3, pp. 171–89.

16. "Bill Taylor: Balancing Your Work and Life," *The Meeting Professional*, April 2000.

17. Southwest Airlines Co. Form 10-K (annual report) for the year ending December 31, 2001, dated February 4, 2002.

18. "An Airline Bailout—with Strings Attached" by Michael Arndt in Chicago, with Nanette Byrnes in New York and Lorraine Woellert in Washington, *BusinessWeek*, October 8, 2001.

19. "Finding and Keeping Great People: More than Pay at Cisco, Southwest" by Vance Cariaga, *Investor's Business Daily*, November 6, 2000, p. A1.

20. "Air Travel Consumer Report," U.S. Department of Transportation, February 2002, Table 5, "January-December Consumer Complaints: Rankings U.S. Airlines," p. 35.

21. *The Microsoft Way* by Randall E. Stross, Addison-Wesley, Reading, Massachusetts, 1996, p. 22.

22. *Europe and the People without History* by Eric R. Wolf, University of California Press, Berkeley and Los Angeles, California, 1982, p. 358.

23. There are a number of books on Albert Kahn, and his work is on display all over Detroit. For a review of his factory architecture online, see "The Factory Architecture of Albert Kahn" by Louis Bergeron and Maria Teresa Maiullari-Pontoi, *ArchitectureWeek*, November 1, 2000, as presented on *ArchitectureWeek*'s Web site at http://www.ArchitectureWeek.com/2000/1101/culture_1-1.html.

24. "Microsoft" by Kathy Rebello in Redmond, Washington, with Evan I. Schwartz in New York and bureau reports, *BusinessWeek* cover story, February 24, 1992.

25. "Key Events in Microsoft History," a document posted on Microsoft's corporate Web site, http://www.microsoft.com.

26. Calculations performed by the author based on Microsoft (MSFT) share price data provided on Yahoo! Finance by Commodity Systems, Inc. (CSI) at http://table.finance.yahoo.com/k?s—sft&g=d.

27. Microsoft Corporation Form 10-K (annual report) for the year ending June 30, 2001, dated September 17, 2001.

28. "Bill Gates Answers the Most Frequently Asked Questions," an undated document posted on Microsoft's corporate Web site at microsoft.com.

29. *The Microsoft Way*, table titled "Number of Employees," p. 20; Microsoft Corporation's Form 10-K (annual report) for the year ending June 30, 2001, dated September 17, 2001.

30. *The Microsoft Way*, p. 41.

31. "Microsoft: The Hiring Machine" by Michele Matassa Flores, *Seattle Times*, February 18, 1996, p. A1.

32. *The Microsoft Way*, p. 42.

33. Interview with Julie Pitta, author's researcher, June 2002.

34. "Microsoft" by Kathy Rebello in Redmond, Washington, with Evan I. Schwartz in New York and bureau reports, *BusinessWeek* cover story, February 24, 1992.

35. "Microsoft: The Hiring Machine" by Michele Matassa Flores, *Seattle Times*, February 18, 1996, p. A1.

36. *Built to Last: Successful Habits of Visionary Companies* by James C. Collins and Jerry I. Porras, HarperBusiness, New York, NY, paperback edition, 1997, p. 207.

37. *Built to Last: Successful Habits of Visionary Companies*, p. 210.

38. "McKnight Principles," posted on the 3M Web site at http://www.3m.com/about3m/history/mcknight.jhtml.

39. For an excellent view of the Roman military's organizational structure and personnel policies, see two books by historian Antonio Santosuosso: *Soldiers, Citizens and the Symbols of War*, Westview Press, 1997, particularly pp. 150–160; *Storming the Heavens*, Westview Press, 2001, particularly chapters 1 and 2, and "Discipline, Pay, and Rewards," pp. 100–105.

40. "They're Not Employees, They're People" by Peter F. Drucker, *Harvard Business Review*, February 2002, p. 2.

CHAPTER 9
The Treasure Box: Secure the Real Assets

1. "Non-OPEC Fact Sheet," Energy Information Administration, United States Department of Energy, June 2002, as presented on the DOE's Web site at http://www.eia.doe.gov/emeu/cabs/nonopec.html.

2. See Chapter 7, "The Getting-Bigger-Faster Box," for a recitation of Samsung's brief foray into the auto business.

3. "Glorious Hopes on a Trillion-Dollar Scrapheap" by Dan Roberts, *Financial Times*, London, September 4, 2001.

4. "Winstar Tainted by CEO, Associates' Pay Plans," Bloomberg, L.P., January 4, 1995, *Bloomberg News*.

5. "Going Wireless Down That Last Local Mile," Newsbytes, a service of Post-Newsweek Business Information Inc., September 7, 1994, New York.

6. Winstar Communications, Inc., Form 10-K (annual report) for the year ending December 31, 1999, dated February 10, 2000, Item 4, "Selected Financial Data," p. 24.

7. Winstar Communications, Inc., Form 10-K (annual report) for the year ending December 31, 1999, dated February 10, 2000, Item 1, "Business," p. 1.

8. Winstar Communications, Inc., Form 10-K (annual report) for the year ending December 31, 1999, dated February 10, 2000, "Notes to Consolidated Financial Statements. Note 3—Property and Equipment," p. F-12.

9. Winstar Communications, Inc., Form 8-K, dated April 18, 2001; *Winstar Bankruptcy News*, edited by Peter A. Chapman, Bankruptcy Creditors' Service, April 19, 2001, Issue Number 1.

10. "Technology: For IDT, the Big Flameouts Light Its Fire" by Ann Wozencraft, *The New York Times*, January 28, 2002, p. C4.

11. "Federal Reserve Board's semiannual monetary policy report to the Congress," testimony of Federal Reserve Board Chairman Alan Greenspan before the Committee on Banking, Housing, and Urban Affairs, U.S. Senate, March 7, 2002, and before the Committee on Financial Services, U.S. House of Representatives, February 27, 2002, as presented on the Federal Reserve Board's Web site at http://www.federalreserve.gov/boarddocs/hh/2002/March/testimony.htm.

12. Ibid.

13. Merrill Lynch & Co., Inc. Form 10-K (annual report) for the year ending December 28, 2001, dated March 14, 2002, "Results of Operations," p. 18 and Item 1, "Business, Overview," pp. 1–2.

14. Merrill Lynch & Co., Inc. Form 10-K (annual report) for the year ending December 28, 2001, Item 1, "Business, Overview," p. 1.

15. "Congress Getting into Analyst Blame Game" by Rachel Konrad and Margaret Kane, CNET News.com, June 11, 2001.

16. "SIA Sets Best Practices ahead of Hearings" by Margaret Kane, CNET News.com, June 12, 2001.

17. "SEC to Investors: Be Your Own Analyst" by Margaret Kane, CNET News.com, June 29, 2001.

18. "Merrill Limits Analysts," CNNmoney, July 10, 2001, on the CNNmoney Web site at http://money.cnn.com/2001/07/10/investing/merrill_analysts/index.htm.

19. "Merrill settles complaint," CNNmoney, July 20, 2001, on the CNN-

money Web site at http://money.cnn.com/2001/07/20/investing/merrill_blodget/.

20. "Affidavit in Support of Application for an Order Pursuant to General Business Law Section 354," Eliot Spitzer, Attorney General of the State of New York, Petitioner; Merrill Lynch & Co., Inc., Henry Blodget, Justin Baldauf, Kirsten Campbell, Virginia Syer Genereux, Sofia Ghachem, Thomas Mazzucco, Edward McCabe and Deepak Raj, Respondents; April 2002, p. 1–2.

21. Ibid., p. 3.

22. Ibid., p. 9.

23. Ibid., p. 10.

24. Ibid., p. 2.

25. Author's calculations based on historical share price data for InfoSpace, Inc. (NASDAQ: INSP) from Commodity Systems, Inc., as provided to the Yahoo! Finance Web site.

26. "Affidavit in Support of Application for an Order Pursuant to General Business Law Section 354," p. 13.

27. "Chairman and CEO Komansky Addresses Research Integrity at Annual Meeting of Shareholders," April 26, 2002, press release issued by Merrill Lynch on its corporate Web site, at http://www.ml.com/about/press_release/04262002-1_komansky_addresses_pr.htm.

28. "Merrill's Apology Fails to Cool Investors' Anger" by Patrick McGeehan, May 1, 2002, *The New York Times*, p. C3.

29. "What If Investors Won't Join the Party?" by Gretchen Morgenson, *The New York Times*, June 2, 2002, p. C1.

30. All quotes attributed to John Strawgfeld in this chapter are from the author's interview with Strangfeld, June 13, 2002, at Prudential Financial's offices in lower Manhattan.

31. "The Mess at Pru-Bache" by Chuck Hawkins, with Leah Nathans Spiro, *BusinessWeek*, March 4, 1991; *Serpent on the Rock* by Kurt Eichenwald, HarperBusiness, New York, 1995.

32. "Deals & Deal Makers: Prudential Securities Takes Tough Stance in Putting 'Sell' Rating on Amazon.com" by Aaron Elstein and Nick Wingfield, *The Wall Street Journal*, February 16, 2001, p. C16.

33. "Kmart downgraded to 'sell'," CNN/Money, January 2, 2002, as published on the CNN/Money Web site at http://money.cnn.com/2002/01/02/companies/kmart/.

34. Kmart Corporation Form 8-K, Item 2, "Bankruptcy or Receivership," dated January 22, 2002.

35. "The Mouse That Ate the Public Domain" by Chris Sprigman, posted

on the FindLaw Web site, March 5, 2002, at http://writ.corporate. findlaw.com/commentary/20020305_sprigman.html.

36. Julie Pitta's interview with Edward Samuels, May 2002.

37. *Eric Eldred et al. v Janet Reno*, United States District Court for the District of Columbia, Case No. 1:99CV00065 JLG, dated May 10, 1999.

CHAPTER 10
The Ends-Over-Means Box:
Results Are More Important Than Process

1. "Colombia Installs New President Who Plans to Talk to Rebels" by Diana Jean Schemo, *The New York Times*, August 8, 1998, p. A2.

2. "Elusive Peace: Struggling Against the Logic of Violence" by Marc Chernick, *NACLA* (North American Congress on Latin America) *Report on the Americas*, September 1, 2000, no. 2, vol. 34, p. 32.

3. "Colombian Guerrillas Kill Popular Official" by Scott Wilson, *The Washington Post*, October 1, 2001, p. A16.

4. "Peace Process Continues—Pastrana," extracts of a television address by Colombian President Andres Pastrana, January 15, 2002, transcribed by the BBC and posted on the BBC Web site at http://news. bbc.co.uk/1/hi/world/americas/1761461.stm.

5. "700 Missing after Jungle Attack by Rebels" by Gabriella Gamini, *The Times*, London, August 2, 2002.

6. "At Enron, 'The Environment Was Ripe for Abuse'" by John A. Byrne, with Mike France in New York and Wendy Zellner in Dallas, *Business-Week*, February 25, 2002.

7. *The War for Talent* by Ed Michaels, Helen Handfield-Jones, and Beth Axelrod, Harvard Business School Press, Boston, 2001, Chapter 6, "Differentiate and Affirm Your People," particularly p. 129.

8. Ibid., p. 127.

9. "How Enron Blew It" by Mimi Swartz, *Texas Monthly*, November 2001.

10. *The War for Talent*, p. 57.

11. *The War for Talent*, p. 127.

12. As of August 2002, numerous Enron executives were under investigation by the U.S. Justice Department for criminal activity, and one, Michael J. Kopper, a senior finance executive, had pled guilty to two felonies. See "Enron Official Is Reported Set to Plead Guilty" by Kurt Eichenwald, *The New York Times*, August 21, 2002, p. A1.

13. *Leading the Revolution* by Gary Hamel, Harvard Business School Press, Boston, 2000, p. 217.

14. *Amalgamated Bank v Kenneth L. Lay et al.*, United States District Court, Southern District of Texas, Houston Division, Civil Action No. H 01-4198, "Plaintiff's *Ex Parte* Application for a Temporary Restraining Order and Order to Show Cause," pp. 3–4, December 5, 2001.

15. "Short Circuit: How Enron's Plan to Market Electricity Nationwide Fizzled" by Rebecca Smith, *The Wall Street Journal*, March 25, 2002, p. A1.

16. *Leading the Revolution* by Gary Hamel, Harvard Business School Press, Boston, 2000, p. 219; "Short Circuit: How Enron's Plan to Market Electricity Nationwide Fizzled."

17. Ten-page printout of an e-mail from Margaret Ceconi to Kenneth L. Lay, dated August 29, 2001. The e-mail was made public by the Committee on Energy and Commerce, U.S. House of Representatives, which wrote a letter to Lay on January 29, 2002, asking questions about the e-mail.

18. "The Talent Myth" by Malcolm Gladwell, *The New Yorker*, July 22, 2002, p. 30.

19. Microsoft Income Statements, 1Q 1998 through 4Q 2002, posted on the Microsoft corporate Web site at http://www.microsoft.com/; Microsoft Inc. Form 10-K (annual report) for the year ending June 30, 2001, "Management's Discussion and Analysis of Results of Operations and Financial Condition," pp. 18–25.

20. Interview by Julie Pitta, author's researcher, week of July 29, 2002. Ms. Pitta submitted written questions to Ballmer, which were answered on a tape recording. Microsoft provided a verbatim transcript of Ballmer's responses.

21. General Motors Corporation 2001 Annual Report, pp. 2 and 48.

22. *Concept of the Corporation* by Peter F. Drucker, John Day, New York, 1972, pp. 305–307.

23. "Unaccountable Management Ethos Breeds Failure" by John Schnapp, *Detroit News*, November 29, 2001.

24. "Straight Shooting: Bob Lutz, President of Chrysler, Tells It Like It Is . . . All the Time" by Paul A. Eisenstein, *Cigar Afficionado*, June 1996.

25. "GM to revamp design system" by Reuters, *Automotive News*, January 25, 2002.

26. "The Results Act Should Be About Results" by Stephen Kelman, *Government Executive*, July 2000, p. 124.

27. "The President's Management Agenda, Fiscal Year 2002," Executive Office of the President, Office of Management and Budget, Summer 2001, pp. 25–27.

28. "The Results Act: Has It Met Congressional Expectations?" Testimony by The Hon. Maurice P. McTigue, Q.S.O., Distinguished Visit-

ing Scholar at the Mercatus Center at George Mason University, before the Subcommittee on Government Efficiency, Financial Management and Intergovernmental Relations, Committee on Government Reform, United States House of Representatives, June 19, 2001.

29. "The Results Act Should Be About Results," p. 124.

30. "Managing for Results," General Accounting Office, July 1999, p. 10.

31. "The Results Act Should Be About Results," p. 124.

32. "Using GPRA to Assist Oversight and Decision-making," statement of J. Christopher Mihm, Director, Strategic Issues, United States General Accounting Office, in testimony before the Subcommittee on Government Efficiency, Financial Management and Intergovernmental Relations, Committee on Government Reform, U.S. House of Representatives, June 19, 2001.

33. "Voulez-Vous Completely Overhaul This Big, Slow Company and Start Making Some Cars People Actually Want Avec Moi?" by Andy Raskin, *Business 2.0*, January 2002; "Saving the Business Without Losing the Company" by Carlos Ghosn, *Harvard Business Review*, January 2002.

34. "Breaking with Tradition in a Foreign Land" by Carlos Ghosn, HBS Working Knowledge, March 18, 2002, posted on the Harvard Business School Web site at http://hbswk.hbs.edu/item.jhtml?id=2836&t= globalization&sid=0&pid=0.

35. "Face to Face: Yarmin Vong Talks to Carlos Ghosn" by Yarmin Vong, *New Straits Times Press*, Malaysia, July 7, 2002.

36. "The Road to Recovery" by Linda Tischler, *Fast Company*, July 2002, pp. 75–86.

37. "Breaking with Tradition in a Foreign Land."

38. "Voulez-Vous Completely Overhaul This Big, Slow Company and Start Making Some Cars People Actually Want Avec Moi?"

39. "Saving the Business Without Losing the Company" by Carlos Ghosn, *Harvard Business Review*, January 2002.

40. "Renault and Nissan Going Dutch" by Tim Burt and David Ibison, *Financial Times*, London, May 29, 2002, p. 15.

41. "Breaking with Tradition in a Foreign Land."

CHAPTER 11
The Renewable Box: Nothing Lasts Forever

1. "Innovation through Applied Technology" on the Vishay BLH corporate Web site at http://www.blh.com/about%20blh.htm. Vishay BLH is the successor of the Baldwin Locomotive Works.

2. *From Steam to Diesel: Managerial Customs and Organizational Capabilities*

in the Twentieth-Century American Locomotive Industry by Albert Churella, Princeton University Press, Princeton, New Jersey, 1998, p. 15.

3. *Industry and Its Relation to Railroads* by Major W. A. Garrett; "Lectures for Supervisory Forces: Pennsylvania Railroad System, Eastern Region," 1923–24; posted at http://prr.railfan.net/documents/Lectures ForSupervisoryForces/IndustryAndItsRelationToRailroads.html.

4. *From Steam to Diesel*, p. 15.

5. *Innovation and Entrepreneurship* by Peter F. Drucker, Harper & Row, New York, 1985, p. 13.

6. *From Steam to Diesel*, p. 13.

7. *From Steam to Diesel*, pp. 13 and 64.

8. *From Steam to Diesel*, p. 15.

9. *From Steam to Diesel*, p. 16.

10. "Railroad History," a timeline prepared by the San Diego Railroad Museum and posted on the museum's Web site at http://www.sdrm.org/history/timeline/.

11. "Celebrating a History of Railroad Industry Excellence" in the "History" section of the corporate Web site of the Electro-Motive Division of General Motors Corporation, August 2002, at http://www.gmemd.com/en/company/history/index.htm.

12. *American Steam Locomotive* by Brian Solomon, Motorbooks International, 1998, p. 8.

13. *Management: Tasks, Responsibilities, Practices* by Peter F. Drucker, Harper & Row, New York, 1973, citing the HarperBusiness paperback edition, 1993, p. 61.

14. *Innovation and Entrepreneurship*, pp. 133–134.

15. "Fresh Start 2002: Weird Ideas That Work" by Polly LaBare, *Fast Company*, January 2002.

16. *Innovation and Entrepreneurship*, pp. 134–140.

17. "IBM to Sell Technology to Cisco" by William M. Bulkeley and Scott Thurm, *The Wall Street Journal*, September 1, 1999, p. A3.

18. International Business Machines Corporation Form 10-K (annual report) for the year ending December 31, 1995, "Notes to Consolidated Financial Statements, Revenue by Classes of Similar Products or Services," p. 76; IBM Form 10-K (annual report) for the year ending December 31, 2001, "Notes to Consolidated Financial Statements, Revenue by Classes of Similar Products or Services," p. 105.

19. "The Fisher Brothers: Their Lives and Times" by Michael Lamm, originally printed in *Special Interest Autos*, 1978; posted at http://www.geocities.com/sponcom26/Life-TimesCover.html.

20. "Waterway Fueled Early Success of Detroit's Auto Industry" by Betty DeRamus, *The Detroit News,* June 1, 2001.
21. "The Fisher Brothers: Their Lives and Times."
22. Ibid.
23. "Fisher Body Craftsman," commemorative 75th anniversary newspaper published by Fisher Body in 1983; posted at http://www.geo cities.com/sponcom26/HISTORYHomePage.html.
24. Ibid.
25. Ibid.
26. "Fresh Start 2002: Weird Ideas That Work" by Polly Barre, *Fast Company,* January 2002, citing ideas advanced in the book *Weird Ideas That Work: 11 12 Practices for Promoting, Managing, and Sustaining Innovation* by Robert Sutton, Free Press, New York, 2001.
27. Corporate history, posted on the 3M corporate Web site at http://www.3m.com/about3m/history/index.jhtml.
28. Timeline posted on the 3M corporate Web site at http://www.3m.com/about3m/history/index.jhtml.
29. "McKnight Principles," posted on the 3M corporate Web site at http://www.3m.com/about3m/history/mcknight.jhtml.
30. *Built to Last: Successful Habits of Visionary Companies* by James C. Collins and Jerry I. Porras, HarperBusiness, New York, paperback edition, 1994, p. 153.
31. *Management: Tasks, Responsibilities, Practices,* p. 798.
32. 3M 2001 Annual Report, "Supplemental Consolidated Statement of Income Information," p. 25; 3M Worldwide corporate Web site, "3M Facts, Year-End 2001," posted at http://www.3m.com/about3m/facts/3Mfacts.jhtml.
33. *American Express: A Century of Service* by Allen Hatch, Doubleday & Company, New York, 1950, p. 48.
34. Ibid., pp. 36–37.
35. Ibid., p. 86.
36. Ibid., p. 93.
37. *Forbes' Greatest Business Stories of All Time* by Daniel Gross and the editors of *Forbes* magazine, John Wiley & Sons, New York, 1996, p. 218.
38. American Express Company Annual Report, 2001, "Consolidated Five-Year Summary of Selected Financial Data," p. 78.
39. *International Directory of Company Histories,* vol. 38, edited by Jay P. Pederson; St. James Press, Detroit, May 2001, p. 44.
40. American Express Company Annual Report, 2001, "Consolidated Statements of Income," p. 48, and "Selected Statistical Information," p. 36.

CHAPTER 12
The Houdini Box: Always Have an Exit Strategy

1. For an interesting view of venture capital exits, see "Venture Capital Exits in Canada and the United States," a research paper by Douglas J. Cumming, School of Business, University of Alberta, and Jeffrey G. MacIntosh, Toronto Stock Exchange Professor of Capital Markets, Faculty of Law, University of Toronto, February 2002, as presented on the University of Toronto, Capital Markets Institute Web site at http://www.rotman.utoronto.ca/cmi/papers/index.htm.

2. "Report of Investigation by the Special Investigative Committee of the Board of Directors of Enron Corp." by William C. Powers Jr., chair, Raymond S. Troubh, and Herbert S. Winokur Jr., February 1, 2002, pp. 2–3.

3. Ibid., pp. 2–3.

4. "Stroh Sells Out: Pabst, Miller Pick Up Brands," April 1999, from the Beer Notes Web site at http://www.beernotes.com.

5. "History of The Thomson Corporation" on The Thomson Corporation Web site at http://www.thomson.com/About_Us/01_1_3_history.htm, July 2002.

6. Presentation by Richard Harrington, president and CEO, The Thomson Corporation, at Credit Suisse First Boston's Media Week Conference, Plaza Hotel, New York, December 4, 2000.

7. "Thomson sells Winnipeg Free Press and Brandon Sun to Canadian Newspapers Co." by the Canadian Press, November 14, 2001, as presented on the Canadian Web portal Canoe at http://www.canoe.ca/NewspaperWars/nov14_thomsonsells-cp.html.

8. "About Us" on *Wired* magazine's official Web site, July 2002, at http://www.wired.com/wired/about/.

9. Author's interview with Peter Rutten, July 15, 2002.

10. Details of *Wired*'s early development come from the author's July 15, 2002, interview with Peter Rutten. Rossetto and Metcalfe, ironically, stopped talking to journalists about *Wired* in 1997.

11. "Can Wired Get Wired Again?" by Linda Himelstein, *BusinessWeek*, November 3, 1997.

12. "Wired Ventures Withdraws Initial Offering for 2d Time" by Lawrence M. Fisher, *The New York Times*, October 26, 1996, p. A38.

13. "Can Wired Get Wired Again?"

14. Ibid.

15. "New Publisher for Wired," *The New York Times*, December 4, 1997, p. D2.

16. "Digital Culture Pioneer Sold to Condé Nast" by Amy Harmon, *The New York Times*, May 11, 1998, p. D2.

17. Details of Control Video's capital and revenue from "Everybody's Wrong" by Robert X. Cringely, technology journalist and writer/host of the PBS miniseries "Triumph of the Nerds," quoting a videotape of Marc Seriff, as posted on the Public Broadcasting Service Web site, dated July 27, 2000, at http://www.pbs.org/cringely/pulpit/pulpit20000727.html.

18. "You've Got Time Warner! How Steve Case Morphed into a Media Mogul" by Kara Swisher, *The Wall Street Journal*, January 11, 2000, p. B1; "Timeline" on AOL Time Warner's corporate Web site at http://aoltimewarner.com/corporate_information/timeline.adp.

19. Marc Seriff's retirement speech was captured on videotape, a copy of which was obtained by Robert X. Cringely, a technology journalist and the writer/host of the PBS miniseries "Triumph of the Nerds." Cringely provided a copy of the tape to the author. Also see "Everybody's Wrong" by Robert X. Cringely as posted on the Public Broadcasting Service Web site, dated July 27, 2000, at http://www.pbs.org/cringely/pulpit/pulpit20000727.html.

20. "On-Line: When Bill Met Steve: A Showdown That Shaped AOL" by Kara Swisher, *The Wall Street Journal*, June 22, 1998, p. B1.

21. Ibid.

22. Biography of James V. Kimsey posted on the Kimsey Foundation Web site at http://www.kimseyfoundation.org/jameskimsey.htm.

23. "America Online: Often Down, But Never Out," a review in *Business-Week*, July 20, 1998, of *AOL.COM* by Kara Swisher, Times Business, New York, 1998.

24. The Nasdaq low in October 1998 was 1343.87; the close in February 2000 was 4696.69. The Nasdaq's daily peak actually occurred on March 10, 1999, at 5132.52, but the February close was higher than the March close. Source: Yahoo! Finance at http://finance.yahoo.com. Data provided by Commodity Systems, Inc. (CSI).

25. Calculated as the increase from the Nasdaq October 1998 low of 1343.87 to the February 2000 close of 4696.69. Using the March high as the end point, of course, produces a higher percentage increase.

26. America Online, Inc., Form 10-K (annual report) for the year ending June 30, 2000, p. 16, discloses just over 2.21 billion shares of common stock were issued and outstanding at June 30, 1999.

27. America Online, Inc., Form 10-K (annual report) for the year ending June 30, 2000, p. 10, shows the company's operating earnings for FY

1999 as $450 million. Net income for the year was actually $754 million (p. 17), but this included $638 million in "other income," mostly gains on securities (p. 34). Even using the net income figure, however, AOL's value was still an equally unbelievable 223 times after-tax earnings.

28. "America Online and Time Warner Complete Merger to Create AOL Time Warner," an AOL Time Warner press release issued January 11, 2001; "Media Megadeal: The Deal; Investors Seem to Want to Keep AOL-Time Warner Asunder" by Alex Berenson, *The New York Times,* January 13, 2000, p. C1.

29. AOL Time Warner Annual Report 2001 for the year ending December 31, 2001, "Note to Consolidated Financial Statements," p. 80; "Dot-Com Era Notions Guided a Huge Merger" by Saul Hansell, *The New York Times,* July 19, 2002, p. A1.

30. "AOL: Just a Cog in Big Media's Wheel" by Jim Hu, CNET News.com, December 6, 2001, as posted on CNET's Web site at http://news.com.com/2100-1023-276709.html?tag=rn.

31. AOL Time Warner, Inc., Form 8-K filed October 23, 2002.

32. "America Online, Inc. Pays $3.5 Million to Settle Financial Reporting Violations," *U.S. Securities and Exchange Commission v. America Online, Inc.,* Civ No. 1:00CV01088 (PLF) (D.D.C. May 15, 2000); Litigation Release no. 16552/May 15, 2000; Accounting and Auditing Enforcement Release No. 1258/May 15, 2000.

<div align="center">

READ THIS LAST
Think Outside the Box

</div>

1. *Marcel Duchamp* edited by Anne d'Harnoncourt and Kynaston McShine, The Museum of Modern Art, New York, and Philadelphia Museum of Art, Philadelphia, 1973, pp. 281–283.

2. *Weird Ideas That Work* by Robert I. Sutton, Free Press, New York, 2002, pp. 7–15.

INDEX

ABOUT THE AUTHOR

A successful businessman and an award-winning journalist, Cheyfitz has built the world's first and largest global custom publishing network for McCann-Erickson WorldGroup, the world's largest advertising agency. After only four years, The Publishing Agency International has full-service companies in New York, Amsterdam, Brussels, London, Madrid, and Seattle. Cheyfitz was a Pulitzer finalist for investigative work at the *Detroit Free Press* and won the prestigious Sigma Delta Chi Bronze Medallion for investigative reporting, among many national and regional journalism honors. He started a city magazine in Detroit in the mid-1980s, making a seamless transition from journalist to self-taught entrepreneur. Next he acquired *Chicago* magazine and built a publishing division with some 1,200 employees and more than twenty operating entities. Cheyfitz lives on Manhattan's Upper West Side with his wife, Ellen, and daughter, Amy.

1566494

Made in the USA